Urban Search

Urban Search

Managing Missing Person Searches
in the Urban Environment

Christopher S. Young and John Wehbring

dbS Productions
Charlottesville, Virginia

All photographs by Christopher S. Young with exception of the following: used with permission from Chris Boyer, p. 13 (industrial), p. 18 (military base); from Langley Air Force Base, p. 14; used with permission from Robert Koester, p. 39; used with permission from Rand McNally, from the Contra Costa Thomas Guide, R.L.07-S-108, p. 42; used with permission from The New Yorker Collection, Arnie Levin from the cartoonbank.com, p. 108; from Contra Costa County, CA, p. 125; used with permission from Marc Silveira, p. 136. Dementia Evaluation Form reprinted with permission from dbS Productions. Urban missing person statistics, initial reflex tasks, and summary behavior profiles are used with permission from dbS Productions.

Cover design by hypertype®
Editor: Emily Powell Koester

Published by dbS Productions
PO Box 94
Charlottesville, Virginia 22902 USA
www.dbs-sar.com

Library of Congress Cataloging-in-Publication Data

Young, Christopher S., 1950–
  Urban search : managing missing person searches in the urban
environment / Christopher S. Young and John Wehbring.
        xiv, 337p. : ill. ; 22 cm.
  Includes bibliographical references (p. 318-323) and index.
  ISBN 978-1-879471-38-2
  1. Missing persons—Investigation—United States—Handbooks, manuals,
etc. 2. Crime scene searches—United States—Handbooks, manuals, etc. I.
Title: Urban Search. II. Wehbring, John, 1935–
  HV6762.U5 Y69 2007
  362.8
                                2007907539

Printed in the United States
10 9 8 7 6 5 4 3 2

To my wife, Peggy, for supporting me when I go out at "O'dark thirty" in the morning.

To my children, Shanda, Evan and Kathryn, who have been great sports and acted as lost and hurt victims all their lives.

And mostly to my father, Fletcher "Fletch" Young, who got me into SAR in the first place!

Chris Young

In loving memory of my mother, Olive Wehbring, who taught me the value of public service.

John Wehbring

Authors

Christopher S. Young has been active in Search and Rescue since 1981. He has managed searches since 1986 and is a Reserve Captain for the Contra Costa County (California) Sheriff's Search and Rescue Team. He also serves as Chairman of the San Francisco Bay Area Search and Rescue Council (BASARC). Chris is a member of the American Society of Law Enforcement Trainers (ASLET) and has been an Instructor for the California Governor's Office of Emergency Services since 1989. Chris has written and published search management papers and presents nationally on "Search Management in the Urban Environment." Chris is a Level 1 law enforcement reserve with the Contra Costa County Sheriff's Department and the Town of Danville, California.

John Wehbring helped organize the San Diego Mountain Rescue Team (SD-MRT) in 1967 and has served six terms as President of SDMRT as well as secretary of the Mountain Rescue Association, which awarded him the Distinguished Lifetime Service Award. He was chief writer and editor of SDMRT's Operations Manual and has written numerous journal articles on SAR. As well, he developed guidelines for adapting wilderness search techniques to urban searching. John has participated in over 1,000 SAR missions in the past 40 years. Since 2002, SDMRT has been involved in 91 urban searches working with the SAR Bureau of San Diego Sheriff's Department.

Contributors

Kimberly R. Kelly is the founder and executive director of "Project Far From Home," a national training program designed to educate law enforcement, search and rescue, fire, EMS, and others who may search for missing at-risk elders. She serves as a Reserve Lieutenant with the San Diego County Sheriff's Department in charge of SAR Training and the annual SAR Academy.

Robert J. Koester is author of numerous books and articles on search and rescue and is an international presenter/trainer. He has contributed seminal research on lost person behavior and created the International Search and Rescue Incident Database (ISRID).

Michael St. John is Operations Coordinator for the Marin County Sheriff SAR Unit. He teaches courses in search management for the California Governor's Office of Emergency Services Law Enforcement Division and has played an integral role in developing the curriculum for abduction search strategies.

Contents

Preface

A Note to the Reader

It would be beneficial to state the assumptions the authors have made in this book so that the reader will know what to expect, what will be covered and what will be left out. These assumptions relate to the position of the reader in the search effort and the reader's knowledge of search procedures.

The reader is assumed to be a person within an agency that is responsible for, among other things, urban search, typically the jurisdictional law enforcement officer in a city or town. He or she may be in a command position where the search function has been delegated or may be responsible for developing the agency's search protocols.

Although the reader is not expected to have a firm knowledge of standard wilderness search procedures, because of space limitations, this book will only mention wilderness search procedures when needed to clarify a point. It is recommended that the reader take one of the many search management courses taught by various entities, both governmental and private, as a way to understand the fundamental principles of searching. A glossary of technical terms is included in the back of the book (Appendix B Glossary of ICS Terms) and the reference list provides excellent references, in particular "The Textbook for Managing Land Search Operations" by Robert "Skip" Stoffel.

While urban searches can be managed in a number of ways, in the United States and many other places in the world, the Incident Command System (ICS) has been adopted as the standard by most agencies. Therefore, it is assumed that the reader has a basic knowledge of ICS, since this system will be the foundation of the management techniques described in this book. See Appendix A (Incident Command System) to become more familiar with or brush up on the fundamentals of ICS.

This book compares factors common to the urban/suburban/rural incident with those faced in a wilderness search, including preplanning, managing the lost person search, special investigation considerations, use of resources, and documentation. Several states have enacted legislation that requires law enforcement agencies to respond to and act on the report of missing children. Because of these requirements the book also includes information on special considerations that are found in child abduction incidents.

It will be obvious to the reader that the procedures discussed in this book lean heavily on the authors' experience in urban search, which has been gained mostly in major urbanized areas of California (San Francisco Bay area and San Diego County), in Virginia, and in parts of Canada. Urban search is still a new subject and other areas of the country may do things a little differently. Thus, we have written this book so that any agency throughout the United States and Canada can utilize these techniques. However, we acknowledge that some readers may find other methods more compatible with their local way of doing things. What we offer are procedures we have found to work in two densely populated urban and suburban areas, based on a combined 100+ years of experience. If you find a better method, by all means use it, and let us know!

Christopher S. Young

Acknowledgments

This has been a work in progress for more than 13 years, first suggested in 1994 by Skip Stoffel at a California Search Management Instructor update. Skip and then Chief of the Law Enforcement Division of California Governor's Office of Emergency Services, Larry Buffaloe, encouraged me to write up a little something on how we search in the San Francisco Bay Area where a large percentage of our missions are urban. The subject was then broached at the first William Syrotuck Symposium on Search Theory and Practice in 1996 when I did a short presentation on searching in the urban environment. This rolled into a full presentation and a paper I wrote called "The Suburban Search Process" delivered at the 1998 NASAR conference. The paper eventually became the outline for this book. Since then, the project has grown exponentially and, through an introduction by Monty Bell, into a collaboration with John Wehbring.

Both John and I received a lot of help, encouragement and support from many colleagues and friends. Much of my source of inspiration came from the hundreds of members of the search and rescue teams from the San Francisco Bay area that make up the Bay Area Search and Rescue Council, and of course from my own Contra Costa County Sheriff's Search and Rescue Team. I would like to thank those who reviewed early drafts and specific subjects, and offered advice: Chris Boyer, Jim Cooke, Paul Lufkin, John Carnes, Cindy Valentin, Jorene Downs, and Ron Seitz as well as Matthew Scharper, California State SAR Coordinator, Governor's Office of Emergency Services Law Enforcement Division, and Lt. Eric Christensen, Contra Costa County Department of the Sheriff.

Additional thanks to my good friends and collaborators Mike St. John for his contribution on missing and abducted children, Kim Kelly for her contribution on persons with Alzheimer's disease, and Bob Koester for his contribution on missing person behavior in the urban environment. And extra special thanks go to Bob and Emily Koester for their support and hard work editing the text.

Chris Young

So many of my fellow members of the San Diego Mountain Rescue Team over the past 40 years have contributed to my understanding of how to find missing persons that it would be difficult to know whom to thank. Rob Bair and Rusty Hoar have been most helpful in consolidating my ideas through their extensive experience in urban searching and their leadership. I especially want to thank the San Diego County Sheriff's Department, its Emergency Services Division, and the SAR Coordinators with whom I worked on urban searches over the most recent years, Sergeants Jim Keenan, Christine Robbins and Mike Munsey.

Most of all, I want to thank the volunteer searchers of the Sheriff's Search and Rescue Bureau who manage the search operations and with whom we mountain rescue types integrate on field teams, both urban and wilderness. Of these, I want to single out Reserve Captain David Kerner and Reserve Commander Chris Van Gorder, who have advanced the concepts of urban searching through their dedicated service.

John Wehbring

Chapter 1. Introduction

In any urban setting around the world at any given time of the day there is a report of a missing person.

Consider the following scenarios:

> ### Scenario One
>
> You are the Watch Commander for the Police Department. It is 8:30 p.m. and you just received a report from the dispatcher saying they have a missing eleven-year-old female, Stacy Costa, who has been missing since 2:00 p.m. The initial investigation reveals that after school, Stacy called her mother at work and told her she was going on her bicycle to a friend's house three blocks away. When her mother got home after work at about 6:30 p.m., Stacy was not there. After calling the friend's house, as well as other neighbors and friends, and then driving around the neighborhood, her mother called the police at about 8:30 p.m. There is no history of the child missing before or running away from home. She likes to frequent a local shopping center, especially the arcade game area. She rides her bike around the neighborhood a lot and takes the municipal bus regularly to visit her father, who lives across town.

> ### Scenario Two
>
> You are the Search and Rescue Coordinator for the County. Dispatch received a call from the City of Martinez Police Department, saying that Walter Czar, an 83-year-old male with a history of stroke and dementia, has been reported missing by his care facility. Walter was last seen about 3:30 p.m. sitting in the garden of Sunny Care Home. One of the attendants of the facility went looking for Walter to give him his afternoon medication and could not find him. The administration checked the entire facility and the streets of the suburban neighborhood surrounding the care facility and turned up nothing. It is now 7:00 p.m. and getting dark.

Questions:

- Is each missing person actually lost or just avoiding the caregiver? How urgent is the search?
- What resources would you use to conduct the search, e.g., who or what would you use?
- Where do you start searching?
- How would you search?
- Would you search at night?
- How long would you search before asking for more help?
- Do you even need to start a search?

These scenarios are typical examples of search missions conducted by search teams around the world. While the scenarios are not out of the ordinary, the theater in which they are staged is not the remote wilderness that people typically think of when they hear of a missing person. Rather they have taken place in the heavily populated and extensively developed stage set of the modern city. Locating someone in these urban areas can be daunting to the agency responsible for finding them. A system is needed. That's where this book comes in.

The reader of this book is either curious about how to go about finding lost people in the city or wants to do the finding. When someone becomes lost, members of the community have a compelling need to help. People who volunteer on search and rescue missions may do so for a number of reasons, but the primary reason is usually to satisfy that need to help someone who is most likely confused, in trouble and needs assistance. Maybe we do it for compassion, to bring closure, or to right what we perceive as a wrong. In any case, finding the lost person isn't always easy, especially in the vast, busy, and confusing infrastructure of our cities and towns where all kinds of hazards exist and the sheer number of people makes it hard to pick out the lost person from the crowd. The need for special procedures and techniques to find that person in the urban environment is the impetus for this book.

The Need for this Book

Most of the world's population lives and works in cities. In 1910, 40% of the United States population lived in urban areas and 60% in rural areas. By 1990, in the United States, the urban population was up to 75%, and in 2000, the count rose again to 79%. As more people move to the city, the possibility of missing person reports increases. Estimates of the number of people missing range widely. For example, the State of California Department of Justice averages over 100,000 missing person reports a year. Most of these are in urban areas and are resolved at almost the same time as they are reported. However, there are many reports that take longer to close or are still open.

People go missing all the time, but they are usually found by friends or relatives, or they return on their own; this is termed "self-rescue." A young child wanders away from his mother at a store. A teenager does not return home when expected. An adult doesn't show up for work. All of these are potentially serious incidents., but they frequently resolve themselves without intervention beyond the immediate family, friends or neighbors. But what happens when the person doesn't return on his own and cannot be found by family, friends or neighbors? The public then calls law enforcement.

The task of searching for missing persons in urban areas usually falls to the local law enforcement agency, although this varies by state and city. Most city police departments have protocols for responding to missing person incidents and that response may include some basic search procedures. When the initial search is not successful and must be expanded, the police department may not have the knowledge, experience or resources to conduct a systematic, thorough area search. Some cities call in local wilderness search teams who know these search procedures. However, these wilderness search teams discover that simply using a wilderness tactic is not appropriate for the urban environment. Both the police and the professional search teams have the best interests of the missing person at heart. Their efforts can be enhanced if they are able to call on search techniques especially designed for the urban environment, which are described in this book

What is "Urban Search"?

"Urban search," as used in this book, refers to the process of finding someone who is reported missing in the urban environment. Before the term "urban environment" is defined, however, it is necessary to differentiate "urban search" from what is commonly known in the United States and Canada as "urban search and rescue."

Searches for missing people in cities have been conducted for years and until recently there has been a need to differentiate them from searches conducted in the wilderness environment. In the 1980s the United States government, under the auspices of the Federal Emergency Management Agency (FEMA), became involved in disaster work. FEMA established local Urban Search and Rescue (USAR) teams and coined the term "urban search and rescue," which meant activities associated with finding and rescuing people who were affected by major, widespread disasters. USAR teams were then called to assist local agencies in disasters, such as earthquakes. Currently, most USAR teams are associated with a fire service. The environment in which these searches typically take place is a collapsed building; thus "urban search and rescue" can be considered shorthand for looking for and evacuating people trapped in collapsed buildings. One could more broadly define the urban search and rescue environment as any major structural disaster. (The Hurricane Katrina disaster of August 2005 added flood search and rescue to the mission of USAR teams, however their primary function is still building search and rescue.)

In this book, however, the term "urban search" is used to represent the ordinary, everyday search for a missing person in any of the areas included within the definition of urban environment. "Urban search and rescue" as defined here involves the unknown and requires further investigation. Urban rescue techniques are not discussed in this book because they are already well developed by local emergency agencies, particularly fire departments. When a missing person is found who needs to be rescued, the appropriate agency is called. This book, therefore, focuses on searching in the urban environment, or simply "urban search."

Who Is in Charge?

In most areas of the United States and Canada, it is the local law enforcement agency's jurisdiction and responsibility to conduct the urban search; however, other governmental agencies may be in charge, depending on state laws and local protocols. In this book, the assumption is that the search function is delegated to the city police department, the county sheriff's department, or to another appropriate law enforcement agency having jurisdiction over the search area. Local laws or statutes dictate who has jurisdictional authority to oversee search and rescue activities with a given area. The term used in search and rescue for this entity is "responsible agency."

Chapter 2. The Environment

Most people have a basic idea of what an "urban environment" means, although the definition can be widely interpreted. At one end of the spectrum is a "pure urban" setting of large, dense cities such as Manhattan and San Francisco. At the other end are the sparsely settled rural regions or recreation areas such as Great Smoky Mountain National Park and Yosemite National Park, which border a "pure wilderness" setting.

The United States Census defines "urban" for the 1990 census as comprising all territory, population, and housing units in urbanized areas and in places of 2,500 or more persons, specifically those places which are incorporated as cities, villages, boroughs and towns.

In terms of ecoregions, "urban areas" are areas where the natural environment has been altered by man to make travel and navigation easier (i.e., the construction of roads) and/or natural vegetation is removed and replaced with structures, pavement or landscaping.

The search scene may encompass "canyons" created by downtown office buildings, suburban housing tracts, open space, city parks, back alleys, easements and rights of way. Many people believe it is not possible to be truly lost in a populated place, but to a very young or a confused elderly person, an urban area can be just as much a wilderness as the remotest regions of the United States.

Thus, the urban environment can be defined by three characteristics:

1. There are a significant number of **people** occupying the land.
2. The area has been significantly developed with **structures and facilities**.
3. There are **roads** and **easy means of travel**.

Whereas wilderness areas have few people and few buildings, urban areas have high concentrations of both. There are gray areas, of course, as most urban areas also have patches of open space such as parks or green belts; however in general the overall density of building is greater than one structure per acre. In this book, the definition of urban environment includes suburban developments as well as such places as campgrounds and second-home developments that may be located in rural or back country areas.

Urban development can be divided into two major categories by function—where people live and where they go to do other things, i.e., residential and non-residential development. Residential areas are important because that is where people frequently go missing. Typical **residential development** will be discussed in more detail later.

Residential areas

- Suburban (bedroom) communities
- Retirement communities
- Multi-family (apartment) buildings
- Redevelopment areas which may include high-crime
- Mixed residential/commercial neighborhoods
- Institutions (care facilities, skilled nursing homes, hospitals, jails, barracks)
- Trailer parks
- Seasonal communities at popular recreational areas
- Temporary housing such as tent or RV camp grounds

Non-residential areas are more varied; for example, employment centers, schools, shopping centers, and recreation areas. Following are examples of typical places where people may be missing from or where they may be found:

Non-residential areas

- Second-home vacation communities
- Shopping centers and malls
- School and college campuses
- Business parks/office buildings or complexes
- Industrial complexes
- Entertainment or sports venues
- Amusement parks
- Urban parks
- Transportation centers and stations
- Temporary events that have large attendance
- Construction sites
- Urban infrastructure facilities
- Mixed-use communities

It is important to keep in mind that among all these urban areas there can be extensive forested or wild, undeveloped areas in which the same search tactics can be used as in wilderness areas. Searchers must be able to quickly adapt their techniques to the terrain they encounter during their search.

The city is an ever-changing complex organism of buildings, streets, signs, cars and, most of all, people. There are many more places in which a person could be hidden from view or be unrecognized among the crowd. In addition, the sheer number of people means more possible scenarios to consider in determining what the person was doing when they became lost. People who become lost in the wilderness are generally in the wilderness area by choice. The searcher will often have enough information to know what the person was doing. However, in an urban environment, the possibilities of what a person would have been doing encompass all manner of human activity, including crime and intentional disappearance. The search manager must be able to sort through these scenarios in order to determine which resources should be utilized in the search.

One last difference between urban and wilderness areas must be noted: urban areas are overlaid with a complex system of streets, roads, paths, and other transportation features that permit easy travel by both the subject and the searchers. The significance of this difference to the search planner will be discussed later.

Experienced search managers are now faced with the challenge of searching in an environment that may be familiar to them yet does not necessarily lend itself to the same tactics used to find people in the backcountry. Searchers may live near or even in big cities but their entire search experience may be limited to the wilderness areas surrounding their community. What would it take to search a suburban housing tract or a canyon of high-rise buildings? The hard surfaces of the city do not yield many clues. Additionally, there are many more natural and man-made places a person could be concealed, which makes searching these areas extremely difficult and time consuming. For instance, every trash bin must be thoroughly investigated. Multi-story buildings add a three-dimensional aspect to the challenge. To search just a single high-rise office building adequately may require several teams working all day. Sewer systems and utility tunnels form intricate underground mazes that defy the best navigational skills. These examples illustrate the complexity of the urban environment.

Common Places for Searches

Listed below are some of the typical areas that might be searched within the urban environment, along with some of their characteristics. Keep in mind that these all could occur singularly or in many combinations.

Downtown high-rise buildings

- City environment with heavy pedestrian and vehicle traffic during the day.
- Easy access to public transportation.
- Most travel ways are in a grid pattern and easy to navigate.
- Buildings occupied during the work day.
- Low population density at night, except around restaurants, bars and night entertainment venues.
- Security access required to some office buildings.

Suburban

- Single-family to high-density multi-family housing.
- Traffic is heavy during the commute hours.
- Highest occupancy during early morning, evening and on weekends.
- Homes occupied during the day, often by families with young children.
- Planned communities with meandering streets and cul-de-sacs.

Retirement communities

- Communities within the much larger city community.
- Population may be as large as 10,000, consisting of mostly retired people.
- Usually contains large open space, golf courses, walking paths, meandering roads, recreational facilities, infirmary/hospital facilities, and gated access to community.

School/college campuses

- Classroom environment for pre-school, kindergarten through high school and college, university, or trade schools.
- Includes large and small, public and private, trade and specialized institutions.
- Pre-school through high school institutions are usually highly monitored and regulated. (Note: teachers and administration can be an excellent source of good information.)

Military bases and government installations

- Usually large, secured complexes for training, housing, equipment storage and logistical headquarters that can cover several acres or square miles. Decommissioned, abandoned facilities can create hazards and become attractive nuisances.

Redevelopment areas

- Usually run-down high-density populous areas.
- Large volume of pedestrian and vehicular traffic at all hours of the day and night.
- Can include encounters with persons carrying and using weapons. Drug dealers and gangs may be present.
- Also includes homeless camps in and around the cities.

Business parks/office buildings or complexes

- Usually seen as clusters of buildings from low- to mid- and high-rise structures.
- Surrounded by large parking lots, green belts, water features, ponds or lakes.
- Low- to non-polluting non-industrial industries.
- Buildings occupied during the normal workday.

Shopping centers/malls

- Retail shops found in strip malls with a few stores, up to large, multi-unit enclosed mega-malls with one or more hub stores.
- Can contain multi-screen cinema complexes, amusement areas (video arcades), food courts and entertainment stages.
- Occupied during business hours.
- Also can serve as a "hang out" for children.

Industrial complexes (light and heavy)

- Small, simple "garage-with-store front" type to large multi-building complexes.
- May have large employee parking lots, secure access, loading docks, warehouses, and intra-building transportation arteries for materials, products and personnel.
- Occupied during business hours or up to 24 hours a day.
- Can pose safety considerations if hazardous materials are stored on site.

Mixed-use communities

- A combination of residential and non-residential occupancies similar to those described above.

- May be difficult to discern the demarcation of the buildings or uses.

Urban parks

- Includes walking, running and bicycle paths meandering through areas of lawns, trees, sports playing fields, pavilions and water features (lakes, ponds and streams).

- Can also be frequented by inter-city homeless persons and serve as sites for their encampments.

Large entertainment and sports venues
- Large parking lots, concessions.
- Occupied during events.
- High security during most events and minimal when not in use.

Amusement parks
- Large temporary and permanent theme parks, water parks, zoos, boardwalks, and county/state fairs.
- Usually associated with a high concentration of people, many from out of the area.
- Family separations ("lost parents") are common.

Transportation centers
- Railways, train stations, bus stations, street bus stops, airports, marinas, shipping ports, subways, freeways and highways. The major difficulty here is that the missing subject may have used any of these modes of travel to leave the search area.

Other large gatherings/events
- Brief, planned or unplanned parades, marches and parties.

Other man-made structures
- These include open drainage ditches, culverts, storm drains, sewer pipes, flood control channels, canals, and water or sewage treatment plants.

Other institutions
- Hospitals, jails, churches, homeless shelters, domestic violence shelters, as well as day care centers for pre-school, after school and the elderly.

Construction sites

- Any of the above-listed environments under construction, including open trenches, foundations, concrete, steel or wood structural skeletons and unfinished interior spaces.

- Construction sites can be attractive hazards (or nuisances) and pose major safety hazards.

Night versus Day Search Operations

Searching at night in the wilderness may be somewhat hazardous to the searcher, but the hazards are usually limited to not being able to see inanimate features such as uneven terrain, trail drop-offs, or tree branches. In the city, the nighttime dangers are different—speeding cars on dark streets, residents who don't expect people to be poking around their homes and back yards, and unfriendly dogs. In addition, the ability to search using typical wilderness attraction techniques such as calling the subject's name or sounding car horns is limited in the nighttime city where such behavior might result in a call to law enforcement. The search team must adjust its tactics to fit the environment.

The night presents an opportunity for a wilderness searcher because the missing person usually stops to take shelter and wait for dawn before proceeding, allowing the searcher to continue tracking or searching while he is hunkered down. In the city, the missing person may continue to travel because the area may be well-lit and accessible. The missing person may also find impromptu shelter when the weather is bad, so the urgency of searching in an urban environment is not as great as it is in the wilderness.

Finally, search operations can affect the neighborhood in which they are conducted. Residents object to the increased traffic, blocked off roads and, at night, the noise from generators and bright lights of the command post. While this should not restrict the search efforts, it can be a public relations problem.

The final decision to search at night rests with the law enforcement agency in charge. Many times the agency will curtail the search at night not wishing to tie up extensive resources based on the assumption that the subject will appear in the morning light like "Little Bo Peep's sheep." However, many times subjects do not show up in the morning. Often, the subject may have been missing an additional 10 to 12 hours, may still be lost and confused, has and may have missed several meals and may not have taken medication. Moreover, the subject may still be on the move and by morning already be many miles away. Therefore, it is vital that night operations be strongly considered when there is any possibility that the lost person is in a life threatening situation.

The daytime urban environment presents a different problem: too many people can distract search efforts, especially if the search takes place where people work, shop or travel. On the other hand, a search can benefit from an abundance of people, who could be enlisted to help in the search for the lost person. These factors must be considered when developing the search plan.

Environmental Hazards and Dangers

Searchers should be aware of and cautious around environmental hazards found in urban areas. Some of the most common urban search hazards were mentioned in the paragraphs above: traffic, people and dogs. Foot, canine and bicycle search teams can suddenly encounter vehicles as they walk or ride along streets or when they try to cross streets while looking to the side of the road for the subject or clues. Gang members can pose a threat if the searcher inadvertently wanders into their "territory." Dogs are everywhere and can be unpredictable. Web resources that offer pointers on how to handle aggressive dogs are listed in the box below.

Other urban hazards include contaminated environments such as sewers and storm drains, trash containers, trash areas, abandoned buildings and cars, homeless encampments, industrial areas, sand and gravel excavation areas, and chemical storage areas. Recognition of the local hazards should be a part of any urban search plan.

Some missing persons, especially children and people with developmental disabilities, may enter dangerous or restricted areas because they cannot read the warning signs or don't recognize the danger. Searchers should be briefed and take extra safety precautions when entering and working in such areas.

Dealing with dogs—Web resources

http://www.ccc.govt.nz/animals/DealingWithAggressiveDogs.asp

http://www.hsus.org/pets/pet_care/dog_care/stay_dog_bite_free/index.html

http://www.dogbitelaw.com/#Dog%20Bite%20Victims

Chapter 3. The Missing Person

Categories of Missing Persons

When a person is missing, it can be useful to try to determine why they are missing, ideally using the reporting party (RP) interview and investigation, which will likely determine how the search is focused. Categorizing a missing person may be difficult, however, because it requires knowing not only what was in the missing person's mind when they disappeared but what events have occurred that would contribute to the disappearance. Following are four basic categories into which most missing persons can be classified, in order of ascending jeopardy to their lives.

Voluntary

Voluntary missing persons intend to be missing, at least in the beginning. (Sometimes they change their mind when difficulties appear.) They include runaway children, runaway adults, suicidal people, fugitives from justice, and those who do not want to be found by the party who reported them missing. Keep in mind that a voluntary missing person is missing only to the person who expects them to be there. The relationship between the reporting party and the missing person should be examined to try to establish if the person is truly missing or just evading searchers.

Not Lost

Persons who are not lost do not appear where and when the reporting party expects them, thus they are reported missing. A person who is missing but not lost may be an innocent victim of miscommunication between himself and the person who reported him missing. Examples of such miscommunication include not appearing at an agreed upon time and place, coming home later than expected, or altering a standard routine and thus worrying the reporting party. The missing person may be in a situation of which the reporting party is unaware.

Lost

A lost person is disoriented to his environment and cannot reason his way out of the predicament that has resulted in him being missing. People with Alzheimer's disease, mental retardation and young children are typical lost persons in the urban environment. Becoming lost in a city is not as risky as it is in the wilderness, but these particular types of missing persons commonly avoid strangers or "hide out" and can be difficult to find. Although they may get their bearings and begin to find their way, they may become disoriented again.

Note: Throughout this book the term "missing person" is often used to refer to the subject. In an urban setting, the search manager usually does not know if the person is lost or not lost until the search is over. Then, in most cases, the missing person is not lost.

At-Risk

A person may be assumed to be at some risk by virtue of being missing, however, in some cases, the missing person may be considered to be at relatively high risk. Additionally, the search plan for an at-risk missing person is different from other types of missing persons. Following are examples of at-risk missing persons (more than one factor may apply).

At-risk

- Children less than 14 years old
- Elderly who cannot care for themselves
- Persons with Alzheimer's disease (or dementia)
- Persons with mental impairments
- Persons with pre-existing medical conditions
- Despondent or suicidal persons
- Persons subject to extreme environmental conditions

---

*The most at-risk missing person is a suspected abducted child
or the victim of a kidnapping.*

*All efforts must be expended to find this missing person
as soon as possible.*

In all cases, when the missing person has a medical or mental condition that requires treatment, his or her doctor should be contacted to establish the risk.

A tool long used in wilderness search and rescue management is the Search Urgency Chart. It was developed to determine relative urgency based on seven factors in a wilderness environment. It has been adapted for the urban environment and is called the Urban Search Urgency Chart.

Urban Search Urgency Chart

If a search condition does exist the following chart will help determine the relative urgency of the situation. Priority factors are rated from 1 to 3 for each factor category. The lower the priority factors, the more urgent the need to respond. At the end, calculate the total and find the sum under the Factors Sum Response. The lower the number, the more urgent the need to respond.

Urban Search Urgency Chart

Priority Factors	Rating
Subject Profile Age	
Very Young	1
Very Old	1
Other	2-3
Medical condition	
Known or suspected ill or injured	1-2
Healthy	3
Known Fatality	3
Number of Subjects	
One Alone	1
More than one (unless separation suspected)	2-3
Subject Knowledge of Area	
Memory Problems	1
New and does not know the area, no map	1
Visits area occasionally, no map	1-2
Experienced, not familiar with area	2
Lives, works and/or intimate knowledge of area	3
Weather Profile	
Existing hazardous weather	1
Predicted hazardous weather (8 hrs or less)	1-2
Predicted hazardous weather (more than 8 hrs)	2
No hazardous weather predicted	3

Equipment (may or may not apply in urban environment)	
Inadequate for environment	1
Questionable for environment	1-2
Adequate for environment	3
Hazards Profile	
Know hazardous area or attractive nuisance	1
Few or no hazards	2-3
Clothing	
Insufficient/Inadequate for conditions	1
Adequate for the conditions	2
Excellent for the conditions	2-3
Time	
Reliable, punctual (rarely late)	1
Usually reliable and on time	2-3
Questionable to unreliable	3
Circumstance	
Missing at-risk (dementia, abduction)	1
Adequate information low risk	2
Questionable information/not in area	2-3
A history of being missing (runaway)	3
Physical Condition	
Physically impaired, no aid equipment	1
Physically impaired with aid equipment	2
No physical impairment	2-3
Factor Sum Response	**Rating**
High priority emergency response	11-14
Moderate response	15-18
Low priority response	19-24
Reevaluate search situation or missing person	25-33

Note: Elapsed time from when the subject "went missing"—along with the "political" sensitivity of the circumstances—will have the effect of increasing the relative urgency. Also, any category with a one (1) may be considered a High Priority Emergency or Moderate response regardless of the total.

Common Types of Missing Person Searches

Search management begins with the preplan and the vulnerability assessment. In assessing the vulnerability of people to become missing within the local urban area, it is useful to examine the most common types of searches that have been previously conducted, based on the type of behavior exhibited by the missing persons. Some types of searches occur more frequently than others, allowing the search manager to preplan for future incidents of the same type.

Persons with Dementia

This type of search includes persons with Alzheimer's disease, developmental disabilities or memory/mental dysfunction. Perhaps the most common type of urban search is for the "Alzheimer's patient," which has become the generic term for persons with dementia or memory loss associated with various diseases and infections, strokes, head injuries, drugs, and nutritional deficiencies. Alzheimer's disease is a type of dementia, related to a number of other diseases that cause memory loss. People with developmental disabilities have a mental and/or physical capacity that was affected at birth or early in their lives. People whose mental capacity is affected are also referred to as having mental retardation. These people form another large group of missing persons.

Missing persons with memory or mental dysfunction have the tendency to walk away from or wander from their care facilities, unnoticed by their caregivers. The health care industry, driven by economics, has moved farther away from in-hospital care toward long-term care ranging from skilled nursing facilities to in-home care. Other missing persons may be living with family members who are not prepared or equipped to deal with long-term around-the-clock care. Many long-term care facilities provide independent and assisted living and thus less restrictive care for the resident. As the symptoms of dementia increase, including the urge to wander, care for these patients becomes more difficult. In addition, decreasing physical ability and health makes it imperative to find the missing person before serious harm befalls them. Searching through extensive residential areas, especially large retirement communities can take a substantial amount of time and resources. In the case of elderly missing persons, half the residents of the retirement community may fit the description and profile.

A more comprehensive description and special considerations regarding missing persons suffering from Alzheimer's disease, other types of dementia and mental retardation are covered in Chapter 11.

Missing or Abducted Children

When children are missing many different scenarios are possible. The child could just be lost, have voluntarily left, have been abducted or worse. According to the FBI's National Crime Information Center (NCIC), Missing Person File, missing children make up more then 85 to 90% of missing person reports. About 800,000 cases are recorded a year; 90 to 95% of these are listed as "Juvenile" (law enforcement enter most missing child cases in "juvenile," including some non-family abductions where there is no evidence of foul play) or "Endangered" (missing and in the company of another person under circumstances indicating that his/her physical safety is in danger). In California, about 100,000 cases are recorded a year; 95% are listed as "Run-Away," cases in which the parent/guardian does not know where the child is, and contacted law enforcement out of concern. The majority of these reported incidents are resolved in minutes by "yelling out the back door," looking down the street or with a few phone calls. Once an official report of a missing child is made it becomes the jurisdiction of the local law enforcement agency.

Attractive hazards (or nuisances) play a part in missing children cases. Children playing in the trunks of old cars, inside refrigerators, or in and around construction sites can become injured or trapped. These hazardous areas may be difficult to recognize or locate and may require extensive investigation and resources.

Probably the biggest increase in requests for search and rescue services in urban areas involves stranger child abduction cases. The Polly Klaas kidnapping in 1993, one of the more publicized cases, was one of about five child abduction cases in the San Francisco Bay area since 1988. After she was abducted from her residence, the search for Polly Klaas continued off and on for several months and involved thousands of hours of searching by trained searchers, not to mention the outpouring of untrained volunteer searchers. Polly's body was eventually found after extensive investigation efforts by specialized teams of FBI investigators and other law enforcement personnel. The murderer was eventually tried and convicted, however other similar cases are still open and the subject of continual investigation and search efforts. Search managers are now expected to be knowledgeable on how to manage a child abduction search. Additional considerations are described in detail in Chapter 11.

Sneak-Aways

Occasionally, we are tasked to look for someone who really is not lost. For example, a parent checks on her child before going to bed and finds the child missing. The parent panics, possibly because of the heightened awareness of abductions. She immediately calls the local law enforcement authority. The search and rescue team will get a call to assist in the search. These searches can last all night with no results. It is discovered later that the child was not actually lost but just did not want to be found. He had sneaked away to meet his friends. In another case, the child may have run away from home for personal reasons such as not wanting to face the wrath of the parents after receiving a poor report card from school. Or an adult sneaks away from his spouse for a "rendezvous" and doesn't want to be found.

These are sometimes called "bastard" searches or non-searches. These incidents will become investigative cases. Good investigation may reveal the intentions of the missing person so that the search effort may be cancelled before too many resources are committed.

Despondent and Suicidal Persons

Lifestyles in large, fast-paced cities have also created stressful environments that have resulted in an increase in missing despondent persons who may be contemplating suicide. Some despondent persons look for open spaces. Others will deal with their troubles in their home or garage. Some want to be found, while others do not. Since it is difficult to know for certain the person's motivation, all such incidents should be treated as "at-risk" emergencies. Detailed information about despondent persons can be found in Chapter 11.

To plan how to approach the search for despondent persons there is a need to determine the intent to commit suicide. This will be revealed through good investigation.

Expressions of intent to commit suicide

✓ An explicit verbal or nonverbal expression of an intent to kill themselves

✓ Implicit or indirect evidence of an intent to die, such as:

• Preparations for death inappropriate to or unexpected in the context of the missing person's life (setting out life insurance policies)

Continued on next page ...

- Expression of farewell (contacting old friends), the desire to die or an acknowledgment of impending death
- Expression of hopelessness
- Expression of great emotional or physical pain or distress
- Efforts to procure or learn more about means of death, practice or rehearse fatal behavior, preparing precautions to avoid being found or to avoid rescue
- Previous suicide attempt, or threat of suicide
- Stressful events or significant losses (actual or threatened), or serious depression or mental disorder
- A means to carry out the intent such as missing medications, weapons, length of ropes

If the missing person left a note, it may be difficult to distinguish whether it signifies a call for help or a true intent to follow through an attempt to end their life. This is where the assistance of those specifically trained in personal crisis intervention will be of help.

In cases in which despondent missing persons choose to travel, it is useful to determine the mode of transportation they used. Walking will limit the search area; if the person drove a vehicle, the search area could be limitless. The search may not be initiated by law enforcement until the vehicle is located.

Inadequate Information Search

Sometimes a search must be initiated with little accurate information. For example, a child tells a parent that he is going for a walk. The parent is so engrossed in his own activity, such as watching a ball game on television, that they do not pay attention to what the child said or ask him where he is going. Time marches on, it starts to get dark, and the parent suddenly realizes the child is gone. The parent looks for the child, having no idea where he might be. When the parent is interviewed he cannot remember what the child was wearing, who the friends are or, maybe the color of the child's hair. Dealing with such incidents can be particularly frustrating, but the search must be undertaken with whatever information is available.

Inactive Search

Consider the following possible scenario where the agency does not take action on a missing person report. The local beat officer investigating the report of a missing person does not recognize the seriousness of the situation and just files the report. The next shift supervisor comes in and finds the missing person report is 12 to 24 hours old and little or nothing has been done. He decides to call in additional resources such as the search and rescue team to avoid any recriminations. Without good information on the missing person and the circumstances of him being missed, the field search concentrates on checking the high probability areas to make sure the missing person is not there. Intensive searching is not undertaken, because of limited resources. Unless the person turns up on his own, the search effort is frustrated and the whole incident must be escalated. The delay has now resulted in a massive search, one that could be unsuccessful and subject the agency to serious charges of neglecting to search.

In the past, some law enforcement agencies have taken little or no action on missing person reports on the assumption that they will resolve themselves when the person returns on his own. Many agencies have waited between 24 to 48 hours from the time of the report before any action was taken. Because of this apathy, lack of action and resulting litigation against these agencies legislation has been enacted. Current legislation affecting most law enforcement jurisdictions, now require an urgency assessment for risk and dissemination of information on the incident through a "Be On the Look Out" (BOLO) report within four hours of the reported missing person. This also requires input into the National Crime and Information Center (NCIC) database within the same time period (see Chapter 5, p. 60).

An immediate hasty field search by available resources should be started if the missing person is determined to be at risk due to age, mental or health conditions. It should be stressed that every missing person report should be considered serious and some action should be taken to determine whether the report is real and whether a field search should be undertaken.

Other Types of Searches

Evidence Search

Another common request that search and rescue teams are increasingly being asked to perform in urban areas is to search for evidence that may have been left behind after a crime has been committed or suspected to have been committed. Typically, this occurs after detectives or police officers have conducted a preliminary search and have not found what they are looking for. Searchers may be tasked to do criminal searches and be required to use Type III (closed grid) search techniques, to look for such things as weapons, shell casings, clothing, stolen goods or even body parts. It should also be noted that any of the other types of searches described above could potentially end up becoming a criminal case and care must be taken to document every phase of the search, both to help solve a case and to provide evidence for a future trial.

Recurring Follow-up Search

Another unique aspect of urban searches is that they may go on for months or even years. After the initial search of neighborhoods, there may be little or no solid clues found. The search is suspended or reduced to a limited level, and management and investigation are continued by the original responsible law enforcement agency. A few days or even months later a tip leads to an area that was not previously searched and the team is recalled to resume the effort. This on-again, off-again cycle can be very discouraging and demoralizing if continued for many months, especially where the missing person is eventually found dead.

Cancelled or False Search

While the aforementioned types of searches can be legitimate, real emergencies, it is also possible that they can lead to cancelled or aborted searches, non-searches that never actually get started, the result of a series of misunderstandings. For example, a missing child call-out was made because the father picked up his child from school and forgot to tell his wife. The wife showed up to pick up the child, could not find him, panicked, called the police, who then called the search team and the search began. The father showed up with his missing son and wondered what all the fuss was about.

Another example of a non-search is the case of misinterpretation by a loved one that the missing person is despondent and has left to commit suicide. The person turns up a few hours into the search and the search team finds that all he wanted to do was to be alone for a while. An unfortunate fallout of these incidents is the "cry-wolf syndrome." After a series of false alarms, search team morale deteriorates and fewer searchers turn up at call-outs. Good investigation may help decrease, if not eliminate, the non-search.

Bastard Search

This term is applied to a search that progresses on the assumption that the missing person is involuntarily missing though it later turns out that he or she voluntarily left to avoid discovery. Usually a bastard search involves adults who are hiding from someone or some situation for personal reasons. They are called bastard searches because they fall within the dictionary definition of an adjective that describes something "lacking genuineness or authority; false."

Chapter 4. Preplanning

The well-known philosopher Snoopy, from Charles Schultz's Peanuts comic strip, once said, "Ten minutes before the party is not the time to learn how to dance." When there is a report of a lost or missing person the responding authority needs to be prepared, ready to go and have a well thought out "preplan" on how to manage the incident. Efficiency, the best use of time and resources, is the key to a successful search. The preplan is a managerial reference document that answers the following questions:

Preplan Information

✓ What authority or agency is responsible for the management of missing person searches?

✓ Who is in charge of the search and what are the lines of authority (e.g., organization chart, chain of command)?

✓ What agency resources, both personnel and equipment, will be utilized?

✓ What search management system and local protocols will be used?

✓ What communication system will be used?

✓ Who will perform the investigation and interviews?

✓ What documentation will be used?

✓ Who will be performing institutional checks?

✓ Who will be putting out BOLO announcements and in what format?

✓ Who will be inputting information into the National Crime Information Center (NCIC)?

✓ Who has the authority to call in outside resources for help in the search effort?

✓ What are the outside resources available in the area and what are their dispatch procedures?

✓ What areas within the jurisdiction may be hazardous and require special resources?

✓ Who will perform the rescue/medical function, if necessary?

This is only a partial list of items that would be included in the preplan. Further information will need to be added as conditions in the area change as new or changed urban environments change. For a good preplan to work it must be read and used. The preplan needs to be a living document that is updated regularly, flexible and adaptable to any situation. See Appendix C for an example of an urban preplan.

Vulnerability Assessment

"The SAR [Vulnerability] Assessment is defined as a systematic investigation of search and/or rescue situations that have [occurred] or may occur in a local area. This report/analysis is usually appended to a jurisdiction's SAR Preplan." (Stoffel 2006, 58). The purpose of the vulnerability assessment is to determine how many and what kind of SAR incidents have occurred, or might occur in the future, in order to properly plan for their management. Taken into account are not only the historic data but an evaluation of geographic and demographic factors that would change the need for SAR missions in the future.

The vulnerability assessment lists all the possible environments and types of searches with which the agency may be involved, including the following:

Possible Environments
✓ Open spaces and parks
✓ Walking trails
✓ Skilled nursing homes
✓ Board and care facilities
✓ Day care centers (both child and adult)
✓ Local transit locations and routes
✓ High crime areas
✓ Common attractive nuisances
✓ Business districts and shopping malls
✓ Entertainment/sport venues and complexes
✓ Schools, hospitals, jails and other institutions
✓ Recurring events (parades, fairs, etc.)

Since so many urban searches originate from residential areas, particularly the person's residence, it may not be possible to specifically identify those areas that may be vulnerable to missing person searches. Experience in past incidents may be helpful.

Note the times of day and the days of the week when these locations will be of greater consideration for searches. For example, suburban residential areas would normally be most vulnerable on weeknights and weekends, when residents are home. Business centers, on the other hand, are busy during the day and vacant nights and weekends. Obtain the phone numbers of security offices, safety offices, special contacts and facility management personnel. (These may be obtained from local police or fire departments.) Remember, the urban environment is constantly changing, so the assessment should be reviewed, updated, added to and corrected with the most current information available.

Additional information can be obtained by tapping into Geographic Information System (GIS) used by many law enforcement jurisdictions. GIS is used to build maps of high crime areas and analyze data collected for use in various operational situations, which would include management tools to aid with better decision-making and the best possible deployment of resources.

Listing all the possible sites and scenarios in a large city can be daunting. For example, within the City of San Diego, there are 170 schools; within San Diego County there are over 500. It would be a monumental task to contact all the schools to assess their vulnerability or to find out if they could be used for a search base in the future. If the information is relatively easy to obtain from the sources, it can be kept in a computer file for reference when an incident occurs. The contact can then be made to the specific resource.

Once the areas and possible types of searches have been developed, start working on the possible scenarios that the search team may encounter and start preparing preplans on how to manage each one. For example, if there is a high concentration of skilled long-term care facilities in a specific area, it would be wise to drive around the neighborhoods, contact the facilities, talk to the staff, and find out their protocol for handling situations where residents with dementia have "wandered." Also, school districts may have district-wide protocols for dealing with missing children that can be incorporated in the preplan. There are several preventative search and rescue programs in place and information available to help alleviate the need to call the search team; for example, Hug-a-Tree (www.gpsar.org/hugatree.html). A Web search under "preventive SAR" or "preventative SAR" will bring up Web sites with materials and educational information on precautions, awareness and survivability. Make notes and include them in the preplanning binder for future reference.

Once the Vulnerability Assessment establishes a need for future search and rescue capabilities, the next step is to prepare the preplan, listing how the agency will handle the missing person search. The question then must be asked: "Do we have the resources to manage a search in any of the environments, situations or scenarios mentioned above?" Following are suggested elements of the preplan.

Resources

In order to run a search many resources are required. The preplan should include lists of resources available locally, regionally and at the state and federal levels. Included in the list would be contact names, alert procedures, phone numbers, qualifications, limitations, availability and typical response times (both during the week and on weekends).

Resources for urban searching can be classified into four categories:

1.   Human and Animal Resources (animal resources always include a handler)

2.   Physical Resources

3.   Information Resources

4.   Specialized Resources

Human and Animal Resources

Off-Duty Personnel and Reserve Officers
These resources, found within the law enforcement agency, can be mobilized quickly. The preplan should include call-out procedures for those full-time and reserve officers who are not currently on duty when the incident starts and who are available for a search. A select group can be trained for search missions and their management and form the foundation of the first unit to be called.

Search and Rescue Teams
Some law enforcement agencies, particularly in the western United States, have supplemented their resources with organized volunteer search and rescue teams. These unpaid professionals are typically associated with the sheriff's department, which has accepted responsibility for search and rescue within the county or the State Office of Emergency Services (OES)/SAR Coordination Office with responsibility for the state. Coordination teams are highly trained in search operations and management and normally work in the rural and wilderness environment. These teams vary in size from a handful of members

to close to a hundred and include specialized resources that are discussed at the end of this chapter.

As the rural environment becomes more urbanized, wilderness SAR teams have found themselves responding more frequently to requests for urban searches because they have been trained as searchers and observers. They know how to find things and organize a search effort. City police departments that do not have their own volunteer SAR teams have begun to call the sheriff's and/or OES/SAR Coordination teams to assist them in searching for missing persons.

We strongly recommend that any responsible agency that experiences a significant number of urban searches (more than 1 per month) utilize a trained, experienced and well-equipped team to conduct those searches. The team must be able to respond quickly and begin the field search as soon as possible after being summoned.

The best solution is to develop a volunteer unit affiliated or associated with the responsible agency. Some agencies may elect to summon a volunteer, non-affiliated wilderness search and rescue group familiar with urban searching. In any case, the unit must:

1. Have a sufficient number of members to conduct a search and be able to respond immediately with personal and unit gear.

2. Have an experienced, professional search management staff, knowledgeable in all phases of urban searching.

3. Have good internal management and leadership.

4. Conduct regular classroom and field training.

Ideally, this primary responding unit should incorporate all the resources needed for a typical urban search, including canine units.

Urban Law Enforcement Agencies
Many urban law enforcement agencies (police departments) are not trained or equipped to manage a large search operation; however, they may be responsible according to state laws or other statutes. When an established search team is requested to assist a police department, it needs to be aware that the police sometimes have a tough time understanding what search management is all about or even how the Incident Command System works. Therefore, it is incumbent on the leaders of the team to approach these agencies and educate them about the team's abilities and resources. For teams made up primarily of volunteers, this task may be difficult. Formal presentations to these agen-

cies, with an emphasis on "we are here to help" and the hat-in-hand are good approaches. Encouraging the agency to call the team when they first get the report of a missing person will greatly increase the chance of success. In some cases, the agencies will recognize the advantages of a trained search team, and will bend over backwards and allow the team to manage the search directly, with the agency—although still overall responsible for the search—providing an oversight or support role.

Outside Resources/Mutual Aid Arrangements
The preplan should also include contacts to obtain outside resources if the search must be escalated or if special resources are needed. These include nearby jurisdictions that could be counted on to provide assistance through mutual aid agreements, as well as state and federal resources. Most western states have a statewide coordinator for these resources. In California, for example, it is the state Office of Emergency Services (OES). It can quickly summon up local, state and federal agencies and coordinate their response.

Spontaneous Volunteers
Occasionally, local unsolicited citizens, sometimes referred to spontaneous volunteers (also called convergent or emergent volunteers), will offer to help search, and the search manager will be faced with a decision about how to handle these volunteers. First, there are several types of volunteers. Some want to actively look for the missing person; others want to help in a support capacity. There are "on-lookers" or "rubber-neckers" found at any disaster. Still others are family or friends who have a special interest in finding the missing person. Many will self-initiate, that is, just show up at the search and start looking on their own. In most cases these volunteers have no formal training or experience in search techniques. It is recommended that a policy and procedure be developed and included in the preplan for managing these spontaneous volunteers. Some agencies discourage or even forbid using untrained volunteers, others utilize them regularly. It may be impossible, legally or politically, to completely prohibit untrained volunteers from going out on their own to search, so there should be a system established to provide them with an answer if they volunteer.

Family and friends, because they are still a good source of information about the missing person after they have been interviewed, should be encouraged to remain available at base. They may be needed to identify clues reported by field teams, to show searchers where the missing person likes to go, or to broadcast messages from the helicopter. They are most useful in this capacity, rather than in the field. It should be noted that after several days of unproductive searching for the missing loved one it will be difficult to keep the family at the base. Sometimes it is useful to establish a liaison with the family such as a family clergyman or a police department chaplain.

People who come to help can be categorized in three types:

1. **People who have a special knowledge or talent** that can be useful, e.g., a neighborhood watch captain who knows the area well and can identify local people, particular hazards or attractive nuisances. These volunteers should be tasked into teams with experienced team leadership.

2. **People who can help with mundane tasks** like making copies of flyers or distributing them in the neighborhood. The activities of these individuals should be well monitored, controlled and documented.

3. **People who want to look for the missing person.** One method is to give them a flyer and tell them to be alert in case they spot the missing person. Do not give them too much information beyond what is on the flyer because they could unwittingly destroy clues. This is particularly true during the initial phase of the search, when hasty search crews are out trying to discover clues or signs that the missing person has passed through an area (sometimes referred to a "picking up sign"). If they want to actively participate in the search, it may be possible to discourage them by citing safety and liability issues and concerns. Some agencies may have a firm policy never to utilize volunteers in the active search, which can be invoked when the search manager is pressed. However, if the decision is to use these volunteers, have them search in unlikely places and make sure they have the appropriate basic equipment.

There is a word of caution that cannot be overly stressed, based on a few recorded missing person search incidents. Occasionally, among the volunteers who show up to assist in the search effort may be the perpetrator of a crime associated with the missing person's disappearance. His only purpose is to divert and detract form the search effort, and to cover up or destroy potential evidence left behind. Thus it is necessary to screen all potential searchers to positively identify them and learn something about their backgrounds and intensions.

If it is decided to utilize untrained volunteers, first identify who they are. They should fill out a release form with their name, address, phone number and driver's license and/or social security number. Request a picture ID and make a photocopy for the record. If no picture ID is available then a take a digital photo. (Note: Any reluctance to giving identifying information by a volunteer should be treated with some suspicion and reported to law enforcement for follow up.) This form should include the following language:

✓ The volunteer is not considered an employee of the agency.

✓ The volunteer will not receive any benefits, including pay.

✓ A release of liability and hold harmless clause in case of accident, injury or death as a result of their search efforts.

✓ Questions about the volunteer's experience.

✓ Questions about the volunteer's health.

Volunteers should be instructed to follow the directions of their assigned leader, stay within the boundaries of their team assignment and do nothing on their own.

Spontaneous volunteers can be assigned to accompany regular search teams (usually one volunteer per team) or formed into teams of their own. In any case, an experienced searcher should be assigned as the leader, and he or she should have volunteers under control at all times. It is best to utilize these teams after professional hasty teams have already covered an area. The tasks could include performing a line search to look for clues, setting up observation posts for containment, or re-searching large areas such as shopping centers. Volunteers should always work in pairs or larger groups. They should never be assigned to any remotely hazardous areas, including canyons and thick brush, and should never be allowed to enter private property except where the public is normally permitted.

It is interesting to note that new research shows the actual searching ability of volunteers is equal to those with basic ground search experience. Searchers with man-tracking experience perform better than both volunteer and basic ground searchers.

It should be noted that young people often volunteer to help look for missing friends or other young people. They tend to be untrained and ill equipped to deal with searching and, more importantly, the emotional reaction if the missing person is found deceased. Special counseling and/or Critical Incident Stress Debriefing (CISD) will need to be planned for in such an incident.

Ad Hoc Organized Volunteer Search Groups

A new phenomenon has begun to appear when the object of the search is a young person: volunteer searchers who are organized by individuals or groups not affiliated with the agency responsible for search and rescue.

A good example is the Danielle Recovery Center: Within five days of 7 year-old Danielle Van Dam being reported missing from her San Diego, California home, a member of the Laura Recovery Center Foundation for Missing Children, based near Houston, Texas, arrived in San Diego to set up a search base for volunteers. The effort continued under the name Danielle Recovery Center for almost a month until her body was found by searchers directed by the group. Similar grass-roots organizations spring up whenever the regular search teams fail to find the missing person within a few days. The question for the authorized agency is how to both utilize them and prevent the problems that could occur with unknown and untrained people. The best answer is to recognize them as a resource, assign a liaison officer with the authorized agency to work with them, and provide them with information about the search efforts to date and suggestions for search assignments. It should be clear that they are operating on their own, not under the direction of the agency.

Other organizations and foundations formed after searches in the name of the missing person (e.g., the Kevin Collins Foundation, the Polly Klaas Foundation) have been formed to support families and law enforcement agencies in locating lost or missing children. These groups have developed networks for disseminating information about the missing child over a large geographic area in a very short period of time. They can be quite effective and should be considered as a resource when the need arises.

Dog Resources and Units

Dog resources, usually called canine units, are classified according to the way they search or their primary use. The following are canine resources that may be used on urban searches:

Air-scent dogs, also called *area dogs,* are trained to run free from a leash in loose search patterns over large open spaces to find any live human scent (and sometimes recent "dead" scent) in the area, utilizing both their sense of smell and their vision. The smell of any human being will alert them to the missing person. For this reason, they are best suited for assignments in places where people are not expected to be present such as restricted areas, uninhabited areas or parks at night.

Trailing dogs are also known as *scent discrimination dogs.* These dogs are trained to sniff an article of clothing belonging to the missing person, find that scent and follow the scent trail of that specific person. These dogs are usually run on a long leash or lead.

Police K-9 dogs are sometimes known as *tracking* and *"sniff and bite" dogs*. These dogs are trained for law enforcement and military use. Some will track criminal suspect footsteps based on crushed vegetation or the suspect's adrenaline scent. These dogs are also trained to protect their handler from any aggressive action by attacking and biting the aggressor. These dogs work both on and off leash. Because of their trained aggressive behavior they may not be always suitable for missing person searches, especially in the urban environment.

Disaster or *confined-space dogs* are trained to find people who are still alive and have been buried by a collapsed building.

Cadaver dogs, sometimes known as *decomposition* or *forensic dogs*, are trained to locate the specific scent of a decomposing body. This may be a body that is buried, even if several years old.

Water dogs are even more specially trained to locate deceased persons underwater. They can work along the shoreline of a body of water or in a watercraft and can provide a general location of submerged decomposing bodies.

Evidence dogs are specially trained to smell out specific objects that could be used as evidence in a court of law. Some dogs are trained to find articles discarded by a criminal while fleeing a crime such as keys, pagers, weapons, bags of money or anything with human scent on it. Others are trained for even more specific evidences such as drugs, bombs and weapons.

Some of the dogs listed above can be cross-trained for more than one skill or discipline.

Equine Resources (horses and mules)

In areas of urban/rural interface or urban parks, horses and mules can be used effectively during a search. They are rarely seen in urban areas, therefore when they are used they attract the attention of residents, who then become aware that a search is being conducted. Generally, mounted search teams have been shown to be superior to foot searchers when searching from roads and trails, and off-road in wilderness, parks and agricultural areas with more open view terrain. Riders can also be successful searching in more challenging terrain or searching at night if they have trained in that environment. In more congested traffic or crowd environments, both rider and horse need training and experience similar to basic mounted police officer training.

Key advantages for the mounted searcher are height, speed, endurance, and the equine search partner's ability to detect clues. Horses and mules can also be used effectively for transportation of other personnel, equipment, clues and evidence. The transportation options include evacuation of a missing person using the methods applied during World War I by medics using Army mules.

Horses and mules provide a higher search platform from which the rider can observe over the tops of fences and other obstructions. This angle of view can also be effective for tracking from the saddle. The mounted searcher is less effective seeing small clues or under shrubs or other overhanging obstructions. Partnering mounted search teams with searchers on bicycles, quads or off-highway motorcycles can provide eyes lower to the ground to effectively utilize the advantages of those resources and balance disadvantages.

The horse normally travels at three to five miles per hour, and can move substantially faster when needed. The mounted searcher moves faster than the human searching on foot, yet is still very effective as a searcher. Horses and mules also have the endurance to travel notably farther than the searcher on foot in a single day. This speed and endurance can be particularly useful in hasty search mode; transporting equipment, clues or evidence; expediting to check a track trap or establish perimeter containment, etc.

In the wild, horses are prey animals and so have developed acute senses of sight, smell and hearing which alerts them to nearby predators. Those senses also allow domestic horses to be able to detect humans. This is a valuable tool for the searcher because the horse or mule is a search partner communicating information. As a specialty available to the mounted searcher, training the horse to air scent and alert improves and focuses the natural detection capabilities. This specialty can be likened to "riding a search dog," complete with various capabilities such as general air-scenting, and scent discrimination for humans, human remains, narcotics, etc.

Basic search management issues related to mounted search teams include:

Mounted search teams

- Rigs transporting the livestock need vehicle access and adequate parking. Staging areas and shared trailers to reduce space requirements can be useful. Adequate space includes locations to secure livestock.

- Driving time hauling live cargo is slower on winding roads.

- Placing mounted search teams on standby allows time to prepare the searcher, livestock and transportation, creating faster response when activated.

- Horses and mules can drink as much as 10 to 20 gallons of water per day, and water may need to be available or provided in the field.

- Per incident, identify expectations for 24 to 72 hours of self-sufficiency for feed and water of livestock.

- Just like any searcher, the training and experience of the mounted search teams in various environments will impact their potential to focus on searching instead of safety in that environment. A team liaison should be able to provide accurate information regarding the abilities of the various mounted searchers.

- Qualified support personnel for mounted search teams can provide assistance providing drop off and pick up services for horses and their riders, or use hauling vehicles or trailers for other logistics needs. Support personnel can also manage any additional livestock not in the field. (Additional livestock can be useful for transportation.)

- With the assistance of local mounted personnel, management should develop and maintain a current preplan for equine-related issues and problems. Maintaining a contact list of local large animal veterinarians is a minimum plan. Many are equipped to respond to the field, but may not be prepared for off-road. Other needs may include resources for horse feed and bulk water for a longer, more remote incident. Also identify resources able to provide livestock extraction in various situations.

Physical Resources

Search Base Facilities and Equipment

Many urban searches are short four- to six-hour incidents utilizing 20 to 30 resources. When searches become extended over a long multi-operational period there is a need to establish a search base command. The base will require suitable space to operate and the equipment to manage it. Some search operations can be run out of borrowed facilities such as school buildings and firehouses (especially the apparatus bays with the fire trucks removed). However, because of the amount and complexity of the equipment needed to run a search, most agencies must have a fully equipped mobile command post (MCP). These range from relatively small trailers to large bus or motor-home type vehicles. Often the MCP is a vehicle that serves the law enforcement agency for other purposes, such as an emergency operations center. Auxiliary vehicles providing such functions as communications, technical rescue, medical standby, food service or rest rooms (e.g., portable toilets) may also be needed. The preplan should identify where to obtain these facilities and equipment.

Following are items needed to conduct an urban search, all of which can be carried in a mobile command post.

Items for an urban search

✓ Maps, map boards and map plotting equipment

✓ Radios—handheld for field teams and base radios for the MCP

✓ Electrical generator to power AC outlets for various equipment

✓ Night lighting equipment—gas lanterns, floodlights, or other types of lighting

✓ Search operation forms

✓ Information library

✓ Photocopier for copying maps, forms and flyers (the larger the format, e.g., 11 inches by 17 inches, the better)

✓ Fax machine

✓ Cellular phone service, phone jacks for outside lines

✓ Computer and printers with LAN to various stations in the MCP; possible wireless link for Internet access

Continued on next page ...

- ✓ Television receiver to check local stations for news of the search
- ✓ Search progress display board (Situation Status, or Sit Stat, boards)
- ✓ Briefing information board, white board for posting information outside MCP
- ✓ Tables, chairs and shelters for work outside the MCP
- ✓ ICS signs, direction signs and identification vests
- ✓ Specialized field team equipment such as GPS receivers, night vision equipment, listening devices
- ✓ Heli-base equipment

Maps

Good maps are essential to any urban search to prepare field team assignments and to keep track of the areas that have been searched. However, finding appropriate maps for searching an urban area can be difficult. In the wilderness environment, the use of United States Geological Survey (USGS) topographic maps is fundamental. Search areas and field team assignments can be described by referring to the trails, drainages, ridge lines, latitude and longitude or Universal Transverse Mercator (UTM) coordinates on the maps. Landmarks seldom change even though USGS maps may not have been updated for several years.

In the ever-changing urban environment, however, USGS maps are inadequate. They are not useless, far from it. They do show topography, which is useful in determining the interface between urban and wilderness areas. Their main drawbacks are that they are not detailed enough and are usually not kept current with the rapid growth in urban areas. These drawbacks can be minimized by conducting area surveys periodically to update local information, mark new trails and enter other pertinent information.

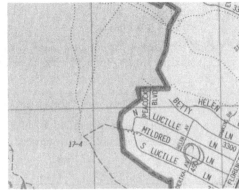

Map© Rand McNally, from the Contra Costa Thomas Guide, R.L.07-S-108

So where can you look for adequate working maps to manage the urban search? Here are some suggestions:

Maps to use in an urban search

✓ American Automobile Association (AAA) maps show streets and permanent features such as schools, churches and fire stations. They are usually readily available (sometimes free) and are updated on a regular basis.

✓ Chamber of Commerce maps show similar detail as AAA maps but usually include additional details such as retail establishments in the "downtown" areas.

✓ Published map books are available in many metropolitan areas: Thomas Guides on the west coast and ADC The Map People on the east coast. These maps take a large metropolitan area, usually a county or city, and break it into modules of greater detail and at a much larger scale than AAA maps. These map books are updated yearly. The books as well as digital versions are readily available and are used by many police departments for dispatching officers to incident calls (usually by street address, cross street, map page and grid). One word of caution—some map book printers may include a purposeful error on each page of a copyrighted map book.

✓ Fire department run maps are usually found on the walls of most fire stations and in each apparatus vehicle. They show each street, with street addresses, within the department's jurisdiction. They are updated regularly but the area of coverage and availability of copies are sometimes limited.

✓ County or municipal tax assessor's maps are used for assessing properties. These maps show every tax parcel by address, including property boundaries and easements. They are excellent maps for planning and executing door-to-door searches of neighborhoods, and are updated periodically. One set of maps can be kept on file for making copies during the incident.

Continued on next page ...

✓   Utility company infrastructure plans, like assessor's maps, show specific lots and house numbers. They also include easements as well as underground utilities and storm drain systems, which may be useful in certain situations. These maps may not be updated regularly and may be difficult to obtain.

✓   Recent aerial and satellite photos are very useful in visualizing the area of the search. Features not found anywhere else can be readily seen. Outlines of homes, backyards and out-buildings can all be seen and may help in planning where to search. Dense tree growth can obscure pertinent details, however, and obtaining these photos may be difficult and expensive.

✓   Internet services such as MapQuest can provide maps and, in some areas, recent aerial photos. Another service is www.Terraserver.com. Terraserver has maps and aerial photos that can be searched by address, zip code, city, county or coordinates and may be purchased online. Google Maps™ provide a similar service and has a hybrid feature, which overlays street maps over satellite images.

✓   Maps that allow GPS coordinates to be downloaded are a recent resource. These digital maps can be loaded directly to a handheld GPS and can locate the user on the viewable map. The data base maps are usually available from one of the commercial map distributors, e.g., Thomas Bros. Maps®, Rand McNally. The detail is limited to simple street maps because of limited storage and memory of the GPS units. These GPS maps, however, are quite useful for downloading the "snail trail" of the search team. They can also be tied into telemetry via digital radio, back to search base, and tied into a digital map on a laptop computer to give the real time location of the search team.

✓   Special maps can often be obtained from the managers of properties being searched. For example, apartment buildings, condominium complexes, mobile home parks, campgrounds, parks or private residential developments may have maps or diagrams that can be readily obtained by search management during the incident. Commercial developments such as shopping centers and downtown business districts may have maps that make searching these areas easier. They can be included in the preplan package or obtained when a search is conducted in the area.

When preparing search assignments, both topographic and street type maps will need to be issued to the search teams. The command post should have photocopying capabilities to reproduce maps as needed.

Communications

Radio communications in an urban environment can be complicated. Even if the search is confined to a single jurisdiction, different radio systems may be employed. Many law enforcement agencies have gone to 800 MHz encoded systems that cannot be monitored by field teams using VHF radios. With multi-jurisdictional operations the potential exists for field units of different agencies operating on mutually incompatible radio frequency bands (VHF, UHF, trunked, etc.). Newer dispatch communication centers can patch multiple radio frequencies together for simultaneous broadcasting during major disasters and events.

The simplest way to overcome these hurdles is to operate a central communications facility at the command post that can monitor all the systems that might be used during a search in that urban area. Messages can then be relayed through the communications unit. In an emergency, where no such coordinated communications are available, handheld radios on the control frequency can be loaned (checked out) to those who need them. For this purpose, it is a good idea to maintain a supply of such handheld radios in the command post. Also, since most urban environments can be noisy it is best to issue radios that have a remote microphone and/or an earphone. Some direct connect communication systems with walkie-talkie features as well as text messaging pagers and mobile phones have been used successfully in the urban setting.

The environment in and around steel and concrete structures will interfere with most established radio systems, as well as pagers and cell phones. Radio repeater systems are often used in areas known to have communication problems. These repeaters can be set up in portable suitcase size containers and used in both inside and outside structures.

Part of the preplan will be designating operational radio frequencies and procedures to be used during the urban search. Established search teams already have these frequencies set up, so it will not be a problem where only that team is operating. Make sure the frequencies chosen have low radio traffic volume or at least can be set up temporarily for exclusive use during the search operation. Incident radio procedures should be included in field team briefings.

Helicopters
Helicopters have limitations in an urban search, but should not be overlooked. When searching a heavily developed area it is difficult to spot a missing person from a helicopter. It is especially difficult if the person is not acting strangely or outrageously enough to draw attention and be spotted by the flight crew (usually consisting of a pilot and at least one trained observer). To be spotted, the person must be out in the open. There are opportunities to use forward looking infrared (FLIR) devices to look for persons moving at night, but again, it is dependent on the person being out in the open. Helicopters can, however, be an advantage in looking into backyards to locate potential search sites like abandoned vehicles and outbuildings.

The main advantage of using helicopters is that they are inherently noisy and attract a lot of attention, especially at night. A helicopter flying low over a neighborhood may generate complaint calls to 911 operators or law enforcement agencies. What has proven successful is to turn the complaint call into a resource by telling the caller why the helicopter is in the area. Have the operator direct the caller to check around her home and yard for the missing person. If the helicopter is equipped with an external loudspeaker, the flight crew can broadcast the missing person's basic description and ask onlookers to check the area around them. A helicopter can also quickly respond to called-in sighting reports before ground searchers can reach the area.

Sources for helicopters, if they are not provided by the responsible agency, include the military, state or local government, and civilian private contractors.

Bicycles
Bicycles have proven to make excellent search vehicles in the urban environment and can search in and about areas inaccessible to most motorized vehicles. Their biggest advantage is that they can cover much longer distances than searchers on foot. Local roads, lanes, trails and rights-of-way can often be quickly searched in a hasty mode by bicycles. They can also be used as containment and traffic control resources. Equipped with saddlebags they can carry emergency supplies and can respond fast to such things as medical emergencies.

All Terrain Vehicles (ATVs)
All terrain vehicles have limited applicability in an urban search environment. They can usually travel in areas that are accessible to bicycles and horses, however they may not be allowed on public roadways if they are not licensed for street use. An ATV makes an excellent workhorse for delivering large pieces of equipment and supplies. They also work well in the interface at the perimeter of urban and open space.

Personal Field Equipment—Uniforms

Professionalism shows in how a searcher presents himself, and urban searches expose the searcher to more civilians than would a wilderness operation. A uniform will help maintain this professional image. If team members are going to be interviewing door-to-door and walking the streets they must present themselves with confidence and a command presence. Having picture identification issued by an agency and/or a badge also will help create a sense of professional authority. If possible, having marked law enforcement vehicles available for transportation or parked nearby can also provide a professional presence. While searchers must be easily identified, search managers should be cautious about putting volunteer personnel in a position of law enforcement authority by using agency markings. Situations could occur where these volunteers are viewed as "cops" and thus inadvertently be put in dangerous positions.

Personal Field Equipment—Urban Field Pack

Urban searching requires the searcher to carry less and different equipment than wilderness searching, where weather and terrain are major factors. Most assignments last only a few hours and the searcher can be confident that food and sleeping facilities will be available at base. The full wilderness pack can be kept in the car with the full complement of search gear. The only personal items needed are clothing adequate for the weather, water, a minimal amount of food and any personal medications. The remaining equipment is required or useful to conduct the search, or to handle common emergencies. Most can be carried in pockets, fanny packs or a small "school book" size pack. Some assignments, such as containment patrols, may require even less. The following recommended list can be changed by local protocols.

Urban Field Pack Contents

✓ Uniform and ID	✓ Note pad and pen/pencil
✓ Food and water	✓ Field interview forms
✓ Appropriate maps (may be distributed at the briefing)	✓ Paper and plastic bags (lunch size, for collecting evidence as directed by the jurisdictional agency)
✓ First aid kit	
✓ Flashlight or head lamp with extra batteries	✓ Rubber examining gloves
	✓ Whistle
✓ Radio	✓ Pocket knife
✓ Cell phone	✓ Watch
✓ GPS receiver	✓ Camera (optional)
✓ Compass	✓ Binoculars (optional)
✓ Extra clothing or foul weather gear as needed	

Information Resources

Many organizations have been established to focus attention and provide information on various "at-risk" populations. Local and national groups specializing in Alzheimer's disease, domestic violence shelters and runaway support groups are just a few.

National Center for Missing and Exploited Children®

The National Center for Missing and Exploited Children® (NCMEC) is a national clearinghouse for information on cases of abducted, runaway, and sexually exploited youth. NCMEC does not investigate such cases, but receives leads and disseminates them to various investigative law enforcement units. In the effort to assist law enforcement, NCMEC offers technical assistance, information dissemination and advice.

NCMEC offers a free consulting service comprised of expert, retired law enforcement officers who are skilled in investigating cases of child sexual abuse and abduction (please note that all travel expenses and costs of resource materials are paid for by NCMEC). NCMEC also has access to the National Crime Information Center (NCIC) and the National Law Enforcement Telecommunications System (NLETS).

NCMEC's Mission

To help prevent child abduction and sexual exploitation; help find missing children; and assist victims of child abduction and sexual exploitation, their families, and the professionals who serve them.

NCMEC was established in 1984 as a private, nonprofit 501(c)3 organization to provide services nationwide for families and professionals in the prevention of abducted, endangered, and sexually exploited children. Pursuant to its mission and its congressional mandates (42 U.S.C. §§5771 et seq.; 42 U.S.C. §11606; 22 C.F.R. §94.6), NCMEC offers the following services, available to law enforcement agencies involved in the search for missing, abducted or lost children:

- technical assistance,
- informational databases, and
- detailed maps of the entire United States.

NCMEC also functions in the following capacities:

- Serves as a clearinghouse of information about missing and exploited children.

- Operates a CyberTipline® the public may use to report Internet-related child sexual exploitation.

- Provides technical assistance to individuals and law enforcement agencies in the prevention, investigation, prosecution, and treatment of cases involving missing and exploited children.

- Assists the U.S. Department of State in certain cases of international child abduction in accordance with the Hague Convention on the Civil Aspects of International Child Abduction.

- Offers training programs to law enforcement and social service professionals.

- Distributes photographs and descriptions of missing children worldwide.

- Coordinates child-protection efforts with the private sector.

- Networks with nonprofit service providers and clearinghouses about missing person cases.

- Provides information about effective legislation to help ensure the protection of children.

NCMEC Hotline: 1.800.THE.LOST (1.800.843.5678)

www.missingkids.com

Weather Reports

The weather situation can be checked by calling the local office of the National Weather Service, or by accessing various weather sources on the Internet.

Specialized Resources

Specialized resources might be used on occasion for certain searches. Specialized resources include dive units, cave or underground teams, confined space rescue units, amateur radio communications units, Critical Incident Stress Debriefing (CISD) debriefers, interpreters, and grid searchers. Specialized equipment such as metal detectors—along with the trained personnel—can be found by contacting local clubs and hobbyist organizations. Food services can be provided by the American Red Cross or the Salvation Army as well as through special donation agreements with some fast food chains. Additional specialized equipment includes night vision equipment and listening devices.

Chapter 5.   Stages of an Urban Search

This chapter provides an outline of the usual progression of an urban search, from the initial report to the actual field search. Some of the material is discussed later in this book; this section simplifies the timeline to help understand the standard procedure.

Stage 1—Initial Report

The first stage of a search is the initial report that someone is missing. Generally, this is precipitated by a call to 911. Why 911? Since its inception, 911 has been the go-to phone number for any emergency. Most 911 calls are routed to a dispatch center for various emergency services (e.g., police, fire, ambulance). Through a screening process by the operator at the 911 center, the nature of the emergency is established and the call is transferred to the dispatch center of the appropriate response agency for action.

The 911 operator will typically ask the following standard list of questions:

- Is this a police, fire or medical emergency?
- Where is the emergency?
- What is going on?
- Is there a time delay?
- Do you have any suspect and/or suspect vehicle information?
- Were/are any weapons seen (e.g., handgun, rifle, shotgun, knife, stick)?

If the nature of the emergency is determined to be a missing person, then the following questions are asked:

- Who is missing?
- Can a physical description be provided?
- How long has the person been missing?
- Where was the missing person last seen?
- Are there any unusual circumstances known about the event?
- What is the callback telephone number for the reporting party?

The caller will also be asked to give his name, address and telephone number. However, the caller may choose not to provide this information. Enhanced 911 systems display the phone number and address of the incoming call to eliminate the problem of locating the emergency when someone dials 911 and cannot speak.

Note: Protocols in many jurisdictions designate 911 wireless phone calls to be answered by the local highway patrol instead of the 911 operator. When cell phones were first introduced they were bulky and carried only in vehicles; thus, most emergency calls came from freeways covered by the highway patrol. With the proliferation of tiny handheld cell phones, calls now come from anywhere and a logistical nightmare has been created—highway patrol must now forward most calls to other jurisdictions. Also, until recently, cell phones could not be traced to specific locations, and callers who couldn't identify their location to emergency workers were at a disadvantage. With the advent of new technology, cell phone calls are located by triangulation from antenna sites. This will allow calls to be routed to the appropriate Public Safety Answering Point (PSAP) for the jurisdiction in which the call originated. Also, newer cell phones themselves are enhanced with built-in GPS receivers that will transmit the caller's location.

What circumstance could have prompted someone to call 911 regarding a missing person? The two scenarios described in Chapter 1 illustrate this point.

In Scenario One, Stacy was not at home by the time she was expected. Her mother called the neighbors and friends, checked the neighborhood and then called the police, via 911. In Scenario Two, Walter was noticed missing from the home. He was reported missing by the home care staff after they searched the facility and the streets in the surrounding area.

Suspicious circumstances also might initiate a missing person report in cases in which the subject has not been reported missing. For example, a patrol officer may notice an unoccupied vehicle in the parking lot of a tennis club at 2:00 a.m. with a bloody towel on the front seat. This would indicate that a crime was committed, and the subject would be sought.

After the 911 operator determines that the incident involves a missing person, the information is forwarded to the dispatch center of the local law enforcement agency which has jurisdiction for follow-up. Up to this point, all that is known is that someone is missing. Local, state and federal laws compel the agency to accept a missing person report, regardless of where the missing person resides or was last seen. The responsibility of the agency having jurisdiction is spelled out in their Policies and Procedures for Missing Persons (see Appendix D Law Enforcement Protocols). Note that some state laws require the agency to initiate an active search whenever the missing person is a juvenile; is at risk due to health, age or mental health problems; is suicidal; or foul play is suspected.

Stage 2—Initial Response

The initial actions taken by the agency depend on its policies and procedures for missing persons. Normally, the agency dispatch center will assign a patrol officer to respond to the scene and interview the reporting party. At the same time, a BOLO alert, with the missing person's description and last-seen location, is broadcast to all local units and adjacent law enforcement jurisdictions. Notification of the incident is also made through the National Crime Information Center (NCIC)—Missing and Unidentified Persons System.

The primary activity of the responding officer is to obtain information about the incident and the missing person. The point last seen (PLS) or the last known position (LKP), such as an abandoned vehicle, should be identified, confirmed and protected, and witnesses should be interviewed.

In many instances, an area search conducted by family, friends and/or neighbors would result in finding the subject with no further action required except for paperwork to close the case files. If these efforts are unsuccessful, the officer will usually perform a hasty search of the immediate environment, such as the residence, hitting more probable areas based on his or her knowledge and experience in the neighborhood. If the missing person is not found within a reasonable period of time, the on-scene officer will contact his or her supervisor, who will then authorize additional assistance of on-duty resources such as other patrol officers and detectives.

Urgency Determination

Sometime during the initial response to a missing person report, someone must decide the level of urgency for finding the missing person. Is this person in imminent danger of dying or is it possibly just a delay in returning from her usual activity? Should an all-out search effort be undertaken or can we wait a while to see what happens? This urgency determination is even more important in an urban search because a high percentage of missing person reports turn out to be false. Therefore, a lot of wasted effort can be prevented by carefully sorting out which incidents require further searching and which can be handled in a different manner.

Often, the first responding police officer or the officer's supervisor can make a quick determination after gathering the initial information and conducting a hasty search. Sometimes, local protocols will specify who makes the urgency determination and when the search should be intensified. In any case, the urgency analysis and determination should be considered as soon as possible, and certainly after the initial search has failed to locate the missing person.

Experienced police officers can often size up the situation from the reporting party interview by using their "intuition," but it is better to do a more thorough investigation and then make a decision. Wilderness search teams sometimes use numerical tables of risk factors to rate search urgency, but these tables are less reliable in an urban setting. One reason is that the survival factors considered important in the wilderness (weather, terrain, experience, equipment carried) are less important in cities, where shelters are everywhere. Another is that the urban subject's mental capacity and behavior patterns vary more than the typical person lost in the wilderness. There are many contributing factors and possible scenarios to consider that such a table would be difficult to create.

The following factors should be considered in analyzing the incident:
- Age of the missing person
- Physical condition of the person
- Medical condition of the person
- Mental condition of the person
- Medication the person may be taking
- Time since last seen
- Method of travel (walking, personal vehicle, public transportation)
- History of similar behavior, or lack of such
- Recent events that might affect the person's behavior
- Incident clues
- Environmental conditions, especially the weather

With this information, it may be possible to make a tentative estimate of the type of search anticipated (see Chapter 3, Common Types of Missing Person Searches). It is important not to assume a specific scenario has occurred or what the missing person might have done. It is better to consider a range of possible scenarios that would fall within reason, take into account all the elements of the situation, and then decide the urgency based on the most urgent scenario. The more risk factors present, the higher the urgency. When unsure, be conservative and elevate the urgency. Search teams do not mind being called for false alarms when the risk factors create high urgency.

The relative urgency can be described as low, medium or high. The recommended response depends on the agency protocols and available resources, but should progressively include the following steps:

LOW URGENCY
✓ Investigation of the incident including interview of appropriate persons ✓ BOLO to law enforcement agencies ✓ Hasty search of area around PLS and likely places the person might be
MEDIUM URGENCY
✓ The above, plus activation of additional law enforcement and search teams ✓ Expanded search effort with additional resources and search teams ✓ Additional public notification, including media and electronic messaging (e.g., AMBER Alert)
HIGH URGENCY
✓ Full search effort using maximum available resources and tactics ✓ Maximum public notification ✓ Expansion of the search area ✓ Calling in mutual aid resources

Be aware that the urgency can change as more information about the person and the incident is received. Urgency tends to increase, especially as time passes. However, it may decrease as the search area is completely covered or mitigating factors are discovered which would tend to place the person in the "voluntarily missing" or "missing but not lost" categories.

Urban Search Urgency Guidelines

The Urban Search Urgency Chart like the one shown in Chapter 3 is designed to give search managers a consistent method of evaluating levels of response to the incident and document the decision-making process.

The following table may also be used to evaluate the urgency of a particular incident. The urgency of the missing person/incident profile listed in each urgency level may be increased or decreased by the factors listed. Missing persons are assumed to be mentally and physically normal for their age, with normal clothing for the situation, unless otherwise indicated. The relative weight of each factor depends on the situation, so values are not assigned to the factors. These are only guidelines and should not be taken as definitive standards.

LOW URGENCY
Runaway/sneak-away adults
Runaway children, 14–18 years old
Fugitives of non-violent crimes
A miscommunication incident
Missing person is late returning from an activity
Little information available on missing person or incident

MEDIUM URGENCY
Mild mental retardation
Alcoholics, drug users
Elderly
Children, 14–18 years old

HIGH URGENCY (At Risk)
Mild to severe Alzheimer's disease (dementia)
Children under the age of 14
Moderate to severe mental retardation
Abducted children (witnessed or suspected)
Kidnapped people (witnessed or suspected)
Despondent or suicidal

INCREASING URGENCY FACTORS
Existing medical condition affecting ability to function
Lack of required medication
Insufficient clothing, food or shelter for the prevailing environmental conditions
Extreme environmental conditions
Increased ability to travel, utilizing urban modes of transportation
Increasing time since missing, onset of night
Progressively younger children
Serious precipitating incident
Information or clues found pointing to higher urgency
DECREASING URGENCY FACTORS
History of running away or erratic behavior
Two or more persons missing together
For suspected voluntary missing person, increasing time with no clues in search area
Information or clues pointing to lower urgency

Public Notification

As soon as it is determined that the search has a medium to high urgency, the responding agency should notify the public—first, all law enforcement agencies within the surrounding areas and then the general public. The timing of notifying the general public is important. Notification may need to take place after some effort has been made to locate the missing person. A premature notification may produce unnecessary concern. One common method of notification is a flyer for distribution with the name of the missing person, a picture, basic physical information and a contact-if-seen phone number (see example on next page). The contact number should be one that is monitored constantly. Reasons for this are discussed in the Media Relations section on page 65. Following are additional methods used to disseminate information.

MISSING PERSON

LAST SEEN FRIDAY, DECEMBER 4, 1998

LYNNE LOUISE CHRISTOPHER

WHITE FEMALE, 8 YEARS, DOB 3/8/90
4'-4", 62 LBS, BLOND HAIR, BLUE EYES
LAST SEEN WEARING A BLUE SWEATSHIRT
BLUE JEANS AND SANDALS

IF YOU HAVE INFORMATION REGARDING THIS DISAPPEARANCE,
CONTACT THE DREDMIL POLICE DEPARTMENT
AT 866 555-1212

Example of public notification flyer

"Be On the Look Out" (BOLO)

"Be On the Look Out," or BOLO, announcements are customary (or mandated) in most law enforcement jurisdictions. A general, wide-area broadcast with a description of the lost person is given from a radio dispatch to all units in the local and adjacent jurisdictions. A beat officer may have seen a suspicious person or someone who just looked out of place before the announcement, but was not compelled to investigate the incident any further. The BOLO announcement may trigger the officer's memory and he may be able to locate the missing person and close the search.

National Crime Information Center (NCIC)

Most law enforcement jurisdictions are required to input lost person information into the National Crime Information Center (NCIC) within 4 hours of notification. In addition to its normal function, NCIC is a collection point of all lost or missing people in all 50 states, the District of Columbia, the Commonwealth of Puerto Rico, the US Virgin Islands and Canada. NCIC works by putting the name and description in a database and then distributing the information throughout the system (see Appendix E California Penal Code Section 14205).

A law enforcement agency may find a person with no identification or who cannot remember who he is or where he lives, for example, a person with Alzheimer's disease. A check in the NCIC database may come up with a match for the missing person. The preplan should include a list of responsible parties within a given jurisdiction for inputting this information. The information from NCIC must be removed once the person is found. Information requested by NCIC is listed in the figure below.

NCIC Data Input

Suggested relevant information is to be gathered relating to a missing person disappearance. The law enforcement agency should gather, at the time of the report, information that shall include, but not be limited to, the following:

1. The name of the missing person(s) (including alternative names used)

2. The date of birth;

3. Identifying marks (birthmarks, moles, tattoos, scars, etc.)

4. Height and weight;

5. Gender;

6. Race;

7. Eye color;

8. Current hair color and true or natural hair color;

9. Prosthetics, surgical implants, or cosmetic implants;

10. Physical anomalies;

Continued on next page ...

11. Blood type (if known);

12. Driver's License number (if known);

13. Social Security number (if known); credit card numbers;

14. A photograph of the missing person(s) (recent full-face photographs are preferable; the agency is encouraged to attempt to ascertain the approximate date the photograph was taken);

15. A description of the clothing the missing person(s) was believed to have been wearing;

16. A description of items that might be with the missing person(s) (jewelry, accessories, shoes or boots, etc.);

17. Information on the missing person's(s') electronic communications devices, such as, but not limited to, cell phone numbers, e-mail addresses, etc.;

18. The reasons why the reporting person(s) believes that the person(s) is missing;

19. Name and location of the missing person's(s') school or employer (if known);

20. Name and location of the missing person's(s') dentist and/or primary care physician (if known);

21. Any circumstances that may indicate that the disappearance of the missing person(s) was not voluntary;

22. Any circumstances that indicate that the missing person(s) may be at risk of injury or death;

23. A description of the possible means of transportation of the missing person(s) (including make, model, color, license plate number, and VIN of a vehicle);

24. Any identifying information about a known or possible abductor and/or person(s) last seen with the missing person(s), including:

Continued on next page ...

a. Name;

b. Physical description;

c. Date of birth;

d. Identifying marks;

e. Description of a possible means of transportation (including make, model, color, license plate number, and VIN of a vehicle);

f. Known associates;

25. Any other information that can aid in locating the missing person(s); and

26. Date of last contact.

Emergency Telephone Notification Systems

Historically, emergency managers have relied on and used traditional methods to deliver notification to the community in the event of a crisis. These forms of communication have included special advisories over the television and radio, the use of warning sirens, emergency personnel driving around the streets making announcements over loudspeakers or going door-to-door advising citizens. These are effective methods; however they require people to have the television or radio on and to be able to hear alerts. As well, they require localities to make extensive use of emergency personnel. Further, 911 systems are taxed with people calling in more for information and clarifications, e.g., "Does this affect me?", "What do we need to do?" or "How long will this be in effect?". In the past, search managers also made use of these methods.

New technology has now been added in the form of emergency telephone notification systems (ETNS). In 1981 in upstate New York, the "Missing Child Network" established the Community Alert Network, Inc. (CAN), the world's first emergency telephone notification service. Still in use, it is a high-speed, emergency telephone notification company, which has the ability to transmit critical information to a large number of people in a short period of time. CAN makes use of the latest in computer, telephone and digitized voice technology to provide these services to more than 600 communities and facilities in the US and Canada. In some communities, CAN is also used to help locate missing persons.

How do emergency telephone notification systems work? Trained personnel call a designated secure "hotline" telephone number and provide a password. Once personnel are verified, they are given detailed instructions that follow a preplanned procedure. The areas to be contacted are defined by geographic locations further delineated by zip codes, street names, street number ranges, Thomas Guides grids, or geographic "zones" that are predefined on area maps. A telephone message is recorded, which will be sent to phone numbers in the selected areas in a certain number of attempts (usually three). Depending on the system and the number of phone lines available, notification calls can go out at the rate of a few thousand to over 15,000 an hour.

Most emergency notification systems will have a printed report that can be forwarded by fax or e-mail to the requesting agency personnel. The report includes the numbers called and the status of each call. The report will also indicate if the system encountered busy signals, no answers, no rings or operator intercepts.

Emergency telephone notification systems have been used successfully in documented missing person cases in urban environments. When used for missing person incidents, the message should include the following information:

✓ Identification of the agency making the call

✓ A brief description of the incident

✓ A description of the missing person

✓ List of areas to search (e.g., backyards, garages, sheds, other outbuildings)

✓ How to respond if the person is located (e.g., emergency phone number, 911)

It must be ensured that if citizens are directed to call a specific phone number, then there are personnel, and in sufficient numbers, to answer the calls.

Although effective, emergency telephone notification systems have drawbacks. It can cost as much as $1.00 or more per call; and in a residential community of thousands, the cost adds up. The timing of the calls should also be taken into consideration—if they are made at night citizens may complain about their sleep being disturbed. Many providers of these systems use only publicly listed phone numbers. Unlisted numbers and/or cell phones need to be added to the data base separately. Some communities that intend to implement ETNS advertise in the media requesting people to submit their contact information for addition into the database if they want to be notified.

A sample ETNS protocol can be found in Appendix F. Following is a partial list of additional services and providers of emergency notification systems:

- Community Alert Network, Inc. (www.can-intl.com); now part of American Emergency Notification (www.aenusa.com/aen.php).

- "A Child Is Missing" (www.achildismissing.org); free to law enforcement

- Dialogic Communication (www.dccusa.com/)

- Reverse 911® (www.reverse911.com)

Child Abduction Alert Systems

In response to a number of high publicity child abductions, local, state and federal agencies developed various systems to instantly notify the public of an abduction. These systems are geared toward enlisting citizens' assistance in locating the child and/or the kidnapper. The most well-known and widely used system is called the AMBER Alert System in honor of Amber Hagerman, a young girl from Arlington, Texas who was kidnapped and killed in 1996. AMBER is an acronym for America's Missing: Broadcast Emergency Response. The federal "PROTECT Act of 2003" established national coordination of state and local AMBER Alert programs, appointed a national AMBER Alert Coordinator and developed guidelines for issuing and disseminating AMBER Alerts. In 2004, the US Department of Justice released a publication entitled "Guidance on Criteria for Issuing AMBER Alerts." The full document can be found at www.amberalert.gov/docs/AMBERCriteria.pdf. The criteria are listed here:

AMBER Alert Criteria

✓ There is reasonable belief by law enforcement that an abduction has occurred.

✓ The law enforcement agency believes that the child is in imminent danger of serious bodily injury or death.

✓ There is enough descriptive information about the victim and the abduction for law enforcement to issue an AMBER Alert to assist in the recovery of the child.

✓ The abduction is of a child aged 17 years or younger.

✓ The child's name and other critical data elements, including the Child Abduction flag, have been entered into the National Crime Information Center (NCIC) system.

The AMBER Alert System is very effective and there have been many success stories in locating missing or abducted children. Although missing adults do not fall under the criteria for activation of an AMBER Alert, the communication and media connections established for the system have also been used success-fully in locating missing persons with Alzheimer's disease. However, as with any system that alerts the public, it can be misused and abused. False reports or hoaxes could jeopardize the effectiveness by desensitizing the public. (Think of the story of the boy who cried wolf.) It is believed that the public will respond better if they know the alerts are issued only after serious deliberation.

Media Relations

For other types of searches, the media must be contacted directly, unless they hear about it through their normal radio monitoring.

Urban searches often will be resolved quickly when the news media are brought in early. Generally, the higher the population density in the search area, the higher the chance that someone other than law enforcement or the search and rescue team will find the missing person. To increase the chance of success, search efforts must take advantage of the media's technology to get the word out. The more eyes that are looking for the lost person, the better the chances are of success. The general public is an important source of clues and infor-mation. People love to help if they are made aware of the need. Be prepared because the response can be overwhelming.

A great help in dealing with the news media is a Public Information Officer (PIO), who usually works within the local law enforcement agency. The PIO has the contacts and skills to help the media disseminate information that the Search Manager wants the public to know.

A contact phone number to report a sighting or any information about the missing person should be included in any media release. This number should be a pre-established number that can handle many incoming calls and be staffed around the clock with live personnel (no recordings). It should also be included in the search preplan. Although 911 operators are equipped to handle such call loads, they cannot take the time to screen every call for accuracy of information. Certainly, the 911 operators can reroute the incoming calls, but this might be logistically impractical. Also, it is difficult to brief the 911 operators if the status of the missing person changes, for example, if they are found. Another phone number should be designated that can either be shut off or play a recording thanking the caller for the assistance and announcing that the missing person has been found.

In the rush to get the word out to the media, a word of caution is in order. Only certain basic information should be released to the public in order to prevent false reports. As phone calls come in, a method for screening the incoming information and clues must be in place. For example, if a call comes in about a sighting in the neighborhood where the missing person was last seen, and another call comes in about a sighting on the other side of the town, a decision needs to be made on where to send the search resources. A preliminary investigation could be made by sending someone to interview the reporting party in order to prevent sending resources in the wrong direction. On the other hand, a simple "lie test" can be devised to screen false reports to prevent wasted effort and increase the success of the search.

A "lie test" could entail withholding a small piece of the missing person's description from the media release. This information should be distinctive enough so that if the person had actually been seen, it would confirm the sighting. Examples include the color of clothing, a piece of jewelry or person's height and weight. When a call comes in about a potential sighting, the lie test question could be: "Was he tall and thin?" If the answer is "Yeah, that was him!" and the operator already knows that the subject was short and overweight, then the reported sighting can be discounted.

How does one deal with possibly hundreds of potential clues? The investigation should be expanded and geared up with enough resources to manage the information as it comes in. Clue logs need to be meticulously kept and reviewed often. Information received at the beginning of the search effort may be linked with new information received from the general public in response to a televised plea. This may further focus the search and result in the missing person being found in a shorter period of time.

Media and general information flyers can be printed in large quantities and distributed. The flyers should contain basic information, a photo and a phone number to call to report any information or sightings. Again, make sure to leave out the "lie test" question information. Members of lost children foundations, civic groups or spontaneous volunteers can distribute the flyers to stores, businesses and neighborhoods.

Searches, especially those for missing children, can be big media events. Reporters want to know everything. Directing their questions to the PIO will help, but there are some "newshounds" that want more. They show up in neighborhoods with microphones and cameras to get the inside scoop. Many have radio scanners and even "big ear" listening devices to pick up conversations. Cell phones are also not immune to eavesdropping. In a sensitive situation, these leaks could be devastating. If there is concern about possible breaches in security and information transfer, search management should establish special radio communication codes for reporting sensitive information (see Communications section in Chapter 4, p. 45).

Another avenue to consider is giving the media what they want. Designate a specific search team for the media to tag along with. This may be a dog team—TV crews love dogs—assigned to search a photogenic area or a vehicle assigned to patrol the area. In extremely large, highly publicized searches with multiple media representation, it may be easier to request that a select pool of reporters go along on the assignment and report back to the others.

It is recommended that someone who is involved in managing the search monitor the media broadcasts. A television in the command post is best. This will confirm that the information that is broadcast to the public is accurate and, if not, can be corrected immediately.

Stage 3—Call Out Additional Resources

At some point, the decision may be made to intensify the search by calling in off-duty officers, reserve officers, detectives, the crime lab and, most important, the volunteer professional search team utilized by the agency for urban searches. The procedure is described as follows:

Notification

The protocols for beginning a field search with additional resources should be incorporated into the agency preplan. As mentioned in Stages 1 and 2, the on-duty officer who first responds and begins the investigation handles the first call. As soon as it is determined that a true missing person is involved, the necessary alerts are broadcast and the initial search begins. When the designated Patrol Commander decides to call in special search resources, they are notified according to the preplan protocol. The protocol should spell out the procedures for determining the number and type of resources, including:

Determining the need for additional resources

Who and how many people are missing—more missing people equals more searchers

The availability of various resources, e.g., ground searchers, dog teams, aircraft

The area to be searched—the larger the area or the potential of the area growing, the more resources required

The number and type of search assignments that need to be filled (These are determined by planning ahead on the areas to be covered and deciding the best resource to use.)

Complete a Mutual Aid Resource request for search and rescue personnel (See Appendix G Mutual Aid Request Form—SAR 141)

The main resource official can be contacted through a phone call, pager (both numeric and alphanumeric), radio or some other medium. If the members of the resource are already on duty, then they can respond immediately. However, most urban search teams are made up of volunteers who are dispersed throughout the community. They may be away from home and thus need time to pick up their gear before responding . Other vehicles or equipment needed for the search can be picked up by designated drivers at the group's storage facility and driven to the site of the search.

The requesting agency contacts the dispatch center for the team (local phone numbers or state resource number) and advises the dispatcher that the local search and rescue team is being requested. The dispatcher pages or calls the team and provides the following basic information that each member will need to know:

What dispatch needs to know

✓ How many people are missing

✓ Who is missing

✓ A physical description

✓ How long they have been missing

✓ The location where the missing person(s) was last seen

✓ Any unusual circumstances known about the event

✓ Any special equipment needed or precautions to be taken (e.g., weather)

✓ A callback telephone number from the requesting agency

✓ The location of the command post

An example of a good call-out system is one used by the San Diego County Sheriff's Department. It works like this: Every member of the Sheriff's SAR Bureau (and the San Diego Mountain Rescue Team) is required to carry an alphanumeric pager. The SAR Coordinator, a regular Deputy Sheriff, puts out a page with a numeric code that a search is in progress. Members then call a hotline telephone number that has a just-recorded message with the information listed in the box above. (A later page goes out with the same information shown in text on everyone's pager. This text message requires access to a computer, so it takes a few minutes to send out.) Members who can respond to the search page their unit leader's personal pager number and leave their personal ID number to identify themselves. This information is then faxed to the SAR office and to the command post (CP) to be used by the Resources Unit.

One advantage is that everyone knows what is going on and can drive directly to the CP. Since the subject description has been included in the message, they can look for the missing person along the way; this has resulted in a find in several cases. Response time is cut to minutes, depending on how far the responder must drive to the CP. Also, a cancellation page can be put out if the missing person is found, allowing searchers to turn around if they have not yet reached base.

The requesting agency is responsible for locating and securing a command post and meeting point for use by the search resources. The command post should have a copier, rest rooms and telephone line. It is preferable that the command post be situated as close to the PLS as possible. Some agencies use a mobile command post equipped with the necessary facilities that can be parked at any suitable site.

In addition, under a multi-jurisdictional incident, a mutually agreeable command structure needs to be established. The Agency Administrator from the requesting local jurisdiction may appoint an Incident Commander. The incident still remains under a single command system. Memoranda of Understanding (MOUs) between the local law enforcement agency and the search teams or other resources can be used to spell out the management structures.

The Initial Call-Out Strategy

The key to successful searching in an urban environment is containment coupled with rapid response and start of the investigation. Time, as always, is the worst enemy. Since it is so easy for the missing person to travel out of the area, initial efforts should be directed towards trying to prevent the person from leaving the search area, thus limiting the size of the area that must be searched. Containment tactics should be started as soon as additional resources become available.

Stage 4—Full Scale Search

Generally, components of the search and rescue (SAR) team start arriving on the scene within an hour of the request. The SAR team is divided into two basic groups: the "overhead team," which administers and coordinates the search effort, and the "search teams," which actually execute the search activities. While search teams are usually on foot, a team can also consist of vehicle patrols, search dogs, air support, as well as equestrian and marine patrol, if required.

When a search is requested, the responding team reports to the CP to coordinate the search, and to arrange for and request mutual aid, if needed. A member of the SAR overhead team is designated as the "Search Manager" or liaison, whose responsibility is to coordinate the search under the Incident Commander (see Appendix A Incident Command System). The agency requesting the search should designate a member to participate in the command structure. Again, the requesting agency retains ultimate command and control of personnel assigned to the incident.

When sufficient SAR assets are in place, a "hasty search" is initiated. The hasty search will concentrate on the PLS and known areas where the missing person is likely to be found. If this search is unsuccessful, a detailed methodical search is undertaken.

Reporting parties should remain available, as SAR will wish to interview them using a prepared set of questions designed to elicit information useful to the searchers. If that is not possible, arrangements should be made to contact them as soon as possible.

Stage 5—Conclusion of the Search

It is everyone's hope that all search efforts will result in finding the lost person in a short period of time. If the person is found alive, the assistance of a rescue unit may be required to extricate him or her from a confined location. A medical evaluation may need to be completed by a paramedic unit and transport to a medical facility may be required. Of course, the person may simply need to be transported back home.

A less positive outcome may also occur: The person may be found dead. Depending on local protocols, the area around the person will need to be secured and an investigation launched to determine the cause of death. The person's body may need to be recovered by trained personnel. Those involved with the search must be debriefed using Critical Incident Stress Debriefing (CISD) protocols.

Despite all search efforts over hours or even days, the person may not be found. At some point, the search will need to be suspended. After a review of all the facts and clues (or lack of clues), as well as input from investigators and the incident command staff, a consensus agreement is eventually made to suspend active search efforts. The local law enforcement agency in charge will continue the investigation and call back resources as necessary (see Suspending an Urban Search Operation below).

> *No matter what the final outcome of the search*
> *for the missing person is,*
> *ALL efforts must be documented.*

Suspending an Urban Search Operation

When the missing person has not been located despite hours or even days or weeks of effort, suspending the search may have to be considered. The decision is never easy. Emotions run high. Intense pressures brought upon by the family, media political figures and the general public can complicate rational thinking. These decisions must never be made alone; rather bring together all the IC section chiefs, the Public Information Officer, a family liaison (such as a clergyman or chaplain) and review the facts gathered from all sources.

Consider all of the following points:

Considerations in suspending a search

- What are the chances of the person still being alive?
- How much time has elapsed since the person went missing and could they have survived during that time?
- How thoroughly was the search area covered?
- Is the environment safe for personnel if the search continues?
- What are the family, media and political pressures?
- What are the chances, or is there increasing evidence, that the missing person is not in the area?
- Would additional searches of the area with the same or different resources make a difference?
- Are there any unresolved clues that require further investigation?
- Are all of the available resources "burnt out" and unable to proceed any further?
- Are there any other missing person searches going on that have a higher priority?

Another consideration is to drop down to a limited search effort. This means suspending the search effort and turning the incident over to full-time investigation, holding the resources on standby, ready to ramp up the search again as new clues or information become available.

Chapter 6. Search Base Considerations

The logistics of an urban search base are different than those of a rural or wilderness base. Seemingly small considerations quickly become complicated. Preplanning potential search bases in the urban area can mitigate some of these problems. Considerations are outlined below.

Location

Urban searches have an advantage over wilderness searches because a search base can usually be set up close to the point last seen (PLS). All communities have public facilities such as firehouses, police departments, community centers, churches, schools or libraries, all of which can serve as a base. Shopping centers, both large regional centers and neighborhood centers, are frequently available. Houses of worship have been utilized. A consideration that must be kept in mind is that the chosen facility may need it back for its original intended use and thus need to be vacated by the search effort. Although the use of a facility during an emergency is temporary, there is no way of knowing how long it will be needed. Once base is established, it is difficult to move it without sufficient notice. Thus, care should be taken early to select a site that can accommodate all the expected activities and functions over the estimated duration of the search.

A primary consideration in selecting a site for base is its possible impact on the community. Search base has high visibility, with vehicles coming and going, helicopters flying overhead, and generators running day and night. This can be advantageous because it alerts the community that something is going on, enabling management to enlist the cooperation of the residents in helping with the search. On the other hand, it can irritate residents who find their access restricted, noise and traffic being generated, and people wandering all over their neighborhood. In general, command posts set up in commercial or industrial areas will have fewer negative impacts than those located in residential areas.

Ideally, the preplan that identifies potential search bases will have contacted the property owners to inform them about what is involved. In most large cities, however, this is not practical, so the authority selecting the incident site should get the owner or manager's permission before moving in the troops. It is preferable that normal activity at the location is reduced or absent; for example, a school that is vacant for the day or a business that is closed for the weekend. They should understand what impacts might occur, with vehicles occupying their parking, rest rooms being used, and possibly some of their buildings being used during the search operation. Whenever possible, the base should be set up away from the normal activity of the property, allowing business to continue as usual.

Parking

The preplan should estimate how much parking will be needed to handle the vehicles responding to the call-out. If large vehicles are expected, such as mobile command post vehicles, space should be reserved for them. Other large resource vehicles like horse trailers will need room to spread out for animals and tack equipment. Access pathways should be established so that vehicles can enter and leave without turning around. Parking should be well separated from staging and the command post (CP), if possible.

If parking is only available on the street, which often happens in residential areas, it can be marked off with yellow tape, traffic cones or signs. Some method of identifying personally-owned vehicles that belong to search team members, such as rear view mirror hangers or magnetic door signs, helps organize the parking. The parking area should be reasonably secure so that equipment is not lost or stolen. The police can usually assist with parking, but the location may end up blocks away from the parking, requiring a shuttle arrangement to transport personnel to base and a security detail to protect the vehicles left at the parking lot.

Shelter and Work Facilities

Unless search base is set up in a building with all the necessary facilities, the search team will need to bring along and set up shelter and work facilities adequate for the operation. A large CP vehicle or trailer will most likely handle these needs; however, if the usual procedure is to work off someone's tailgate, it will quickly become apparent that this will not suffice on a long or complex search. Depending on the weather, pop-up type canopies or large tents work well. Folding tables and chairs furnish the "office" for search management.

Communications

The incident command post should be set up in a place that has good radio communications. In general, this means a location that has clear space around it, preferably on high ground. This isn't always possible in a large city with tall buildings, but most urban searches take place in low-density residential areas that accommodate a tall radio antenna. When setting up the antenna, be careful not to hit overhead lines or trees.

VHF radios work best when the receiver is within line-of-sight of the transmitter. VHF systems will not tolerate tons of concrete between the base and field teams, therefore multiple repeaters or relay stations may be needed. Teams working underground or inside structures may need someone above ground to relay for them. Small details like phone numbers for base and cell phones for field teams can make a difference. If all else fails, most 911 systems will allow toll-free call-ins to a dispatch center and call transfer to base. Other hybrid communication with combination cell phone and direct two-way radio (e.g., Nextel) are effective in urban environments.

Many agencies have Mobile Data Computers (MDCs) that are effective for communicating text information of the search and provide an electronic record of the incident.

Rest and Sleeping Areas

Searchers who want to nap between tasks may have to improvise. Space sometimes can be set aside in parks or grassy areas, however in a more concrete environment, nappers will have to use their vehicles or sleep on equipment. What about overnight sleeping? During urban operations, searchers released at the end of the day usually go home for the night and return the next day. For those who stay over, or just want to catch a few hours of sleep, their vehicles are the obvious choice. Sometimes space can be found inside the facility where the base is established. Local fire stations can usually make some room and some police departments will cover the cost of motel rooms (maximum occupancy, of course). Some hotel chains may be willing to donate rooms. Another possibility is a school gym floor, which offers the added benefit of locker rooms and hot showers.

Rest Rooms

Any search operation of more than a few hours needs some kind of rest room. In the wilderness, searchers can go behind a tree, but in the city it is not appropriate to use alleys as a bathroom. Often the permanent facility being used for base will have rest rooms. Local commercial establishment may make their bathrooms available, but they must understand what they are getting into. Muddy boot tracks all over the plush executive washroom might cause some terse comments. Many large police departments have portable toilets that can be towed to the site, or they can be leased from local suppliers.

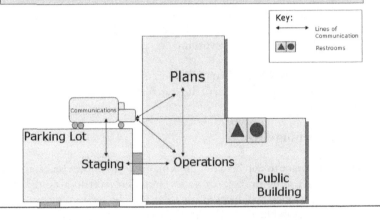

Example of a typical urban search base layout, including areas for the
Communications, Plans, Staging and Operations Sections

Chapter 7. Search Planning

Investigation and Interviewing Techniques

Overview

The best way to find a missing person in the urban environment is NOT to send out an armada of search teams and personnel hoping to find clues, but to place heavy emphasis on the initial investigation and prepare a search plan that focuses on places the person would likely be found. Information on where to look can be best obtained by good investigation. Build a profile of the missing person as if he or she is someone you already know. Get to know who the person's family, friends, business associates or schoolmates are. By doing this you can better predict what the missing person will do in a particular situation. For example, you may find that the initial call about a possible child abduction is determined later, through investigation, to be a runaway or a case of the child forgetting to call home.

This is not to say that all search activity should wait until a thorough investigation is completed. In most cases, the initial information on the missing person will be enough to begin assigning field teams and sending them to the prime areas. They can then be reassigned, or newly-arrived searchers can be assembled into teams and dispatched, if new information is obtained.

Investigation as used in a search context is the continual process of gathering information about the missing person and the circumstances under which he or she is missing. Information gathering includes interviewing people who have pertinent knowledge of the person. This process commences with the first report of the missing person and is completed at the end of the search operation. It includes the interview with the person after he or she is found to determine what happened.

Besides usefulness in search planning, investigation gathers historical and statistical information, which can be useful in future searches for similar missing persons. The investigation report should include post-search information on the effectiveness of the resources utilized in locating the missing person. In addition, the complete report of the investigation and the management of the search incident can later be incorporated into a training exercise.

Interview and Interrogation

It is helpful to understand the difference between interview and interrogation. Law enforcement agencies are tasked with investigating incidents to determine whether crimes have been committed and, if they have, to arrest the perpetrators. Established rules and techniques have been developed to complete these tasks, which include interview and interrogation. For law enforcement these are defined as:

> **Interview:** A structured, non-accusatory process to obtain useful information from someone who may or may not have knowledge of events or circumstances of the incident. Specific techniques may be used to aid recall or elicit behavior useful in determining the veracity or involvement of the interviewee. It should be noted that the interviewee might not have any knowledge of the crime or the perpetrators. Interviews may also evoke lies and themes to use against the uncooperative. In some instances there will come a point in an interview where the interviewee may become a suspect of a crime. The interview will then become an interrogation.

> **Interrogation:** A structured, accusatory process during which a suspect of a crime is confronted in a confident manner and then convinced that the best decision would be to admit responsibility. The techniques used in obtaining useful information are designed to apply pressure to or intentionally trip up the interviewee.

In law enforcement interview and interrogation, there are laws and codes to protect the interviewee and define when a person is considered free to walk away from the questioning at any time, if they are being detained or in a custodial environment. It may be necessary to read the person the Miranda rights. An attorney may need to be present before any questioning occurs.

In law enforcement interviews and interrogations a great deal of the time is spent preparing for the actual session. Questions are carefully crafted and well thought out to induce a specific response. During the sessions the first hours are devoted to general conversation, which the investigator uses to develop a rapport with the person and identify behavioral changes that accompany a change in topic.

In missing person incidents involving law enforcement and/or search and rescue personnel there is a more specific definition:

> **Search Interview:** A structured but informal questioning process to obtain useful information from someone who has first hand and/or pertinent knowledge of the missing person. The tone of the interview is such that there is no condoning or condemning the action of the missing person, the interviewee or the circumstances surrounding the person's disappearance. Questions are structured to aid the interviewee in recalling specific details and events leading up to the disappearance of the missing person. The information gathered is used to develop a missing person profile, to collect lists of other persons to interview and to aid in planning where to look for the missing person.

In this type of missing person interview, the questions are nearly the same for all types of searches and missing persons. A rapport is developed almost immediately because of the common goal of the interviewer and interviewee to find the missing person and bring them home safely. In most circumstances the interviewee is free to walk away from the questioning at anytime, but is encouraged to stay and help.

Some techniques used in search interviewing and investigations are designed to solicit full and accurate information about the missing person. Some questions may even be designed to trip up the interviewee so the answers can be corroborated with other interviews in order to find out who has the most credible information.

Whom to Interview

The person (or persons) who reported the person missing is the best place to start. Anyone with first hand knowledge or potentially important knowledge of the missing person can give the investigator the best information to help develop the missing person profile.

Potential Interviewees

- ✓ Parents
- ✓ Spouses
- ✓ Children
- ✓ Siblings
- ✓ Other relatives
- ✓ Close friends
- ✓ Co-workers
- ✓ School teachers
- ✓ School administration, counselor, nurse
- ✓ Classmates
- ✓ Family physician
- ✓ Mental health professional
- ✓ Missing person's caregiver
- ✓ Other health care or welfare worker
- ✓ Business associates
- ✓ Members of civic groups to which the person belongs
- ✓ Local law enforcement personnel familiar with the missing person and/or familiar with the area
- ✓ Person or persons who last saw the missing person
- ✓ Eyewitnesses to the incident
- ✓ People who have seen the person since he or she was first missing

An important aspect to understand is that those with direct personnel knowledge of the missing person implies direct emotional ties. These emotions are expressed in many ways—being upset and angry with themselves for "allowing this to happen" or at the interviewers (statements such as "Why are you asking all these stupid questions?" and "Why aren't you out looking for my Kathryn?"). Or they might have a "panicky" feeling, which can lead to irrational thoughts and actions. Understandably, someone close to the missing person is worried and frightened by the fact that the missing person is gone and something bad might have happened to them.

It is essential to keep in mind and understand these emotions and the subsequent effects on the interview. Interviewees may be preoccupied and not always listening to what they are being asked. They also may be slow to respond. Therefore, the interview must be adjusted to compensate for these distractions.

Information to Obtain

The initial report of the missing person initiates information gathering. The 911 operator establishes the nature of the emergency by using a standard list of questions, based on the classic who, what, where, when, why and how.

If the nature of the emergency is established to be a missing person then the following information is collected:

Initial Information Checklist

✓ Name of missing person (or persons)

✓ Physical characteristics

✓ Clothing

✓ Mental, emotional and physical condition

✓ How long the individual has been missing

✓ Place where the missing person was last seen

✓ Any suspicious, special or anomalous circumstances known about the event

✓ Availability and mode of transportation

✓ Suspect information if it is a possible abduction

✓ Call back telephone number for the reporting party

✓ Relationship to the missing person

The dispatcher forwards this information to a "beat" or duty officer. The officer is dispatched to investigate the missing person incident and prepare a report, called the Officer Response to Missing Person Report.

Items to address during initial investigation

✓ Get the name, nicknames, aliases, date of birth (age), race, gender of missing person.

✓ Find out if the missing person can communicate; if he/she knows his/her own name and address; if he/she speaks English.

✓ Establish and secure the physical point last seen (PLS) of the missing person and determine how long the person has been missing.

✓ Determine who saw the missing person last and have that person available for further interview.

✓ Get a detailed physical description of the missing person, including clothing and any information about their footwear.

✓ Obtain a recent photograph of the missing person.

✓ If the missing person is a child or an elderly person, and the PLS is a house, check the interior and exterior of the residence yourself, paying particular attention to the space under beds and to closets or cabinets. A check is essential even if family members assure the officer that the house has already been checked.

✓ Obtain information from family members and/or friends who may have conducted any searches in the area. Anyone who has been in the area of the PLS should remain on site until the search and rescue team arrives and records their tracks/footprints.

✓ Have dispatch contact local hospitals, the jail and local shelters to determine if the missing person is in any of those facilities.

✓ Find out if the missing person has ever been missing in the past and under what circumstances.

✓ Locate and secure any clothing, bedding or other items that belong to the missing person that can be used as a scent article for trailing dogs. Keep others away from any such material until the arrival of the search and rescue team. (Some trailing dog handlers may want to collect these scent articles themselves.)

Continued on next page ...

> ✓ Get a list of addresses and phone numbers of any friends or relatives.
>
> ✓ Try to get information on the mental state of the missing person.
>
> ✓ If the missing person is a child, find out what school he or she goes to and the name of the teacher and school administrator.
>
> ✓ If the missing person is an adult, find out the name, address and phone number of the employer or caregiver.
>
> ✓ Complete the standard missing person form as department procedure manual and protocol dictate.

The initial report information will be used to determine whether the missing person is lost, runaway, suicidal or any other possible scenario, and if the search and further investigation needs to continue.

The initial investigation by the responding officer generally leads to a more in-depth and expanded investigation by trained investigators/interviewers. In addition to confirming such basic information as name, age, sex, clothing description, shoe size and point last seen (PLS), the interview should look at the following incident variables.

Mobility and ability to travel

Missing persons can move in a straight line in an urban environment and if unrestrained could travel out of the local area, thus expanding the search area quickly. This could lead to a complete rethinking of where and how to search for the missing person.

> **Example questions:**
>
> - Can the person walk, ride, hitchhike or drive?
> - Does he have access to a vehicle, bicycle, horse, boat or airplane?
> - Does he have knowledge of and access to public transportation, rapid transit, trains, buses or taxis? (Some bus operators may allow on elderly person to ride a bus without paying.)
> - What type of money or credit cards does he carry?

Ability to survive
Survival in any urban environment is not as challenging as it is in the wilderness. However, some missing persons may be unable to recognize or utilize the facilities, services or resources that are required for basic survival, e.g., food or shelter. They may be unwilling, afraid or too independent to ask for help. These attitudes could affect their chances of survival and increase the urgency of the search effort.

Example questions:

- Does the missing person have any money with her?
- Does she have a pager or cell phone?
- Does she know how to call home?
- Is she familiar with her surroundings?
- Does she live in the area?

Mindset and intent
Did the missing person have an idea of what he was doing, where he was going and what he intended to do when he got there? For example, is the missing person with Alzheimer's trying to "go home" to a former residence? Is the missing person contemplating suicide and does he have the means to carry out his plan?

Example questions:

- Was he just going for a walk?
- Is he trying to find something or someone?
- Did he leave a note?
- Does he have a diary?

Ability or tendency to respond
The tendency of the person to respond to attraction techniques, such as calling her name, may be very normal when she is in a normal situation or state of mind. However, circumstances in the urban environment or in her life may preclude her from doing so. For example, someone who does not want to be found (e.g., runaway or despondent) may avoid searchers or not respond to attraction techniques.

Example questions:

- Was the missing child taught not to respond to strangers unless they know the secret password? Was a password established?

- Did she do something that would make her feel guilty? Will she avoid responding because she is afraid of punishment?

- For an adult, is there a mental, physical or language problem that could hinder her ability to answer searchers' calls?

Likes and dislikes and what attracts the person's attention

The missing person may have a fondness for a specific activity, a place to "hang out", a special pet or animal that he enjoys being around. The converse should also be asked: What would cause him to turn away, shun or hide if he were exposed to an unpleasant activity, crowded environment or specific type of person or thing?

Example questions:

- Does he like to play video games at the local fast food store?

- Do crowds bother him?

- Does he prefer solitude?

- Does he like animals?

- Is he afraid of someone in a uniform?

- Is he attracted to water?

Past and recent behavior and life history

Is there anything influencing the missing person in the recent, not so recent or distant past that would account for her behavior? Does she long to return to a better time or place in her life? For example, people with Alzheimer's disease often are living in the past and will try to return home to a former residence. Or did she just decide to go visit a friend she has not seen in a long while?

Example questions:

- Did a pleasant or unpleasant event just occur?

- Did something occur in her life recently or in the past that would affect her current mindset?

- Where did she grow up? Does she return there often?

- Who are her friends, peers and relatives?

- What was her life's work and where?

- Did she just return from a trip; where did she go?

Frequently, after collecting this information from one source, a list of additional sources of information is developed, including names of friends, family, teachers, relatives and clergy—all the people who know the missing person. The list could include places and attractions. More information may be available from outside agencies and jurisdictions frequented by the missing person. Institutions such as hospitals, domestic violence shelters, homeless shelters and jails should be contacted.

The Interviewers

The law enforcement agency that called for search team resources may have already completed a good background investigation and interview. Sometimes this is not the case because of the rapid development of the incident and/or the unavailability of trained personnel. Law enforcement personnel routinely deal with formal interviews and interrogations in criminal cases, but may not be skilled in search interviewing. Additional information to develop search strategies must be obtained. If the requesting law enforcement agency does not have the resources or skills for search investigation, then the information gathering may fall to the search team managers.

Two investigators should be assigned to an interview team. The interviewers should have a background in search and search management. Alternatively, the interview team could consist of one SAR member and one law enforcement officer trained in search and rescue. Prior to sitting down with the interviewee, interviewers should determine which one of them will ask the questions and which one will be the scribe or note taker. This is to establish which interviewer the interviewee will focus on and build rapport. During the interview, it may become apparent that the roles should be reversed; for example, the interviewee may prefer to talk to the other member of the team who is a woman.

The scribe can also ask follow up or clarification questions but should not dominate the interview. The scribe should be listening carefully to the questions and answers, as well as observing the interviewee's demeanor and body language, and looking around the room for clues.

When conducting the interview the interviewers need to be aware of their own demeanor and attitude as described in the following principles:

Interviewing Principles

✓ First and foremost, *be a good listener.* Be attentive to what interviewees say and how they are saying it.

✓ *Stay calm.* Interviewees may be under a lot of stress; interviewers who are emotional, anxious or restless may cause unnecessary pressure.

✓ *Be non-threatening.* This may require a change of uniform or appearance. The mere fact that an interviewer is wearing a uniform may be enough to intimidate interviewees, making them uncomfortable and less inclined to provide information. Law enforcement personnel are well advised to take off their duty belts and weapons.

✓ *Do not be patronizing or condescending.* Tone of voice and word choice should not convey that you condone or condemn the actions or lack of action of the missing person(s) or the interviewee. For example, a pointed question such as "Why did you let them do that?" might offend the interviewee. *It is not the interviewer's responsibility to judge*; such an attitude could lead interviewees to distrust the interviewer's sincerity in using the information obtained to only find the missing person.

✓ *Be respectful and polite.* Use "please" and "thank you." This goes a long way to build trust and rapport.

✓ *Be reassuring* and let interviewees know what is happening. Remember, interviewees may be under a lot of stress. Tell interviewees about the number of teams that are out looking for the missing person. Let them know that they will be notified as soon as any new information becomes available. Emphasize how important the information being gathered in the interview is and how helpful it will be in the search effort.

Continued on next page ...

✓ *Do not give false hope.* Be wary of saying "Sure, we will find him" as it will be difficult to recant if the person is not found. This false sense of hope could be devastating to the family of the missing loved one.

✓ *Do not lie,* but do assure interviewees that every effort and resource is being used to find the missing person.

✓ *Do not ask leading questions,* especially if you already know an answer from another source that may be contradictory. For example, do not ask the parents of a missing child, "Is he a good boy?" when the boy's teacher has described him as a "bad boy" and a disciplinary problem.

✓ *Some questions may be sensitive.* They should be prefaced with a statement such as "I know this is a sensitive question, but we need to ask if the missing person has tried to commit suicide in the past." In addition to suicide, questions about drug and alcohol abuse, sexual activity and even religious and ethnic beliefs can be sensitive. An interviewee may not want to give such information for fear of tarnishing a reputation, not wanting to accept the possibility or truth, or fearing retribution or other repercussions. *Focus on gathering facts* and each piece will help put the puzzle together. If the interviewee seems uncomfortable with the question, the interviewer should *emphasize that the information is confidential* and shared only with those who need to know.

✓ *Do not rush the questioning along or interrupt a response.* Wait for the full answer to a question. Some people do not process questions quickly, especially the elderly. When under stress it can take them even longer. Allow time for thinking and, once they have answered, allow time for more thinking. Most people cannot sit silently for more than six seconds in an interview without saying something. That six-second pause can allow for additional information to be presented. It may be necessary to break the questions down into smaller pieces in order for the interviewee to better understand and respond appropriately.

Continued on next page ...

> ✓ *Project a sense of positive urgency.* The interview is being conducted to help find the missing person. The interviewee may not see the need or understand the urgency of the situation. It is important to reassure the interviewee that the search effort has started and that the information they provide will help in the search planning on where to look.
>
> ✓ *Be professional.* Interviewing is a serious job. Sit up straight, keep your feet off the furniture—all the things your mother (or drill sergeant) taught you.

The Interview Setting

A good interview can take more than two hours. Therefore, the location for the interview is also very important: it should be someplace quiet, comfortable and non-distracting to help put the interviewee at ease. It may be difficult to find a quiet spot considering the circumstances and activities of the search effort. The best location is a place with limited foot traffic and people coming in and out. A busy area is distracting and can be detrimental to the interview, destroying the momentum of the interview or train of thought and concentration of the interviewee. Law enforcement personnel may also be a distraction to the interview process as they go about their jobs in the space where the interview may be held. In such cases, it may be necessary to find a "hiding place" to conduct the interview.

Other considerations for the interview setting are the residence or the search site. Interviews at the residence are usually more productive. It is a place that the interviewees most likely know well and where they feel comfortable and safe. An additional benefit is that the home is where resource information such as addresses, phone numbers and other potential documentation or clues are located.

Friends, family or loved ones can also be distracting. Although they may provide comfort to the interviewee during the interview, they may also divert the interviewee's attention from the interviewer, or worse they may answer a question rather than allowing the interviewee to answer. This is especially true of divorced parents. The dominant "ex" may answer the question and may not allow the other "ex" to answer. In such a scenario, the solution is to conduct separate interviews with different interviewers.

It may be necessary to have food and drink available during a long interview. Beverages containing caffeine or alcohol should be discouraged as they can affect judgment and cloud responses to questions. Smoking can also be a problem for both the interviewee and interviewer, causing a dilemma: if the interviewer must smoke and is not permitted to, he or she may become nervous and uncooperative; if smoking is permitted, the smoke may be distracting to the interviewer. The issue of smoking should be discussed with all parties prior to the interview. A simple adjustment of location to allow for ventilation may resolve the dilemma.

The room itself should have comfortable chairs in the living room or kitchen, for example. The important thing is to sit down. A writing surface for note taking is helpful. The interviewer should face the interviewee; the note taker should sit to the side of the interviewee.

A list of questions or a special set of questions made up for the particular incident or interviewee is extremely helpful. Examples are accessible on the Bay Area Search and Rescue Council (BASARC) Web site at http://www.basarc. org/forms/BASARCForms/InterviewShort_V.9-2000.doc and http://www. basarc.org/forms/BASARCForms/InterviewLong_V.9-2000.doc. The forms found on the Web site are designed in a long and short format. The short format list of questions is used by the interviewer; the scribe uses the long format, which includes space to write the answers. The interviewer can use these as a guide to make sure all pertinent questions are asked and to keep everyone on track.

Interviewers must pay attention to the surroundings and environment. Is it safe to be there? Are there kitchen knives or other potential aggressive weapons within arm's reach? Should the interview be conducted in a different location? Is the home well kept or messy? Are there any visual clues to be seen that might aid in building a profile of the missing person? Both interviewers should be making written and mental notes.

The Questions

The Start

In building a profile of the missing person and establishing rapport with the interviewee, it is prudent to start with a statement similar to the following:

"We don't know your missing father (or child or whoever the missing person is) and we need to know as much as we can about them to better understand and figure out what they would do in a given or particular situation. This will also give us an idea of where to search and make the best use of our resources."

Tangential Questioning

In all questioning it is important to take advantage of tangential questions that spin off the basic questions. An initial question could be: "Does the missing person smoke?" If the answer is "yes", one might ask the following questions.

Example questions:

- What brand does he smoke?
- How many packs does he have with him?
- Why does he smoke? Is it to reduce stress?
- When does he smoke?
- How many cigarettes does he smoke a day?
- What would happen to his smoking consumption if he were under stress, such as being lost?
- What would happen to him physically and/or mentally if he ran out of cigarettes?

Tangential questions could go on indefinitely, depending on the subject matter. The interviewer must think outside the box and take tangential questioning as far as it will go. However, the interviewer must be aware that interviewee may also go off on tangents not relevant to the missing person. The interviewer may then have to redirect the interview to maintain focus. Additionally, the interviewee is usually under a lot of stress and may have a difficult time focusing on the questions. The interviewer may then have to paraphrase or break the questions down into manageable parts for clarity.

Variables in the person's life could affect the outcome of the incident. Dividing up the questions into the following categories will add control to the interview and help keep everyone focused and on track.

Health Status

Questions similar to those taught in first aid, first responder or Emergency Medical Technician (EMT) courses use the mnemonic device SAMPLE:

S	Are there any *Signs* or *Symptoms* of illness of injury?
A	Does he/she have any *Allergies* to insect bites or medications we need to be aware of?
M	Is he/she taking any *Medications*? If so, what for and where are they? What happens if he/she misses her medications? What happens if he/she takes too much of her medications?
P	Are there any *Past* medical conditions we need to be aware of? Is he/she under a doctor's care?
L	When was the *Last time he/she had food or water?*
E	Were there any *Events* leading up to his/her current health condition?

Mental Status

Following are questions related to the missing person's past and current mental condition and what changes could occur in his condition.

Past and current mental health status

- Is he happy or sad? Is he depressed? Is he feeling guilty or fearful? Has he turned inward and withdrawn or has he become more outgoing and friendly? What is making him this way?

- What are his likes and dislikes about people and things?

- What is his level of responsiveness? Has he been or is he disoriented to his surroundings?

- Would he give up the fight to find his way home?

- Would he become fatigued and unable to move on?

- What are his good and bad habits? Does he have something he uses as a "security blanket?" If so, what is it?

- Is he outgoing and friendly to kids, adults, strangers or animals?

Despondent/suicidal

- Has his sleep been disrupted?

- Has there been a stressful event or significant loss (actual or threatened) in his life?

- Is there a history of serious depression or mental disorder?

- Has he expressed feelings of guilt, hopelessness or depression?

- Has he been expressing great emotional and/or physical pain or distress?

- Has he been putting things in order, e.g., paying up insurance policies, calling old friends, giving away possessions?

- Has he talked about planning to commit suicide?

- Has he attempted suicide in the past?

- Has he shown efforts to learn about means of death or rehearse fatal acts and precautions to avoid rescue?

- Does he have the means (e.g., gun, pills, rope) to complete his intent?

Mental Retardation

- Did he learn to sit up, crawl or walk later than other children?

- Did he learn to talk later or have trouble speaking?

- Does he find it hard to remember things?

- Does he have trouble understanding how to pay for things?

- Does he have trouble understanding social rules?

- Does he have trouble seeing the consequences of his actions?

- Does he have trouble solving problems?

- Does he have trouble thinking logically?

Psychotic Behavior

- Does he show signs of sedation, depressed respiration, a semi-hypnotic state, contracted pupils, depressed reflexes and/or intoxication?

- Has he shown a lack of pain or fatigue?

- Is he showing signs of lack of coordination, restlessness, excitement, disorientation, confusion and/or delirium?

- Is he experiencing hallucinations, pupil dilation, increased blood pressure and body temperature, depressed appetite, and on occasion, nausea and chills?

Dementia

- Are there signs of memory loss that affect his job skills?
- Is he experiencing difficulty in performing familiar tasks?
- Is he having problems with language?
- Is he disorientated to time and place?
- Is he showing signs of poor or decreased judgment?
- Is he having problems with abstract thinking?
- Does he place items in inappropriate places?
- Is he showing signs of rapid changes in mood or behavior?
- Have there been dramatic changes in personality?
- Is he experiencing a loss of initiative?

Historical Information

History

- Has something like this happened before? If so, what happened and what were the results?

- Has the missing person walked away from other care facilities before? Where was she found?

- Does she have a history of running away?

Outside Influences

There are outside influences that could hamper or change the outcome of the search. In urban areas, weather and terrain are less of a factor than in the wilderness; however, they can be significant if they are severe. Rather, density of both people and buildings are stronger influences. Additionally, when fewer people are looking for the missing person (this typically happens during night searches when people are inside their homes) there is less chance of the missing person being seen. Similarly, the more buildings, streets and houses there are, the more places there are that must be searched.

Past and Current Search Activity

Questions to ask once the person has been noticed missing.

Search Activity

- What efforts have you (the reporting party) made to find the person? This will help determine if search areas have been missed or require searching again.

- What efforts have others made to find the person? What searching is still going on? Again, this will help determine if search areas have been missed or require searching again. It also determines who else might still be looking for the missing person.

Note: Most people are poor at estimating distances—they tend to overestimate, and are likely to give unreliable information. The most reliable information on locations and distance should be plotted on a map.

Time When Noticed Missing

- When did you (the reporting party) notice him/her missing?

- What were you doing or what activities were you engaged in prior to the time you noticed him/her missing? This question can be revealing because there can be a considerable difference from the time the person was reported missing and the actual time he or she was last seen.

Time Since Last Seen

- When was the last time the person was seen and what was he doing?
- When was the last time he took medication?
- When was the last time he had sleep and for how long?

Keep in mind that questions which require an estimate of time can produce a variety of responses. Make use of "activity association" to estimate time, such as "What program was on television at the time?" and "Was the sun just starting to go down?"

Sensitive Questions

Some questions may be sensitive. Thus, before asking sensitive questions, it is helpful to make the following statement: "The next set of questions may be sensitive, but we need to ask them to better understand the missing person's state of mind or possible impairments."

Example questions about an adolescent:

- How is she handling puberty ("the hormones on the run")?
- What are her sex habits?
- Does he or she have a girlfriend or boyfriend?
- Has he or she ever sneaked away to see a boyfriend or girlfriend?

Example questions about an adult:

- Could she be experiencing postpartum (after birth) depression?
- Is she going through menopause and how is she handling it? Is she taking any medications?
- Has she been diagnosed with or do you suspect that the missing person has dementia or Alzheimer's disease?
- Has there been any past criminal behavior?
- Is there a possibility that she is having an affair?
- Is the marriage in trouble?

Example question about someone of any age:

- Could he be using or have a problem with drugs or alcohol?

Final Questions

The most important questions are saved until the end.

Final questions

- Is there anything we should know that would help us locate the missing person?
- Where do you think she is?

These questions—at the end of an interview—produce surprising results. One effective technique is to ask if there is anything else and then give a pause; this will give the interviewee time to think and usually come up with one or two pieces of information that could prove important. The response to the last question above can be very accurate, as the following example shows.

A German couple came to visit a brother in the United States. The visiting wife went for a walk and did not come back. Law enforcement was called and a very difficult interview was conducted with the husband. Because of the language barrier, the brother interpreted the interview questions and the husband's responses. Interviewers learned that the wife was depressed and had a heart condition. However, the interviewers sensed that the brother was altering the questions and responses.

A non-law enforcement interpreter was brought in and coached on the questions to be asked. This interpreter took a walk with the husband and asked the final question, "Where do you think your wife is?" The husband gave a detailed response, stating that he thought his wife would walk for a while, find a secluded spot along a road, smoke one cigarette, take all of her heart medication and lie down to die.

Later that day some sightseers spotted the missing wife alive but unresponsive, just barely visible from an overlook. Upon investigation of the site, a single butt of a German brand of cigarettes was found along with the empty blister pack of her heart medications.

This story illustrates that the people closest to the missing person may have the best insight into the person and what has happened. At the beginning of an interview there may be many possible scenarios explaining why a person is missing. The hope is that the outcome will be simple. After interviewing for a few hours, however, the interviewee may realize and even be resigned to the fact that the final outcome may not be so simple. During the time spent in the interview, rapport between interviewer and interviewee should have grown stronger, which may help the interviewee to open up and describe, even in great detail, what they think happened to the missing person.

In some situations, the interviewee's answers to the questions may seem vague or untruthful. Unfortunately, some caregivers at nursing homes may not to give straight answers if a resident has wandered away; they may fear punishment for neglecting the person and allowing them to wander away. As the interviewer, it is wise to have a certain level of suspicion without the suspicion being obvious. Asking the same question in a different way later on in the interview will confirm or alleviate this suspicion. People under stress become easily confused and may give two different responses to the same question without realizing it. This technique is used in an interrogation of a suspected criminal in order to trip up the suspect. The early rapport building questions during an interrogation are designed to establish the interviewee's truth response mode. During a missing person interview, if it is felt that the interviewee is being less than truthful, it may be necessary to bring in law enforcement personnel skilled in interrogation in order to discover the truth.

Additional Considerations in Interviewing

Body Language

Research indicates that 93% of communication is non-verbal, i.e., body language, tone of voice and gesture (Mehrabian 1981). Posture, hand gestures, eye contact, licking of the lips, and fidgeting in a chair are all examples of non-verbal communication. The interviewer should be aware of the interviewee's body language and record what he or she sees. This may help later when there is a need to determine truthfulness. The interviewer's own body language, of course, should convey understanding, trust and professionalism.

How Long Will the Interview Last?

A good interview can take as much as two hours in order to be thorough and to take advantage of tangential questions. The time should be broken up into a short interview to obtain initial information that will be passed on to search management, followed by a longer, more in-depth interview. The interviewee should be informed about the interview length and process, including that there will be frequent breaks to gather up thoughts and make use of the rest room or obtain refreshments. The first interviewee will generate a list of other people to interview, each of whom could conceivably require another two hours. Investigation staff will need to gear up to manage more interviews and interview teams.

When Is a Good Time to Stop the Interview?

A good time is when you have exhausted the prepared list of questions. When sufficient crucial information has been gathered, it can be transmitted to the search planners during a break. However, if a particularly hot item of information is shared, then stop briefly and transmit the information immediately. For example:

> *At the start of a search for an elderly person who has walked away from a nursing home, searchers were told that the missing person used a cane to walk. From tangential questions during the interview of the reporting party, interviewers learned that if the person lost or dropped the cane he would fall and that he did not have the upper body strength to get up. At this point, the interview was interrupted and the information was transmitted to the field. Searchers were then advised that they should look for someone lying down or walking. Indeed, the missing person was found lying down after he lost his footing and cane. His first words were "I fell and can't get up."*

Inevitably, after reviewing the interview data with others, there will be more questions. The interviewers should tell the interviewee that they will be back with more questions and arrange a place to meet again. Someone should stay with the interviewee to keep them from leaving, as well as to have someone to talk to and perhaps continue an informal interview.

The Use of Tape Recorders

Many interviewers are not able to write down responses to questions quickly and may want to use a tape recorder. However, many people may find a tape recorder intimidating. Interviewers should ask the interviewee if they may tape the interview. Even if the interviewee agrees, he or she may not be as forthcoming with full or truthful responses. An alternative is to not tell the interviewee that the conversation will be recorded. However, this brings up the following issues. Interviewers need to be aware of the laws governing recorded conversations. Many law enforcement jurisdictions allow recording as long as one party is aware of the recording or if one party is under the direction or is an agent of law enforcement (Reference: California Penal Code Section 633 and 633.5). Further, as mentioned above, most interviews are lengthy and most tape recorders will not record continuously without having to stop and turn the tape over. Most recorders have an end of tape audible signal. If the interviewee notices this, the interviewer's credibility and rapport will be gone or severely diminished, which will cause irreparable damage to the interview.

Dealing with Parents of Missing Children

It goes without saying that the parent of a lost or missing child is experiencing tremendous emotions. In addition to being upset, feelings of shock and horror, denial and doubt, anger and aggression, agitation and restlessness, and guilt are common. These emotions are directed at themselves, other family and friends as well as the interviewer. It is important for the interviewer to understand these emotions and know how to deal with them. Voicing concern and understanding is important. It is very difficult to be empathetic unless the interviewer has personally experienced a child being lost; however a sympathetic "I understand how you feel" voice is appropriate.

Parents are under a lot of emotional stress and will have a tough time focusing on the interview. If interviewers notice that the parents are not focused, they may help the process by stating: "I know this is difficult, but in order for us to help find your child we need to get through these questions. Let's see if we can answer a few more and then we'll take a break." They may have difficulty understanding and answering complex questions; thus, breaking down questions if necessary may be helpful.

Another challenge occurs with divorced or separated parents. Accusations may be hurled from both sides in order to place blame or cause hurt. One ex-spouse may be hiding something from the other. In this situation, the interviewer should not try to mediate. Parents not on friendly terms should be separated into different rooms and have different interviewers. A good guideline for dealing with parents of missing children is described in "When Your Child is Missing: A Family Survival Guide," which can be accessed at http://ojjdp.ncjrs. org/pubs/childismissing/contents.html. See References for other guides.

Document, Document, Document

Take notes or use an interview form to record the conversation. Good documentation is imperative for several reasons. The most important reason is to be able to pass on information obtained in the interview to search management or the responsible law enforcement agency for review and evaluation and ultimately use it to improve the search. Another reason is to keep track of who talked to whom and when. Still another is for the legal record in case the missing person case turns out to be a criminal one. Things said and documented in the interview can be used in court. With this in mind, interview records should be written up as soon as possible while the information is fresh. Questions asked by the interviewer and the interviewee's responses should be included in the report. Subjective information such as "they seemed uneasy" should not be included as it could be subject to interpretation and questioning by a lawyer.

Post-Search Interviews

If the outcome of the search is positive—the missing person is found alive—then it is a good idea to conduct a post-search interview. Consider what the person has been through. It may not be appropriate to talk to them right away due to medical or mental conditions. However, try to get the information first hand from the person, not from a third party who could misinterpret a response. When a time and place for the post-search interview has been established, try to find out the following information:

Post-search interview information

- Where did the missing person go?
- How long he was mobile?
- What did he do?
- Why did he do what he did?
- How did he survive?
- Did he see the searchers, helicopters, signals, or hear his name called?
- Was there anyone else with him and what happened to that person?
- Confirm any possible clues found or items dropped and not found.

Then, plot the information on a map to show:

- Where he was found
- Where he got lost or disoriented
- The direction and paths traveled

Obtain the following additional information:

- Who made the find?
- What was the find environment?

This information can then be used to confirm the effectiveness of the search planning as well as resources such as dogs or a helicopter. The information gathered can also be used for statistics and future training.

Telephone Interviews

It may be necessary to conduct interviews over the telephone or even a radio in some circumstances. The important thing to keep in mind is that all of the interview and investigation techniques discussed so far also apply to telephone interviews. However, interviewers will lose the following important aspects of a face-to-face interview:

- Ability to observe body language (55% of non-verbal communication) (Mehrabian 1981)

- Show and discuss maps or diagrams to clarify information

- Obtain physical evidence or items that could be helpful in the investigation

---

Tips for telephone interviews

✓ Be a good listener.

✓ Be more descriptive and colorful in questioning, but use plain language that the interviewee will understand. This will require more time.

✓ Have marked-up maps faxed, transmitted by other electronic means, or by messenger.

✓ Speak slowly. Many people subconsciously interpret speech by listening as well as reading lips. When the interviewee is unable to read lips, you must slow down your rate of speaking, even more than you would typically to accommodate for stress factors.

✓ Lower your voice pitch, which will help prevent the problem of higher frequencies being filtered out through the telephone.

✓ Speak directly into the telephone transmitter to prevent muffled and unintelligible speech.

✓ Use the interviewee's name often to convey that you care and are paying attention.

Continued on next page ...

> ✓ Listen for overtones in the interviewee's voice. This is like reading between the lines and is a substitute for reading body language.
>
> ✓ Listen more intently to the responses to questions.
>
> ✓ Listen to your own voice. Does it convey warmth, sincerity, confidence, interest, and professionalism?

Phone interviews should be documented just like an in-person interview, as described earlier. There may only be one interviewer to record the information. Additional interviewers can listen in on an extension phone or use a speakerphone, although this can be intimidating to the interviewee. If cell phones must be used, the batteries should be charged and/or extra batteries available. It is disruptive if the call is dropped because of a low battery or if there are several breaks to change the batteries.

Interview Practice

In order to learn and reinforce any new skill one must practice. A simple technique to learn interview skills is to set up simple scenarios between three people—one interviewee and two interviewers.

Example scenario

The interviewee (who is also the reporting party) is told to think of an elderly relative or friend they know and can describe both physically and mentally.

The scenario
The elderly person has come to visit the interviewee for the weekend. The interviewee left alone to go to the grocery store and was gone for about an hour. Upon returning home from the store, the elderly person was gone. It is not known why the person is missing.

The interviewers conduct an interview using a prepared list of questions and try to build a profile of the missing person. After about 20 to 30 minutes, interviewers stop the interview and discuss the following:

Discussion questions

- How many questions (including tangential questions) were completed in the given time period?
- What did you learn about the missing person?
- What did you learn about the interview process?
- What questions would you add?
- What would you do differently?

Switch roles, change the scenario, make the missing person a juvenile, and discuss the results.

Field Interviews

As field teams progress on their search assignments they will come upon people living, working and traveling within the search area. Specific search assignments might be established to set up a trail or road block for the sole purpose of interviewing people going in or out of the search area. In all cases, searchers should take the opportunity to stop and interview these people to elicit information that could be useful in the search. An interview can be as simple as showing a picture of the missing person and asking if they have seen him.

Procedures and tips for effective field interviewing

The location of field interviews may be any frequently traveled routes into and out of the search area. If the specific assignment is to be a trail or road block, it should be set up to make it difficult for users to pass by the interview team, but not so difficult that it would impede two-way traffic. The area should be marked so it is easily seen. Enough personnel should be available to handle a large volume of traffic in order not to miss anyone who could have potential clues.

First, careful selection about whom to interview and under what circumstances is important. People need to feel they are not threatened or inconvenienced. Searchers also need to feel they are safe. Time of day, the surroundings, and the urgency of the search should be taken into account. People who live in or frequent the area are usually the best sources.

Second, searchers should approach each potential witness in a friendly manner and identify themselves and the reason for wanting to ask questions. If the person is reluctant, explain that his cooperation is completely voluntary but may be very important to the success of the search. For example, it is helpful to explain the importance of relevant negatives—such as the fact that no one was seen at all in a given area—to be better able to focus the search efforts.

Initial, basic field interview questions

- Have you seen (or "Do you know ...?") this person? Show a photo of the missing person.

- How long have you been here?

- Would you have seen him if he were in this area?

- Who else might have seen him?

- Did you hear or see anything unusual?

- What did you notice along the way?

All negative responses should be recorded to keep track of places where the missing person was NOT seen. If there are positive responses, more questions should be asked to find out what else the potential witness knows. If the information seems particularly important, an experienced interviewer should meet the person, either in the field or at the base. Name, address, e-mail, home, work and cell phone numbers should be collected for follow up. If a group of people are being interviewed, contact information should be collected from at least two people. Interview notes should be reviewed before releasing the witness. All witness information must be legible, unambiguous, accurate and complete. As well, contact information for the Investigations Unit (e.g., phone, e-mail, Web site) should also be provided in case the interviewee remembers any additional information at a later time.

A brief description of the person(s) interviewed should be documented—for example, number of adult males, number of adult females, approximate ages, appearance (race, ethnicity, equipment that might stand out). In rare cases and at the direction of the incident command, a digital photograph of each person interviewed may be taken with permission.

If searchers are asked about what is happening, only non-sensitive information about the missing person and the conduct of the search should be shared. Searchers in the field must not speak to the media. Members of the media should be referred to the Public Information Officer (PIO) at base.

Summary of Interviewing

The process of investigation and interviewing in a lost or missing person incident is a continual process of gathering information to better understand what the missing person might do in a particular circumstance and plan how to make the best use of resources. Success depends on the following key points:

Key elements of a successful interview process

✓ Understand that interviewing in a lost or missing incident is different from interviewing in the context of a standard law enforcement interview and interrogation.

✓ Interviews are in-depth and designed to paint a mental picture of the missing person.

✓ Interview anyone who has direct knowledge of the missing person and/or direct knowledge of the circumstances leading up to the disappearance.

✓ In addition to gathering basic descriptive information, include the person's:

　° Mobility and ability to travel
　° Ability to survive
　° Mindset and intent
　° Ability or tendency to respond
　° Likes and dislikes and what attracts her attention
　° Past and recent behavior and life history

✓ Understand that the interviewer is building rapport while conducting an interview. The interviewer's demeanor can make the difference in the amount and quality of the information she receives.

✓ Be a good listener.

✓ Select an interview location and setting that will reduce stress on the interviewee.

✓ Have a guideline or list of questions prepared prior to conducting an interview to keep the interview on track.

✓ Take advantage of tangential questions.

✓ Practice, Practice, Practice

Internet Search

As technology and the information super highway advances so has its use in the search for a missing person. Recent documented cases have shown that pure investigation using the Internet have resulted in the location of missing persons, thus preventing unnecessary use of resources in the field. For example:

A backcountry packer crew came across an abandoned campsite fully set up with a tent, sleeping bad, cooking area and proper food storage. A luggage tag inside of a bear canister revealed a name and contact information. A review of the backcountry permits confirmed that a Mr. Smith (name has been changed) did enter the area but was not technically overdue. The trail was non-existent because of snow coverage at the time. Because there had been past experiences with abandoned sites of this nature, the local authorities felt that a search was warranted.

That night, a Google™ search on the Internet revealed that Mr. Smith was an Information Technologies Professor at Lancaster University in England. Further searching uncovered his office phone number, where his voice mail stated he was on holiday in the United States. Using the Lancaster University phone directory listed on the Internet, investigators were able to contact Mr. Smith's co-workers to conduct interviews and determine his travel plans. The University Web site also had a photograph of Mr. Smith. Sometime early the next morning, investigators discovered that a co-worker had received an e-mail from the Mr. Smith a few days earlier.

Investigators obtained Mr. Smith's e-mail address and sent him notification regarding the search efforts. He wrote back several days later to confirm his well being, and informed them that he was in a nearby town at the time.

Further interviews with Mr. Smith concluded that he set up camp and spent one night. The morning of the second day he hiked to a nearby lookout point to "get my bearings." He traveled along a ridgeline for what turned into a short day hike. He attempted to re-trace his steps and he quickly realized that he had become disoriented. He spent some time trying to find his camp and, after several hours of no success, he decided to hike out. He bivouacked that night and the next day stumbled across a well-traveled trail and was able to exit on the fourth day. He then took a bus to the nearby town.

As illustrated above, Web sites of employers can yield valuable information that can be used to resolve the case of a missing person. Web sites of organizations of which the missing person is known to be a member can also produce valuable information. Additional sources of information can be found by typing in the missing person's name in a search engine (e.g., Google™, Yahoo™). Many people, especially the young, have established their own Web sites and post journals sometimes referred to as personal publishing or "blogs."

Blogs (also called web logs or weblogs) are a frequent, chronological publication of personal thoughts and web links. Essentially, a blog is a Web site where a person writes content on an ongoing basis. As one adds content to the blog, new posts are automatically positioned on top of previous posts so a visitor can see "what's new." The visitor can leave comments or link to another blog or e-mail to others if they choose. A blog can be a personal diary, a daily pulpit, a collaborative space, a political soapbox, a breaking-news outlet, a collection of links, or one's own private thoughts. There are literally millions of blogs, in all shapes and sizes, and there are no real rules. A blog is often a combination of what's happening in someone's personal and business life as well as what is happening on the web—a kind of high-tech, hybrid diary/guide site. The trend has gained momentum with the introduction of automated publishing systems, most notably Google's Blogger™ at www.blogger.com or www.livejournal.com. Thousands of individuals use services such as Blogger to simplify and accelerate the publishing process. These personal Web sites will also include photos of the blogger, names and photos of friends and family and even people they dislike. Journals posted on the blog can reveal the missing person's innermost thoughts and help further develop the missing person profile.

"First, they do an on-line search."

Other Investigative Techniques

In addition to interviewing, search management should consider other ways of gathering information about the incident, the missing person and the environment in which the search will be conducted.

Records of the missing person
- ✓ Family photographs
- ✓ Yearbooks
- ✓ Medical reports
- ✓ School or work records
- ✓ Computer files
- ✓ E-mails
- ✓ Credit card tracers
- ✓ Video security camera records
- ✓ The person's phone calls or answering machine recordings
- ✓ Missing clothing, shoes or personal items
- ✓ Criminal records
- ✓ Automobile registration
- ✓ Sales receipts
- ✓ ATM withdrawals

The list can go on indefinitely. All the possibilities should be considered, based on what interviewers have learned about the missing person.

Institution Checks

Call all the likely public or private institutions where he missing person might be. A description of the missing person should be left at the institution, in case he is admitted later.

Institutions
- ✓ Hospitals
- ✓ Care centers
- ✓ Mental health facilities
- ✓ Jail
- ✓ Detox centers
- ✓ Domestic violence shelters
- ✓ Homeless shelters
- ✓ County Protective Services

Clues

Collect and analyze all clues discovered during the course of the search. Follow up on any pertinent clues. Forms to keep track of clues are found in Appendix H.

> **Clues**
> - ✓ Items found by searchers
> - ✓ Canine alerts
> - ✓ Human or vehicle tracks
> - ✓ Eyewitness sightings
> - ✓ Reported unusual noises or smells

Knowledgeable People

Use people who are familiar with the neighborhood or area to help identify hiding places, attractive hazards, and popular gathering places. They can tell what is normal or abnormal about the area, who lives where, and general information that may be helpful in the search. Familiar people include police who patrol the area and other public employees who service the area. They should remain in the command post to be available to instantly respond to questions during the course of the search.

It is important to center the investigation, including the interviewing, in one functional section of search management. Under ICS, typically, it would be the Planning/Intelligence Section, which correlates all the information gathered from different sources. Equally important is for the Planning Section to pass on its analyses to the Operations Section so that immediate action can be taken on vital information. There should be a continual flow of information between the two sections so each knows what the other is doing.

Chapter 8. Search Management

Assembling an overhead team immediately at base should be the first concern of search management. A contingent of key personnel and multiple resources will provide the best means for rapid containment and gathering of clues before they are distorted or lost. Resources should include overhead managers, investigation and interviewing personnel, a public information officer, trailing and air scent dogs and vehicles. After establishing the overhead command structure, the first assignments will need to be focused on investigation and containment.

It is assumed that the Incident Command System (ICS) and the standard procedures taught in search management courses worldwide will be used to conduct the urban search incident. These procedures work equally well in either urban or wilderness settings. Refer to Appendix A on the structure of ICS. This chapter will focus on procedures that are particularly applicable to urban searches.

Setting Up a Search Base

When the search effort moves beyond the initial response to a full field search and the operation moves from the tailgate of a vehicle to a large, busy command post, a search base must be established. Refer to Chapter 6 (Search Base Considerations) for selection of the site. The arrival of the Logistics Section before other searchers simplifies the setup and organization of the search base, as described below.

The location of the command post should be established first. If it is in a fixed structure, all other functions follow from its layout. If it is a mobile command post (MCP), the vehicle should be parked in a prominent place accessible to the staff. The search base area should be cordoned off or at least restricted to those involved with the search, if possible. In some cases, it may be necessary to close a street or narrow a travel lane to permit the base to be set up or to allow vehicles to enter and leave base with ease. It is essential to obtain the cooperation of the law enforcement agency controlling traffic for this purpose.

Some agencies prefer to handle check-in at the entry to the search base in order to make sure everyone is accounted for. Others conduct check-in at the staging area or near the command post (CP). In any case, someone should be available to direct vehicles to the designated parking spaces and to answer questions of people coming to the operation. A space near the CP or staging area should be created to allow pickup and drop-off of search teams, preferably utilizing a one-way circulation plan that does not require them to back up. As well, an area should be designated for the media, especially television trucks.

Other base functions should be situated as normally recommended. Eating and sleeping should be done away from the CP. The staging area can be located close to the CP if it is a small search; for a larger search, this area should be placed a short distance away, with the Staging Manager in communication with the CP by radio or cordless phone. If the particular ICS function is not evident from the facility itself, signs should be posted to indicate the locations of each function. Command staff personnel should wear vests or other means of identifying their function, particularly during mutual aid searches.

Personnel Control

While ICS uses a check-in list (ICS Form 211) to record participants in an operation, many search and rescue teams use the T-card, a more flexible and useful method of keeping track of personnel. T-cards are small card-stock disposable cards a few inches wide and about 4 inches long, cut with a T-shaped top. Some search teams provide members with blank T-cards well before a search which they fill in with their name, team or unit name, rank, qualifications, medical conditions and emergency contact number. When they get to an operation, the rest of the card is filled in with incident information, e.g., date and time arrived, time available until (end of shift), and special equipment carried. The T-card is given to Check-in, which passes it on to the Resources Unit of the Planning Section. The Planning Section uses T-cards to put together field teams and make other assignments.

T-cards

Once staff and field team assignments are given, the T-cards are placed in the appropriate slots on a display board so that one can see where all searchers are located. Units or personnel can be identified on the board as being "In Service", "Available", "Assigned", or "Out of Service." A searcher's card can be moved around from slot to slot on the board as the searcher is moved from place to place or assigned new duties. At the end of the operation, when the searcher checks out, his card is pulled and put into the Out of Service slot. The ICS 211 form should still be filled out to keep a separate record of all participants.

Display board

Mapping

An important function in search management is the utilization of maps to plan the search, keep track of the progress of the search, and record the efforts of search teams. This function can be handled by the Planning Section or the Operations Section or shared. The preplan should set forth how mapping will be done within the urban areas under the responsible agencies' jurisdiction.

If the urban area is small, the agency may be able to use only one map, which can be mounted on a map board or table in the mobile command post (MCP). In most cases, however, many maps will be needed to cover the city at the large scale (1 inch=2000 feet or less) required to adequately identify streets and prominent features. These maps should be available on the MCP or at some central location easily accessible during a search. The map(s) appropriate to cover the search area is selected and mounted on map boards. A Mylar, other plastic overlay cover, or an unsupported vinyl sheet should be placed over the paper maps and secured to protect them from water and general wear and tear.

At least three information overlays representing the "before," "during," and "after" phases of the search are placed over the map. Alternatively, separate paper maps may be used.

1. Plan—The first overlay or map shows the search plan, e.g., search base, search sectors, team assignments, attractive hazards, the PLS, and other information necessary for planning.

2. Status—The second overlay plots the locations of field teams and includes information, e.g., clues, as teams report in by radio.

3. Debrief—The third overlay is used during each field team's debriefing to indicate which areas they actually searched and the probability of detection (POD) of each area.

For overlays, 8½ x 11 clear plastic copier (overhead projector) film is used and held down with adhesive double-sided poster tape. All overlays should contain registration marks indicating which map they correspond to and how they line up with the map features. Overlays can be removed and replaced as needed. Multiple overlays can be left on the map, however it may be confusing. New overlays can be made for each operational period or when they get too confusing; these overlays should include the date and time.

Permanent marker pens in different colors should be used to mark the overlays. Keep a small bottle of ethyl alcohol and cotton swabs handy to make corrections or erasures.

Instead of paper maps many search teams use computer mapping programs. They enable the Planning Section to perform all the above functions in an easier and more accurate fashion, including plotting search team UTM coordinate positions as they are reported from GPS receivers. Maps can be printed with the selected information.

Computer mapping programs also have limitations. As search managers need other information from the computer, the map will not be visible on the computer monitor. Also, the command post display screen should be projected so several people can see it at the same time. In addition, field teams must work with maps printed from the computer, usually 8½ x 11 size; thus they will carry several maps during most urban searches, which can be cumbersome. Nevertheless, computer mapping programs seem to be the wave of the future.

Strategies

Before search teams are sent into the field, search managers must consider the information from the investigation, despite the fact that the information may be incomplete or sketchy at the time the initial search plan is developed.

Essentially, search managers are faced with the question "Where and how do we search, given the resources available or anticipated?" Various strategies or tactics can be employed by search planners, depending on the incident circumstances. These will be described below, and in Chapter 9 (Tactics) and Chapter 11 (Missing Person Behavior).

Scenario Analysis and Subject Profiling

It has been said that a missing person search is like a classic mystery. When a person is reported missing the first thought is: what happened and why is the person missing? Naturally, people come up with stories to explain what happened, i.e., they develop scenarios. Missing person scenarios are developed for two purposes. The first is to assess the urgency of the situation in order to determine the level of searching required, including whether to call out a search team. The second purpose is to plan the search, as discussed below.

Scenarios start to emerge with the first call to 911, while the operator attempts to make sense of the story being told by the reporting party. Thereafter, the search manager receives more information from the initial response and begins to put together a story of what might have happened to the missing person. Unless the case is straightforward, additional scenarios may develop. With new information, the search planning team can sort out which scenario is most likely so they can begin to plan where to search first. Other contingencies or scenarios can be included in the search plan as resources become available to investigate them.

The scenarios presented at the beginning of this book are examined in the next two pages. Possible explanations are put forth to show the kind of scenarios that may be developed to explain about what might have taken place.

Scenario One

You are the watch commander for the Police Department. It is 8:30 p.m. and you just received a report from the dispatcher reporting a missing 11-year-old female, Stacy Costa, who has been missing since 2:00 p.m. The initial investigation reveals that after school, Stacy called her mother at work and told her she was going on her bicycle to a friend's house three blocks away. When her mother got home after work about 6:30 p.m., Stacy was not there. After calling the friend's house, as well as other neighbors and friends, and then driving around the neighborhood, her mother called the police about 8:30 p.m. There is no history of the child missing before or running away from home. She likes to frequent a local shopping center, especially the arcade games area. She rides her bike around the neighborhood a lot and takes the municipal bus regularly to visit her father, who lives across town.

Possible explanations:

- ☐ Stacy is at a friend's house.
- ☐ Stacy is hanging out at the mall.
- ☐ Stacy has been injured and is unable summon help.
- ☐ Stacy is in the hospital as the result of an accident and is unconscious.
- ☐ Stacy has run away from home.
- ☐ Stacy is with her father.
- ☐ Stacy is with another relative.
- ☐ Stacy is hiding in her room.
- ☐ Stacy has been kidnapped and taken from the area.
- ☐ Stacy's mother is not telling the truth about the circumstances of her daughter's disappearance.

Scenario Two

You are the search and rescue coordinator for the county. You have just received a call from the City of Martinez Police Department reporting that Walter Czar, an 83-year-old male with a history of stroke and dementia, has been reported missing by his care facility. The information you received is not much to go on. Walter was last seen about 3:30 p.m. sitting in the garden of Sunny Care Home. One of the attendants of the facility went looking for Walter to give him his afternoon medication and could not find him. The administration checked the entire facility and the streets of the suburban neighborhood surrounding the care facility and turned up nothing. It is now 7:00 p.m. and getting dark.

Possible explanations:

☐ Walter is still somewhere in the facility.

☐ Walter is wandering the neighborhood.

☐ Walter is downtown and has wandered into a store or office building.

☐ Walter has taken public transportation to try to get back to the home he lived in 20 years ago.

☐ Walter has been injured and is unable summon help.

☐ Walter is in the hospital as the result of an accident and is unconscious.

☐ Walter is in a shelter.

☐ Walter is in police custody.

☐ Walter's family picked him up and did not notify the facility.

☐ The facility personnel are not telling the truth about the circumstances of Walter's disappearance.

All possible explanations should have some basis in reality given the information available. The point is to make a list of plausible theories on where the missing person is and the situation he or she may be in. Next, the list is prioritized from the most likely to the least likely. As with any mystery, the final step is to investigate the incident through interviewing and searching for physical evidence that will substantiate the theory, rule it out or lead to a new theory.

In most urban searches the more obvious or likely scenarios are the ones that usually prove true. If the missing person is not found the case can best be summed up by Sir Arthur Conan Doyle's Sherlock Holmes' classic statement, "When you have eliminated the impossible, whatever remains, however improbable, must be the truth." It may be that the true scenario—what actually happened—places the subject outside the targeted search area. Further physical effort by search personnel will continue to be fruitless and the search will be suspended. (See also Chapter 5, Suspending an Urban Search Operation, p. 71)

Missing Person Behavior

An obvious first step to finding a missing person is to guess where he or she might be. A profile of the missing person can be developed using information provided by informants or other sources to help focus efforts in areas where the person would likely go. However, often the search manager must put together a hasty search plan based on little specific personal information. In such cases, behavior studies are useful.

Several researchers have analyzed the behavior of various types of missing persons in order to arrive at tendencies for that type of person. "Lost person" studies examine the behavior exhibited by a representative sample of people who are reported missing and are pursuing a common interest or activity (e.g., hiking, fishing, climbing, berry picking) or share a common condition (e.g., young children, people with Alzheimer's disease or mental impairments, people who are suicidal). The theory is that, on average, people tend to behave in a certain predictable way. This information can help focus search efforts when a person in a certain category is missing.

Behavior patterns are usually expressed in terms of what the person did when he got lost, i.e., did he stay put or try to "walk out" (self-rescue). If he walked out, the data would include the amount of time he spent walking, the distance he walked, and how far from the PLS he was when found. Some studies also include a statistical breakdown of how the person was found—whether by ground searchers or other search techniques—or whether he walked out.

In the city, however, the situation is different. First, a missing person could fit into so many more activity categories that it would be difficult to select the one that solely represents the subject. Second, because a city is complex, the number of possible scenarios increases exponentially. Third, with the exception of children, despondent people and people with Alzheimer's, few studies of urban missing persons have been conducted—until now.

This book presents new statistics for the field of urban search that will greatly assist the search manager in searching for ten categories of missing persons in the urban environment: dementia, children (in age groups 1-3, 4-6 and 7-12), abducted children, despondent, mental retardation, mental illness, autism, and substance abuse. The data comes from the International Search and Rescue Incident Database (ISRID), the most comprehensive study conducted to date on where missing persons are found, how far away they are found from the initial planning point (IPP), and the specific behaviors associated with each category of missing person. Missing person behavior data and profiles specific to the urban environment are provided in detail in Chapter 11.

Chapter 9. Tactics

In the initial stages of the search (see Chapter 5), management typically starts with the first person on scene, for instance, over the hood of a car in front of the residence of the missing person; and the initial or hasty search centers around tasks. This chapter outlines tasks, assignments and tactics that are essential in running a search.

The first person on the scene will need to do the following tasks:

1. **Gather information**

   ✓ Obtain information and circumstances surrounding the missing person.

   ✓ Find out what has already been done to locate the missing person.

2. **Prepare for search**

   ✓ Establish search urgency, i.e., if it is a missing person, despondent, etc.

   ✓ Send out a BOLO (Be On the Look Out) to all local law enforcement agencies in the area.

   ✓ Secure point last seen (PLS) or last known position (LKP), such as the vehicle or residence.

   ✓ Protect any obvious clues and potential scent articles for search dogs.

3. **Begin initial search**

   ✓ Conduct a hasty search of immediate area.

   ✓ Check on leads produced by the initial investigation.

   ✓ Start to write up "reflex tasks" or obvious field assignments.

When planning the assignments, start with the following tasks:

1. Thoroughly check within a ¼ mile (300 meters) radius around the PLS.

   ✓ Use established checklists included in the Field Operations Guide (FOG) manual and past experiences in the area.

   ✓ Look for clues and interview contacts in the field.

   ✓ Include areas based on information about the missing person's travel plans.

2. When using search dogs:

   ✓ Gather scent articles.

   ✓ Use trailing dogs from the PLS.

   ✓ Use area dogs and/or cadaver dogs around the PLS.

Document initial efforts, collecting the following information:

Use established forms or just a standard pad of paper to record:

   ✓ List of who is in the field

   ✓ List of what they are doing in the field

   ✓ List of who is scheduled to arrive

Conduct initial briefing for resources as they arrive at the search, including:

1. General information:

   ✓ Circumstances

   ✓ Description

   ✓ Medical history (if relevant)

   ✓ Intentions (if known)

   ✓ Radio Channel

2. Objectives and goals of the search assignment including the limits to search assignments

It is during this initial phase that 70–80% of missing persons are found and the search ends just as it is getting started. If the person is not found immediately, then more formal and systematic searching tactics are necessary.

Containment

One of the first tactics to use in an urban search is containment—the effort to prevent the person from leaving the search area without being noticed or leaving a clue. The longer it takes a loved one to report a person missing, and the longer the requesting agency waits to call the search and rescue team, the harder it will be to set up any sort of containment. If they wait too long the missing person could be miles away, past several jurisdictions or even in the next county. A quick response to a missing person report may be able to set up containment procedures that could confine the search to a relatively small area. But it needs to be done quickly because the missing person can travel far in a short period of time. Even walking is easier and faster in a city than in the woods, and there are a great many more options as far as route and method of travel.

In urban areas, natural barriers to the person's travel are limited. Streets and roadways make it easier for the person to use private transportation (cars, motorcycles, bicycles, etc.) to leave the area. The same holds true for public transportation (buses, trolleys, subways, taxis, etc.). Busy streets or highways are not boundaries, even for small children. All these limitations should be taken into account when planning a containment strategy.

Most containment in the hasty search mode can be handled by vehicle patrols, with a trained observer in the passenger's seat. Observers will require good briefings and information with accurate descriptions and a good profile about the missing person they are looking for. Here again, the investigation information is critical. There are many people out there who might look like the missing person. The better and more accurate the information, the better the chances of success. Updated information needs to be given out as it becomes apparent through investigation.

Bicycle units are another hasty search technique that combines active visual searching with a containment component. Both vehicles and bikes can cover a lot of streets in a short period of time. Helicopters can also be employed to search a large area very quickly in the hopes that the missing person can be spotted from the air.

Another containment tactic is to position personnel at critical "escape route" locations where the person might leave the area and to watch for signs of passage. Examples of these routes would be security entrances to gated communities or housing developments or the main entrances and exits to buildings. Interviewing people who enter or leave the area might also turn up valuable information. Except under very unusual circumstances, however, it is impossible to seal off any large urban area to prevent the person from escaping.

Public Transportation and Public Corridor Considerations

Containment in urban areas is made more difficult because of the ready availability of public transportation. Public transportation such as trains, buses, trolleys, subways and taxis should be checked to see if the missing person used any of them to leave the area. Designated pathways for pedestrians, bicycles, mountain bikes, or roller bladders can be investigated by interviewing people using these routes. Find out if the missing person frequently uses these modes of transportation. Latchkey children (independent children where parents are not at home during the day) are very adept at getting around the neighborhood. Determine if the missing person has money and a means of access to transportation. Knowing these details can better help develop plans and strategies.

The route of the public transportation possibly utilized by the person should be treated as a separate path or trail. For example, a bloodhound may trail the person to a bus stop. A bus can travel over a wide urban and rural area, even out of the containment area, but it does follow a fixed path. An investigator will need to contact the bus company and the bus drivers who drive the routes in the defined search area. It is critical to interview the bus driver earlier on in the search rather than waiting to determine if the missing person got on the bus and, if so, where he or she got off. Also inquire what clothing the person was wearing and if he or she was with someone. If the driver does not remember the person, then a list of all bus stops will determine where further investigation needs to take place.

A proven technique to pick up the trail along public transportation routes is called leap-frogging. Trailing dog and/or investigative teams jump from bus stop to bus stop looking for the missing person's scent or other clues. (See Chapter 4, Dog Resources, p. 37)

Many mass transit systems have their own police services and, most importantly, video surveillance. Videotapes can be reviewed to see if the missing person may have entered or exited a transit station or train. Some people with Alzheimer's have been known to get on transit systems and ride all day and night.

Attractive Destinations and Hazards

What things are likely to attract the missing person? Each urban area has its own special "hang-outs." For children it may be the local convenience store with its video games or other places like culverts, ditches, canals, creeks, and utility easements. Children may have a "fort," a tree house or other special hiding place in or about their residence. Identify hiding places like backyards, abandoned cars, old refrigerators, out buildings, sheds and woodpiles. Investigations will help establish the high probability areas based on the missing person's profile and behavior pattern.

Malls, stores, churches, and community centers are possible attractive destinations for missing persons with Alzheimer's. One should not discount any place where a person could hide. For example, there is one documented missing person case of an elderly woman in the early stages of dementia who would go out in the yard and cover herself with fallen leaves. In the case of someone with Alzheimer's, it is important to remember that the person is living in the reality of his or her past. People with Alzheimer's cannot remember recent events and are often disoriented to time and place, i.e., they do not know what day, month, year or season it is, and they do not know where they are. It is helpful to know where the person is in his or her own personal lifeline. Knowing this history can help search management prepare a plan that takes details of a person's life into account and targets likely destinations. For example, if searchers learned that the person grew up on a farm and was accustomed to taking naps outside or in the barn, a search of likely outbuildings or comfortable sleeping areas should be considered.

Search Area Delineation and Segmentation

Once the appropriate maps have been attained the search area must be delineated and broken up into manageable search areas. If historical information is available for searches conducted in a particular geographic area, then it would be prudent to conduct a preplanning statistical analysis. Lacking such information, standard search area delineation techniques used in the wilderness setting can be adapted to urban searches. One way to estimate overall search area delineation is to judge the distance the subject could have traveled during the time elapsed since the last sighting, using whatever mode of transportation would have been available, and draw a circle on the map with that distance as the radius and with the point last seen (PLS) as the center (theoretical search area). That circle can then be modified to take into account any barriers or impediments to travel (subjective search area). The resulting line will then delineate the search area boundary. Obviously, the more time that has elapsed since the person went missing and the speed at which they could travel, the larger the area will be. Adjustments can be made based on locally available knowledge of the area.

Given this, what is the best way to segment urban search areas? The size of each segment depends primarily on what types of search assignments are contemplated. In the first phases of the search, the plan may focus on vehicle search with possibly a few canine teams or foot teams assigned to specific targets. Vehicles can typically cover about a half square mile of medium-density residential development in 30 to 60 minutes. The canine units may need an hour or two to complete their assignment. It is rare to need more than a few hours to completely search a segment using Type I searching, before either expanding the search area or going to Type II techniques.

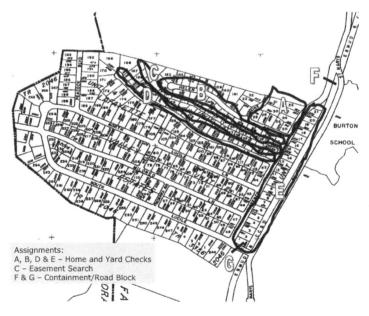

Assignments:
A, B, D & E – Home and Yard Checks
C – Easement Search
F & G – Containment/Road Block

Example of urban segmentation

Urban search segments can be broken down into blocks, using as the dividing line streets, alleys, property boundaries or easements, as long as they are clearly visible to search teams in the field. This all may be contingent upon the density of development around the PLS. Streets can be laid out in grid patterns, meander in curves or dead-end into cul de sacs. Boundaries may have to be delineated arbitrarily based on the area to be covered with the resources available. Wilderness searches use creek drainages or ridge lines as the edges of search segments. Additionally, hiking trails are treated as separate segments. In an urban search, streets are the center of a task, with the field teams searching both sides of the street as they progress. Fence lines that run along the backs of housing lots or easements of property also may be appropriate sector boundaries, and may be used instead of the street. The segmenting process will become apparent in the discussion of door-to-door canvassing tactics in the next chapter.

Clue Management

In the wilderness environment, where few people have recently passed, clues left by the lost person may be easy to find. A candy wrapper in a green meadow is easy to spot and can be corroborated with additional nearby clues such as footprints, broken twigs, etc. The urban environment, on the other hand, is rich with evidence of people's passage. However, the majority of the physical clues that are found will often have little or nothing to do with the missing subject. Just as broadcasting the missing person's description to the public will elicit numerous false sighting reports, so will finding many possible physical clues confuse search management. A separate function should be established by managers to keep track, sort through and handle the multitude of clues searchers find. Pertinent clues should be logged in (see Appendix H Interview and Clue Forms) and tagged. It is not uncommon for physical clues gathered during a search to become evidence of a crime, if the missing person incident turns into a criminal case. The search management team should, therefore, be well-versed in the laws of evidence in their jurisdiction and in their responsibilities regarding the chain of custody for that evidence.

Documentation

Detailed and thorough door-to-door interview logs, as well as other investigation reports, should be analyzed by search management for use in search planning. These logs may produce more pieces to the puzzle and may lead the search in a totally different direction than originally anticipated. Accurate maps of areas both searched and not searched need to be kept. Proper documentation can be used to back up the decision to drop to a limited search operation, or to suspend a long search. In an urban setting, a limited search means that all avenues have been exhausted and there are no clues. If search coverage is thorough, it may be acceptable to say the missing person is out of the area. The responsibility for the search is then turned over to the agency with jurisdiction. Documentation is kept together in the event that the search resumes. If the missing person is eventually found deceased, the documentation may help clear up the case.

Chapter 10. Search Operations

Field Team Assignments

Field team assignments are usually made by the Planning Section after team assignments have been put together by the Operations Section. Hasty foot teams, including canine teams, are made up of two, three, or sometimes four searchers. Two- or three-person teams are preferable because they can move fast and can be transported in one vehicle to their drop-off point. Foot teams should have at least one radio on the designated frequency, a map or maps covering their search sector, and subject information, including a flyer, if possible. Teams should have a GPS unit if the maps being used have UTM coordinates on them.

Communications

The agency preplan should include protocols for setting up and maintaining communications between the command post and field teams, as well as inter-team communications. In accordance with ICS protocols, plain language should be used during radio transmissions rather than codes, e.g., "Copy" vs. "10-4" or "What is your location?" vs. "What is your 10-20?". However, in some cases, special private codes or specific phrases can be used to transmit sensitive information when certain parties are present and such information is not intended for them to hear. For instance, news media monitor radio frequencies used by searchers. In addition, family members may be within earshot of the command post radios; it can be devastating if the family accidentally hears that their missing loved one was found dead. Searchers as well as radio dispatchers should be briefed on these codes prior to the start of an assignment. Examples of codes and their meanings:

Code	Meaning
15-D-1	One subject found dead
15-G-2	Two subjects found in good condition
15-H	Possible homicide
15-S	Secure scene
15-T-2	Two subjects in need of transportation
15-E	Medical on scene
15-M	Medical needed

It is best not to transmit a message over the radio concerning dead bodies or possible law enforcement concerns, such as a homicide; rather instruct the searcher to request a police officer to meet them or to use a more secure method, such as a cell phone, to transmit the information. Spontaneous volunteers who will probably not have radios should specifically be informed on this point.

Because cell phones are so common and searchers are likely to have them, it is important to designate specific numbers for specific purposes, e.g., IC, Plans Section, Investigation, Transportation. These numbers should be included on the search team briefing forms. Wireless phone coverage is almost always adequate in an urban area. Thus, cell phones are a good way to provide backup communications to the radio system.

Briefing

The briefing of searchers will require more detail in an urban setting than in the wilderness. The more information about the missing person, the better. A detailed description of the person's clothing will help the teams spot potential subjects in large crowds. This detail would also include layers of clothing that might be shed by children or a person with Alzheimer's. Information about the missing person's personality is also helpful to give team members an insight into what he or she might do in a particular situation. Anything unusual about the person should be mentioned. The "lie test" question should be discussed and agreed upon. As noted in the section on media relations, specific information is withheld and known only to the searchers. This type of information—usually something distinctive about the missing person such as a piece of jewelry—would confirm the subject's identity if he or she were actually seen. The briefing must also instruct searchers what to do when dealing with media contacts. (See Media Relations, p. 65 and Door-to-Door Canvassing, p. 141.)

Safety issues about the neighborhood must be emphasized and understood prior to leaving for the assignment. These issues should be written out in a safety/hazard risk assessment. Instructions on how to handle the inevitable media contacts and to whom the media should direct their questions should be included.

Team assignments should include team call sign; communication, medical and safety plans; description of the missing person, and maps of the assignment. All team members must understand what they are to do before leaving for their assignment, including whether they are authorized to search private property. It is important to constantly reinforce and emphasize that thoroughness, as well as being meticulous in all team efforts, is the ultimate goal. Team members must be given sufficient searching data about the missing person to be able to recognize a clue when they find one. For example, an assignment might be to look for the butt of a specific brand of cigarette. In such a case, searchers should be instructed to find a compromise between reporting every cigarette butt and reporting nothing. Searchers should expect that there will be a lot of unrelated trash and false clues.

Before teams are sent out, the initial briefing can be done for the entire assembled crew; however, subsequent briefings are usually done by the field team leader. The team leader must receive the same briefing information at the same time he or she receives the team assignment to be able to pass it on to the team. All briefing information should be written down so copies can be given to the field teams.

Institution Checks

As noted in Chapter 7 Search Planning, a procedure for checking area institutions should be established. Local jails, alcohol or drug detoxification and rehabilitation centers, homeless shelters, and domestic violence shelters should be checked. For instance, someone who is disoriented due to Alzheimer's might be construed as having a mental illness or other problem and be transported to one of these institutions. Or an unconscious person admitted to an area hospital with injuries or a suspected mental illness could turn out to be the missing person.

Field Searching

Once the search management team has basic information about the subject and the search area, it can develop an initial search plan based on that information and the available resources. This can often be done with minimum equipment, without waiting for the mobile command post to appear. If the responding search team's personal equipment includes the appropriate maps and radios, a temporary command post can be set up, field teams assigned as personnel arrive and the actual search can begin without delay.

Hasty Search (Type I)

The first search tactic is usually a hasty search, using vehicles, ground searchers and canine units sent out as quickly as possible.

Vehicle Search

Vehicles lend themselves to the urban environment. They can cover more area with less effort than ground teams. Vehicle searching offers a means of possibly containing the search area while also searching it. The objective is to visually look for the subject while driving all the accessible public streets in the search sector, and to conduct field interviews of likely people in the area who might have had the opportunity to see the person. The area of view will be limited to the street itself, sidewalks, and private properties on either side of the street that are accessible to the public. Vehicle searches have proven surprisingly effective if they are begun as soon as possible. Remember, the initial search effort, conducted by law enforcement officers before the search team is called, was probably done in vehicles.

Although public vehicles such as police cars can be used for vehicle searches, more likely they will be the privately owned vehicles of the searchers. It helps to have some kind of identification visible on the car, but it is not necessary. A vehicle team is usually comprised of two people—a driver and a navigator/radio operator. Special equipment for a vehicle patrol includes a clipboard to hold the map and write on it and, at night, two powerful flashlights or spotlights, one for the driver and one for the navigator. A car GPS also comes in handy. The navigator should also have a means of recording the path of the vehicle (possibly by using a highlighter to mark the map) and any field interviews they may conduct. During the course of the search, the vehicle team may want to get out and check likely areas such as parks, canyons, school yards, and fast food or convenience stores.

Teams are usually assigned a search sector comprised of a grid of streets. It is up to the navigator to decide how to cover them. With a rectangular grid pattern, the easiest way is to cover all the streets going in one direction (e.g., north-south), then the perpendicular streets (e.g., east-west). Boundary streets should be viewed on both sides, if possible, so the adjoining sectors "overlap." Drive as slowly as needed to adequately view all the possible areas; however, be aware of the ambient traffic and avoid dangerous situations resulting from impeding traffic.

Ground Search

In a hasty search, foot teams of ground searchers or canine units go where the missing person would most likely have gone; it is an effort to actually see the person or pick up a clue of his or her whereabouts. The criterion for hasty searches is speed. However, with speed, there is greater likelihood of a relatively low probability of detection (POD). In a hasty search, the idea is to quickly cover the area with trained searchers who might have a chance to spot the subject, talk to someone who has seen the subject, or better yet, find a good clue. This tactic has proven successful in urban areas because of quick action while the person is still moving through the area.

Search assignments for hasty search teams focus on areas identified as being likely destinations of the missing person. In instances where the Logistics Section has enough dedicated vehicles and drivers, field teams can be transported to their assignments and picked up later by means of a shuttle system. In other situations, field teams may want to work from their own vehicles, carrying only necessary equipment and water. This speeds up the mobility of the team, but may require an additional person, such as a dedicated driver.

Another technique is to quickly check the attractive hazards where the missing person might go, as identified in the reporting party (RP) interview.

Efficient Search (Type II)

Search teams running Type II searches in the wilderness environment use an open grid pattern to find clues. In the urban environment, the Type II search is typically more careful and thorough; all accessible areas are searched more slowly and deliberately, with searchers looking in every possible hiding place within the designated search area and expecting a high probability of detection (POD). It should be clear to the field team which type of search they should do knowing that a Type II search takes more time than a Type I search.

During a Type II or III search, each search team member must remember to slow down his or her pace and thoroughly search all possible hiding places. This is especially true in a crowded area. Look at each potential hiding place and decide if there is any way possible, or even probable, that the missing person could have entered it, even by crawling. If unsure, then thoroughly search the space. Locked trunks of vehicles, piles of laundry, under beds, inside camping ice chests have all been used as hiding spots. Do not fail to search a place just because no "rational" person would be there. If it is possible, people will do it. Additionally, don't take just one person's word that an area has been searched. It is up to all team members to make sure the area is carefully searched to a high POD.

Thorough Search (Type III)

Closed grid searches are done typically as a re-search method, or where searchers look for very small clues. Normally Type III searches in urban areas are done only in places where the missing person is suspected to have gone and after the area has already been searched using other techniques. A Type III search requires a large number of searchers, who line up shoulder-to-shoulder and then sweep across the designated area as a unit. It has a high POD, but has limited applicability in the urban environment.

Attraction

Attraction is the tactic of attempting to have the conscious and alert missing person respond to the searchers. It is very effective in the wilderness. In fact, a high percentage of successful wilderness searches end with the missing person seeing or hearing searchers and answering with a call.

There are two basic types of attraction techniques—visual and audible. In the wilderness, night visual attraction includes shining headlights or spotlights on an object, leaving lanterns or light sticks at prominent landmarks, the use of head lamps by searchers, and illuminating the search base. Day visual attraction includes stringing trail tape or string lines across likely routes, searchers wearing bright clothing, or using a helicopter to fly over an area. Audible attraction includes the obvious technique of calling the missing person's name, as well as blowing whistles or sirens, using a loudspeaker, or driving up and down roads (often the subject will hear the vehicle and head for it). These visual and audible attraction signals depend on the missing person being able to identify them from the background sights and sounds of the present environment.

The urban environment is much different. First, many subjects are not actually lost and would not necessarily respond to an attraction signal. Second, the urban environment is a complex swirl of activity, lights, sounds and people and thus tends to drown out attraction techniques. Attraction methods could be misconstrued by people in the environment. For example, sirens and whistles mean something besides "search" to a city dweller; and calling out a name is not a safe tactic in some neighborhoods. For this reason, most urban search field teams are reluctant to use attraction. However, it is still a viable tactic when used judiciously, as in the instances described below.

Calling out the missing person's name can be done in quiet residential neighborhoods during the day when most people are at work or during the early evening hours when people in the neighborhood are aware that a search is going on. It can also be used in specific areas or locations where the subject might be lying down but is unable to move, regardless of the neighborhood situation. Sometimes the sounds of radio transmissions and loud talking between search team members will be enough to alert the person. Visual methods include uniforms and police vehicles driving through the streets. Search dogs wear vests to identify them. Even if these tactics do not attract the missing person, they will let the neighborhood know that a search is going on.

Canine Search

As mentioned in Chapter 4 Preplanning, canine resources may consist of trailing dogs, air-scent dogs, police K-9 dogs, disaster dogs, cadaver dogs, and evidence dogs. See pages 37–38 for definitions.

Of all canine resources, *trailing dogs* may be the most effective. Trailing dogs determine the missing person's direction of travel, especially if there are no obvious footprints to follow. The bloodhound is the classic trailing dog, but is certainly not the only breed capable of scent discrimination. Trailing dogs start at the point last seen (PLS) or last known position (LKP) where they sniff a scent article that is been in contact with the missing person, e.g., a pillowcase, T-shirt, hat or the inside arm of a jacket. The dog handler collects the scent article in a paper or plastic bag and offers it to the dog. The dog will then sort out all the scents in the area, pick the one that matches the article, and proceed in the direction of that scent, thus narrowing down the search area by focusing efforts in the direction indicted by the dog. It is important that the scent article be collected and handled as evidence under the rules of evidence (chain of custody). It is important that few people handle the article to prevent scent contamination. Those who handle the article should be near the dog while they are being "scented" so the dog can sort out the scents.

In reality, the use of trailing dogs in an urban setting is much more complicated. If the trailing dog starts at the missing person's residence, the person's scent is everywhere. The trick is for the dog to work his way out of this scent pool and find the strongest, most recent scent. If the missing person frequently takes walks in the neighborhood, the dog may follow the wrong trail. Thus, it is important during the investigation to find out where the person normally travels. For example: Where does the child play? Where does the elderly person take their daily walk? Knowing this information will help interpret the dog's trail and may prevent misleading the search effort.

Other obstacles arise when employing trailing dogs in the urban environment. Safety of the dog and the handler is paramount. The handler has to pay close attention to the dog in order to "read" what the dog is doing. Since the handler's focus is on the dog, other search personnel need to be on the alert for dangers and distractions. The handler needs at least one other searcher to handle the radio and navigate, although two people are better. These searchers—known as runners—stay to the side and just behind the dog. Scent trails usually run along roadways heavy with vehicle traffic. The runners are responsible for alerting or stopping vehicle traffic if the scent trail leads across the roadway. Marked police vehicles with overhead warning lights can also follow behind and in front of the dog team and assist in traffic control. If possible, drivers should shut off their engines as the dog team passes. Excessive vehicle exhaust fumes can desensitize the dog's sense of smell. Other distractions include people who want to pet the dog, small animals and other dogs that want to socialize.

As the trailing dog follows an urban trail, the handler and runners should make note of the direction of travel by calling in their location by street name or address. If the dog becomes alert and shows interest in a specific location due to scent pooling (an area where the subject's scent is strong because they stayed in one place for an extended period), this should be noted for further investigation. If the trail leads past a pay phone, then someone should check the phone company records for outgoing calls that might lead to a clue.

Training in the urban environment on a regular basis can mitigate some of the drawbacks mentioned above. Have a training subject walk through a large populated area like a shopping mall, theme park or fair grounds so the dog becomes accustomed to working through large crowds. Another technique is to teach the dog to indicate if the missing person got in a vehicle and left the area. Scent will still be emitted from a moving vehicle. Some dogs can be trained to follow this weak scent.

Trailing dogs can be combined with air-scent dogs to form a task force. The trailing dog may indicate on a garage or out-building. Rather than using searchers, an air-scent dog can quickly clear the building.

Air-scent dogs can be used to search large areas where people are not allowed or are not normally present, e.g., industrial areas or residential neighborhoods late at night, closed parks. As long as people are not out and about, air-scent dogs can be useful. A word of caution to handlers in urban areas: there may be other dogs in the area that could bark or attack if the air-scent dog comes upon them.

Another unique technique is the drive-and-sniff task, a free-form search by an air-scent dog team. Instead of searching a large area , the team searches locations where they think the subject may have stopped, such as small patches of woods, empty lots, culverts, businesses or parks. The dog is directed to search the immediate area and return to the handler. This is more efficient than drawing up large quarter-acre search segments, but requires very careful mapping by the team and an exacting debrief back at base.

Most *police K-9 dogs* have been cross-trained to track and have been used successfully in lost person urban searches. Caution is suggested when considering the use of K-9s because of their aggression training.

Cadaver dogs are very effective in locating a person when foul play is suspected or in cases where the missing person is believed to be dead. The search area must be much smaller than an air-scent dog's in order to work effectively. If a trailing dog trail leads to a dead end, or an investigative lead points to a specific area, a cadaver dog can be brought in to locate the missing person.

Evidence dogs can be used to locate items, such as a weapon, discarded by a fleeing suspect.

Disaster dogs are usually only used when there is a major disaster such as an earthquake in order to find people trapped in collapsed buildings. They would not normally be used for a missing person search.

Helicopter Operations

If helicopters are readily available and the crew (usually a pilot and one observer) is on duty, they can be sent immediately to the search area to begin the search and try to establish containment. The very presence of a helicopter circling low over an area alerts people that there is something important happening. If it is a night search, the helicopter can use spotlights, night vision equipment or FLIR units. At any time it can use its loudspeaker to request assistance from citizens on the ground in looking for the subject, and it can coordinate ground searchers via radio. In rare instances the helicopter can transport personnel or equipment. It may be possible to set up a heli-base near the search base, in which case it may be prudent to appoint a helicopter coordinator to manage takeoffs and landings.

Pilots should land and along with the observer be briefed on the incident and shown their assignments. Pilots work with maps in longitude and latitude coordinate systems. However, most urban law enforcement helicopter pilots know and work with street names and prominent landmarks.

Helicopter Assignments

- ✓ Fly over and check the city park.
- ✓ Fly over the area bounded by 12th to 27th St. and Adamson to Vermont Ave.
- ✓ Fly in ever widening circles out from the residence.
- ✓ Fly the perimeter outside of the main search area.
- ✓ Check the backyards and alleys on the 2000 block of Maple.
- ✓ Fly low over the immediate area of the missing person's residence and announce over the load speaker to the neighbors that we are looking for a missing child and to check in and around their homes.
- ✓ Hover over the bridge and light up the creek on the north side to aid recovery efforts.

Vehicle and Bicycle Search

Vehicles and bicycles are most useful as a hasty search resource or to provide initial containment of the search area. To use police vehicles, usually during daylight hours, a searcher rides as an observer and covers the right side of the street, while the driver covers the left side. During nighttime, it may be necessary to add a second observer to sit behind the driver to cover the left side of the road so the driver can devote attention to navigation and safety. Both observers would make use of flashlights or spotlights. Also, the police can be asked to stand by at the command post for special assignments or in case they are needed for any law enforcement aspect of the search. Personally owned vehicles may be used in the same manner.

Bicycles are just coming into their own for urban searching. Mountain bike units have been formed for wilderness searches but also prove useful in hasty searching in the city. Two-person assignments work best.

Man-tracking

Man-trackers are well utilized in a wilderness environment when ground surface conditions are amenable to tracking and where few other people are walking in the same area. The urban environment can take advantage of the tracker's skills. Man-trackers are detail-oriented, sensitive to clues and know how to find subtle differences in the surroundings. An urban tracking team may look for disturbances in the dust in a room, on the floor or on counters and doors, which may indicate that someone, perhaps the missing person, has passed that way. If the missing person has very distinctive footwear (e.g., he wears only socks) that may leave unique enough clues to follow. A highly skilled tracking team is usually the first resource sent to the PLS in an attempt to find signs. Even in urban areas, man-trackers can frequently find something useful. In any case, they can identify the PLS and protect it from disturbance by others.

Building Searches

There may be times during a search when it is necessary or prudent to search a building systematically. The decision to search a building depends on the circumstances surrounding the subject and the incident. Often, this can be done by using the urgency determination guidelines (see Chapter 5, p. 57). For example, a task during the initial investigation is to search around the PLS, and if it is a residence, to make sure the missing person is not hiding or asleep there. Reporting parties sometimes overlook children and people with dementia, even if they say they have searched the house.

Most of the time, people become missing because of their own innocent actions, and search tactics rely on standard procedures that do not extend to searching buildings. Occasionally, searchers may receive information that indicates the missing person may avoid being found, or is the victim of abduction or other criminal act. The missing person may be in danger, and hasty searching has turned up nothing. In such cases, the search manager may authorize teams to search buildings that are likely hiding places.

There are legal considerations to searching buildings which depend on applicable laws. Searchers should be made aware of these laws, either during the assignment briefing or when advised by the local authority while the search is in progress. In general, teams can search private residential property when granted permission by the owner, manager, or authorized agent. Usually, a cooperative resident or business manager grants permission, but if there is hesitation or refusal, search personnel should try persuasion. Where the grantor imposes restrictions, it should be reported to command for further instructions. If all else fails, authorities can get a court order to search the property. Furthermore, if the authorized agency determines there is a life or death emergency, and it falls under the definition of "exigent circumstances," it can order the search to extend into closed areas. It is important to understand the use of exigent circumstance, and in the preplan spell out who has the power to authorize warrantless entry into a building.

Public and commercial properties, which are normally open to the public, are also open to searchers during operating hours. Vacant and open buildings that may be an attraction to the missing person can usually be searched without permission. Remember to search outbuildings, such as sheds and garages. In any situation where the search extends to private, occupied property, permission must be obtained first. All of these scenarios should be considered during urban search training, and applicable guidelines should be established by the authorized agency.

Firefighters and police SWAT teams have long used special tactics for searching buildings, from single-story houses to high-rise offices. They operate under emergency provisions of the law, however, which allow them to use dynamic (forced) or covert (secret) entry, tactics that consider the probability of high risk and possible hostile subjects. The urban searcher does not typically face such scenarios, thus they are not considered here; however, the method of searching once the team has gained entry may apply to non-threat searching.

The procedure for searching the interior of a building is simply a systematic, careful room-by-room sweep. The search plan depends on the urgency of the situation, the probability of finding the subject in the building, and the resources (i.e., people) available for the search. For example, if a child is reported missing from his home by his parents, and there is no indication of foul play, the initial investigation team (usually two searchers) could conduct the search accompanied by one of the parents. Other residents should be kept in a central room to avoid contaminating the scene and possible evidence, such as scent articles for trailing dogs.

If it is suspected that the missing person is avoiding searchers or an abduction has occurred, the search plan should incorporate more safeguards, one of which is perimeter containment. Perimeter containment would hopefully prevent the subject from leaving the building unnoticed and would keep track of other people going in. This is accomplished by positioning observers at diagonal corners of the building where each can watch at least two sides of the building. Obviously, if the base of the building is multi-faceted, or there is a basement, additional personnel are needed. Exit corridors, such as elevator lobbies or stairwells, also need to be watched. All personnel should have radios.

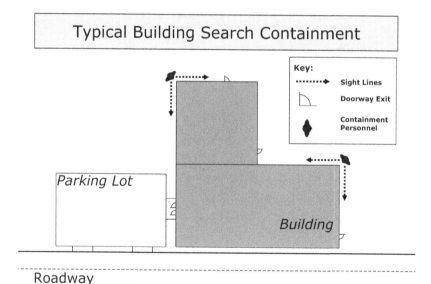

Next, search teams sweep each floor systematically, starting at the upper-most level (or roof), checking each room behind every door. By following a set pattern, searchers can avoid missing areas or not finding a subject who is well hidden. The search should run from the floor to the ceiling and should be conducted either in a clockwise or counterclockwise direction. This includes rest rooms, janitor closets, mechanical rooms, electrical rooms, storage cabinets, and lockers, under and around furniture, and through all of the assorted clutter that is usually underfoot. Make sure all of the lights are on for maximum detectability. If feasible and plausible, it may be necessary to search above dropped-ceiling spaces or crawl spaces.

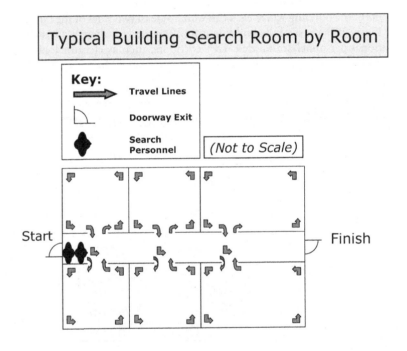

Although this description assumes a minimum two-person foot team, another technique is to use dogs to clear rooms. *Air-scent dogs work well for this task.*

If it is an office or commercial building, a building manager who knows the layout of the building and has a master key should accompany the team. As each room is checked, the doors should be relocked or sealed. If a building floor plan is available, it can provide a good map and means of recording which rooms have been searched. In a multi-story building, as each floor is secured, the teams can then move down to the next level. The process is repeated until the entire building is swept and secured. Exterior perimeter containment should continue until the entire building is secured to prevent any unauthorized entry into the building.

The most common mistake made by building searchers is that of speed. Methodical searches are done at the rate at which the room or structure can be controlled and thoroughly searched. There is no need to go faster than that. This can take a long time with extensive resources and should probably be limited to thorough searches conducted after less intensive searching has turned up nothing. Finally, please note that building search is an extremely perishable skill that should be practiced during annual maintenance training.

Neighborhood Door-to-Door Canvassing and Interviewing

The technique of door-to-door canvassing and interviewing in residential neighborhoods generates many clues. Door-to-door interviews may help answer the question "Did the missing subject pass by this way?" The task is simple. Two-to-three person teams go down both sides of a street, stopping at each house to ask questions. Interviewing is labor intensive, taking as much as 15 minutes per house depending on how on the level (or type) of search. There can be as many as 250 to 300 single family homes in a suburban neighborhood and possibly several hundred more in multi-family high-density housing. Doing the math, it is easy to see the need for extensive resources.

Levels of thoroughness in a neighborhood canvass search have been defined by Michael St. John of the Marin County (CA) Sheriff's Search and Rescue Team:

Level I

The most thorough and detailed. Consists of an interview with all residents. This is followed by a complete search, with permission of the residents, of the front and back yards and any out buildings. A request is also made of residents to complete an interior search; or, with the permission of the residents, the field team may conduct an interior search. In a suspected abduction, the interior search should be conducted by the interview team, preferably without the residents present.

Level II

Consists of an interview with all residents and a request of the residents to search their property.

Level III

Residents are not contacted or are absent during the search. An information flyer can be left at the door.

Have a plan on how to draw up the assignments, and the appropriate maps that best describe the neighborhood to be searched. Maps may be a combination of street maps and assessor maps showing individual properties and addresses.

Neighborhood canvassing should be done when it is safe. Knocking on doors and disturbing the residents at one o'clock in the morning may make it difficult to get positive responses to your questions (assuming they even answer the door at 1 a.m.). It is also advisable to have a Safety Officer assigned for the door-to-door interviewing. The Safety Officer looks out for the searchers' welfare and safety. A working knowledge of the neighborhoods to be searched may prevent someone from getting hurt. For example, a searcher may inadvertently walk up and knock on the door of a "crack house." The Safety Officer should be from the local law enforcement agency, if possible. Some agencies have a policy of only having uniformed officers conduct door-to-door searches. The officers might be accompanied by a volunteer searcher.

Upon knocking on the door announce who you are clearly and politely, who you represent (e.g., police or sheriff's department), and why you are there. Searchers should look professional by wearing some sort of clean uniform and carry identification cards. There is no need to carry a full backpack and wear climbing helmets, multiple radio harnesses or other essentials normally required in a wilderness search environment. Cleaning the mud off boots and a clean shirt and pants will add to the professional look.

Find out and then clearly define and brief teams on what authority team members have to enter private property to check out back yards or out buildings.

Safety briefing instructions are the same as the officer safety training for law enforcement deputies when they approach a residence in response to detail call. The information should include:

Safety Briefing Instructions

1. *Be alert* when approaching a house. *Be aware* of your surroundings. When you go up to a house, look at what and who is around you.

2. *Have an escape plan.* If something happens, how are you going to retreat? Who needs to be contacted?

3. *Listen at the door before knocking.* Do you hear people talking? Are you going to be interrupting a domestic dispute? Is there a dog barking behind the door that may jump out when the door is open.

4. *Do not stand directly in front of the door.* No one wants to be in the line of fire in case an irate citizen decides to shoot a bullet through the door and ask questions later. On the other hand, no one should appear to be trying to conceal him or herself. Just stand to the side.

5. *Knock on the door hard.* Do not use the doorbell. Knocking commands authority. Do not knock on the door with your flashlight.

6. *Stand far enough away* to encourage the occupant to come out.

7. *Do not go in the house,* even if invited. Ask the interviewee to step outside.

8. *One member of the team should place themselves in front of the door.* They will ask all of the questions and give the resident one person to focus on. *The other members of the team should stand to the side* recording the responses to the questions, observing the inside of the residence and being alert to safety issues.

9. *When leaving, back away until the person is inside and has closed the door.*

Continued on next page ...

> *9. If the interviewee is uncooperative, thank them for their time,* make a note in your log to come back, if necessary, and advise the Safety Officer.
>
> *10. Additionally, a radio person should be standing at the sidewalk observing* the interview at the door. A prearranged panic signal from the interviewers will alert the radio operator to summon help.

Interviewing requires good interpersonal skills. Getting used to the task requires practice. Field team practice scenarios on how to go door-to-door and ask questions should be set up in basic training. Use of forms and a list of appropriate questions will help alleviate the tension and anxiety search team members may feel. A standard interview dialog should consist of:

> **Interview Dialog**
>
> Identifying yourself and your affiliation clearly and with authority:
>
> *"Hi, my name is _____ with the Sheriff's search and rescue team and we are looking for Jane Doe who is missing. Can you help us?"*
>
> Have identification ready to show the person you are interviewing.
>
> Determine if they have seen the missing person:
>
> *"Do you know Jane? Have you seen her?"*
>
> Compile a list of possible witness:
>
> *"Who lives here? Were they home at (time)?*
>
> *Was there someone else at home when you/they were gone?"*

Interview teams should have a picture of the missing person available. Have the ID test question available to corroborate the interviewee's statements. Finally, depending on the level of the search, ask the residents if the team can check their backyard and outbuildings and if the residents would check the interior of the residence.

Try not to take the residents' word that they have searched their own property. It may or may not be accurate, or their idea of a thorough search may be to look out of the back window. Always ask permission to search the property yourself. If they are reluctant, ask them to assist you, pointing out possible hiding places or clue locations.

A useful tool for documentation is an Urban Interview Log (see Appendix H Interview and Clue Forms).

An urban interview log lists the following:

✓ All the addresses where teams went

✓ Whom you talked to

✓ Phone numbers

✓ Whether anyone was home

✓ Whether any pertinent information (clues) were obtained

The log also lists places like attractive hazards around that particular area such as abandoned cars, out-buildings, and places that the search teams did not get a chance to check but should be checked later. If the incident is a suspected abduction, list the license plates of all vehicles in the neighborhood for future reference.

Occasionally, a resident may become belligerent, refuse to talk to the teams or even chase them off. In this situation, back out and apologize for the interruption. Note the address and the circumstances and pass this information on to law enforcement personnel who will contact the person later.

It is important to find out what is out of the ordinary, but it is equally important to consider what is NOT out of the ordinary, or what is normal for the neighborhood. Often this information can be obtained by interviewing people who are in the neighborhood on a regular basis. They may have unwittingly seen or heard something pertinent regarding the missing person.

People to interview
✓   Mail carriers
✓   FedEx and UPS drivers
✓   Newspaper delivery persons
✓   Utility workers, trash collectors, city workers
✓   Familiar walkers, joggers, neighbors in the area
✓   Bus drivers, taxi drivers

Handouts or "leave behind" flyers are an excellent idea (see Chapter 5, p. 59). They will encourage the public to continue looking for the missing person and provide information on whom to contact if the person is seen or found.

While walking from door to door, teams will inevitably come across people on the street. These people should be interviewed. Simply put out a hand, make eye contact and say, "Excuse me, may I have a moment of your time?" Ask them where they have been, what and whom they saw, and about conditions in the area. Have a map available to confirm routes they traveled. Give them a handout and ask them to report anything that they see or might remember about the missing person.

A technique to accelerate a door-to-door interview is to stop at houses where it appears that someone has been home most of the day. Homes with toys in the yard are a good clue that children and a caregiver might have been home.

Other sources of information are Neighborhood Watch Program participants. Such programs motivate neighbors to be alert for strange or abnormal incidents and activities in the neighborhood. Find out who is the point-of-contact and how that person can be reached.

Dumpster Diving

As unpleasant as the task sounds, there may be an occasion when it is necessary to do a thorough search of a garbage dumpster. The task usually requires turning the dumpster over and emptying the contents on a large floor area. How deep the searcher needs to dig is determined by the assignment, e.g., looking for evidence or a body. Essential equipment includes good rubber gloves (preferably covering up to the elbows), good rubber boots up to the knees, a rubber apron, eye protection and a face mask. Tools include shovels and garden rakes; however if searching for very small items, a screen and wheelbarrow may be required. Finally, an adequate source of water with a hose and spray nozzle to wash down personnel and equipment is a must.

Missing Vehicle Search

Occasionally, there may be a request to search for a person who was last seen driving a vehicle but did not arrive at his or her destination; all indications are that he or she is not purposely avoiding the family. In other words, something happened between the departure and arrival that prevented the person from arriving at his or her destination. The plan is to search for the vehicle.

The first step is to put out a BOLO to see if any officer has spotted the vehicle. If the route is known or obvious, officers can be dispatched to search along it. A helicopter may be used if the vehicle is not found in the first search. If these techniques are unsuccessful, a more intensive search may be warranted depending on how long it has been since the person was missing and how many hazardous conditions exist.

Bicycle units are particularly useful for an intensive search if the route allows them. Any areas where the vehicle might have left the roadway should be carefully searched, possibly even by foot teams. Consider scenarios where the vehicle has crashed off the road and is hidden from searchers looking down into the bushes. These are rare in urban settings, but they can occur. Check stores or other places along the way where the person might have stopped. After this, revert to investigative techniques to find out more about the person as well as any relevant factors that might have caused the person to be missing.

Re-searching

A normal procedure during any search is to go over areas that have been searched by Type I or hasty teams. This is even more important in the city where the person may have been missed by the hasty team or may have returned to areas already searched. Type II or thorough searching would have a higher probability of detection. However, covering an area with dense urban housing has proved difficult at best. It is therefore preferable to be as thorough as possible during the first, and perhaps the only, search in the area.

Debriefing

Debriefing teams is important in order to document the areas searched and provide information for planning future searches. Team leaders should debrief their own team members before reporting to the Planning Section for debriefing. They should also compile all information, maps and areas that couldn't be searched and why. Addresses of interviewed residents should be logged, as well as areas where searching was difficult and coverage was not as good as the rest of the area. Team leaders should be prepared to give an exact accounting of what was done and what was not, and to identify areas that must be checked later.

> *It is not a crime to fail to complete a task,*
> *but to report an assignment as complete when it is not,*
> *is unforgiveable.*

If an urban door-to-door interview is taking place simultaneously with a search of an adjacent open space, a separate debriefing may be required to prevent confusion or missed information.

Calling Outside Resources After First Operational Period

One unfortunate downside to searching in an urban environment is the high burnout rate of search personnel. There is high intensity in managing and performing many different tasks with many different resources. An operational period can run longer than ten hours without relief, and it takes time to obtain additional resources. Some search teams have a large pool of members who can be rotated into the operation to relieve those going off duty; others may have to call in outside resources as soon as participation dwindles. In urban searches, spontaneous volunteers sometimes show up to help out. The decision on when to call in these resources takes the following factors into consideration:

Resource factors to consider

What is the current urgency of the incident?

In the previous section on Urgency Determination, it was mentioned that the urgency may change as the search goes on. If the search has gone on for some time without success, outside help should be considered.

How much more searching needs to be done?

Because of the complexity of urban areas, there are almost an infinite number of assignments that can be made, however it may be possible that the available personnel can conduct the remainder of the assignments within the established operational period.

What kind of outside resources are available?

Many U.S. cities have worked out mutual aid plans and agreements with their adjacent jurisdictions, which allow them to draw on these nearby resources with a direct request. In many areas, under the Mutual Aid Plan, the state Office of Emergency Services (OES) and the state SAR Coordinator, specifically, can provide professional volunteer search teams to any municipality through their computer system database. The SAR Coordinator can also provide other state resources, e.g., State Trooper or Highway Patrol helicopters, a communication van staffed with a professional specialist(s), and can call in resources from adjacent states and/or the federal government. It is important that the requested resources be familiar with urban searching and experienced enough to be integrated into the operation without friction.

How much longer can search efficiency be maintained?

Some agencies use a system based on an eight-hour shift to estimate when mutual aid should be requested. If the search has been going on for four hours and it looks like the subject will not be found in the next two hours, call for mutual aid. This decision, including what additional resources are needed, is made during the first planning meeting held four hours into the search. Replacement overhead personnel arrive at hour eight into the search and the field teams at hour nine. The hour gap is to provide enough time for the new managers to be briefed before the field personnel arrive. This cycle continues. A timeline chart has been developed to graphically show the transition from one operating period to the next (see page 152).

Continued on next page ...

Unfortunately, some teams use a longer operational period of 12 hours and wait until the end of that period to call for outside help when it becomes apparent that search efficiency has deteriorated and management staff is exhausted. Urban searches allow personnel to return to their homes and rest up before returning to the operation. In addition, the response times for most searchers are shorter because they usually reside close to the operation. Even most mutual aid calls are from nearby cities, resulting in shorter response times.

Suspending an Urban Search

When a missing person is not found, there comes a time when physical search efforts must cease. An effective way to handle the decision to suspend or continue the search is to hold a meeting of the incident command staff and carefully evaluate all the evidence. The following personnel should be in attendance:

✓ Jurisdictional Agency Incident Commander

✓ Section Chiefs (Planning, Operations, Logistics)

✓ Public Information Officer (PIO)

✓ Liaisons from allied resources participating in the search

✓ The family liaison officer (It is not recommended to have a family member present at the meeting as the decisions made and items discussed may have repercussions after the fact.)

Everyone should be free to speak to the matters at hand. The tasks of the meeting are to conduct a final scenario analysis and compare it with all previous analyses, and to review the results of the investigation.

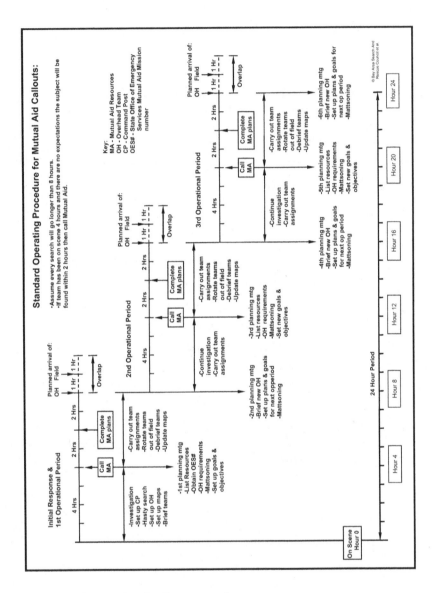

Example of mutual aid call-outs timeline

Chapter 11. Missing Person Behavior

Kimberly R. Kelly, Robert J. Koester, Michael St. John

Lost person behavior is a powerful tool that helps determine where to look for the missing person. It is also appropriate to use the term "missing person behavior" given that in urban settings the subject is often not "lost" in the traditional sense of the word; thus, the term "missing person behavior" is used in this book. Behavior can guide the search planner in determining the search area and where to send teams within that search area. It can also help field personnel know the most likely areas the subject would be within their particular search segment. In the end, missing person behavior is just a tool, based upon probability, statistics, and likely behavior. Every missing person is unique, with a different set of circumstances and behavior. Investigation is the tool that helps determine the specifics of an individual person. However, good investigation takes time, and resources still need to be deployed. Missing person behavior gets the search moving.

Missing person behavior contains two separate but equally important elements:

- Statistics that give probabilities of where the missing person will be located, and
- A general overview of the types of behaviors, actions, and goals of the missing person.

From these two elements it is possible to make strategic and tactical recommendations. The recommendations can guide both the initial search effort and the extended effort.

International Search & Rescue Incident Database (ISRID)

Missing person behavior descriptions and statistics are only as good as the source of information they are taken from. In the past, the only statistics and descriptions available came from wilderness search incidents. Any urban search planner should look upon this older information with great suspicion. The urban environment is considerably different than the wilderness environment. However, wilderness search and rescue resources are now being called to search in the urban environment more frequently. These teams are contributing information on urban incidents, and thus a large body of incidents has been slowly developing. Many urban incidents have now been captured by ISRID.

The International Search & Rescue Incident Database (ISRID) project began in 2002 and has collected data on search and rescue incidents from around the world (United States, Canada, Australia, New Zealand, United Kingdom, Ireland, and South Africa). Over 50,000 SAR incidents have already been collected. ISRID combines over 35 separate databases. It also includes previously published incidents from Dennis Kelley, William Syrotuck, Barry Mitchell, Ken Hill, Don Heth & Ed Cornell, Dave Perkins, Pete Roberts, Jed Feeny, and Robert Koester. In addition, several previously unpublished databases are included. All of the databases represent responses from a search and rescue resource. Robert Koester leads the project with funding from Fronterra Search and Rescue Software. The project is expected to continue to collect incidents on an ongoing basis. Therefore, some statistics will change as more incidents are added to the database. Current information is available at www.isrid.net.

All of the statistics provided in the summary tables in this chapter come from the ISRID database. All of the incidents were searches (as opposed to rescues or evidence-only searches) at the onset. All incidents were also identified as occurring either in an urban or suburban environment. As of the beginning of 2007, 1144 urban incidents met the above conditions.

Who gets lost in the urban environment?

While almost all of us have gotten "turned around," been "not quite sure where we are," or even admitted we were "lost" in a strange city, few of us have required a formal search. Getting lost in an urban environment requires more than simply not knowing where you are; it requires not knowing how to seek help. In order for a formal search to be initiated, somebody needs to miss the subject. Until the publication of the ISRID database, we knew children and persons with dementia (Alzheimer's disease) were involved in urban searches although not to what degree. By following the news we might also perceive that child abductions occur on a frequent basis. Based on 1144 urban incidents, it is now possible to have a much better idea of who becomes the subject of an urban search.

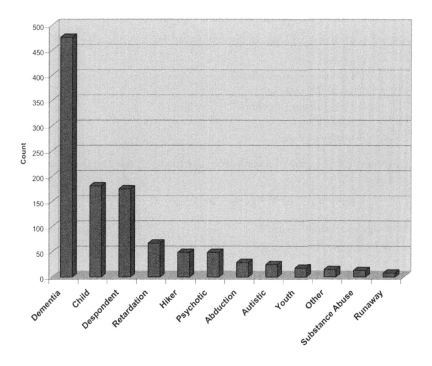

The bar graph above shows that the most common type of person to become lost in the urban environment is someone with dementia; those cases account for 44% of the incidents. Lost children and despondents each account for 16% of the incidents. Lost children are defined as those age 12 and under without any other mental disorder. Children who are abducted, or who have autism or mental retardation are placed into separate, respective categories. Youth are defined as adolescents age 13-15 who do not fit any of the other categories nor are they involved in a runaway type of incident. ISRID surprisingly contains 4% hikers in an urban environment, perhaps because some urban environments contain large parks or extensive greenbelt trail networks where it is possible to hike and actually become lost. Abductions, which receive extensive national media attention account for 3% of the incidents in the urban database. This still represents a significant number due to the dire outcome associated with these cases.

Types of missing person cases in the urban environment

Altered cognitive (thinking, judgment, social skill, etc) levels—73%

- Dementia
- Depression (Despondent)
- Mental Retardation
- Mental Illness (Psychotic)
- Autism
- Substance Abuse

Have not fully developed responsible cognitive abilities and decision making—18%

- Children Age 1–3, Age 4–6, and Age 7–12

Investigative in nature—4%

- Runaway
- Abduction

The ISRID database collected several different types of statistics about each of these types of cases. The statistic best known to wilderness search planners is the distance from the point last seen (PLS). Searches can start either from a direct eyewitness and truly be at a point last seen or, in some cases, from substantial evidence (car parked at trail head at urban park), which represents the last known position (LKP). The broadest term that includes both starting places—PLS and LKP—is the initial planning point (IPP). ISRID collected data termed "distance from the IPP," which measures the crow's flight distance in miles between the IPP and the find location. ISRID data presents the actual count (n) of cases that included distance information.

The data tables report the distance from which 25% of the missing persons are found, followed by 50% or the median. The median represents the distance at which half the subjects were found closer than that distance and half the cases were further out. It is common to plot the median distance ring onto a search planning map. However, many planners have made the mistake of searching only to the median. This is an unfortunate method which essentially ensures that search managers will fail in almost half the cases. The 75% or third quartile is the next distance reported. It often represents the practical distance where sector or area searching is possible. The final distance is the 95%, also referred to as the maximum zone. This is considered the largest practical distance; cases beyond the 95% represent statistical outliers. The table below shows data from dementia incidents to illustrate.

Distance from IPP n=336 cases		
	Miles	Km
25%	0.2	0.4
50%	0.7	1.1
75%	2.0	3.2
Max zone	7.8	12.6

The table above shows 336 urban dementia incidents that reported distance from the IPP. This can be considered highly reliable since previous lost person data were often based on as few as eight cases. The distances are given in both miles and kilometers. Many searchers are now familiar with kilometers since the Universal Transverse Mercator (UTM) grid system is based upon a kilometer square. It can be seen from the data that a quarter of the subjects were located within 0.2 miles or 400 meters, while half of the subjects were found within 0.7 miles or 1.1 kilometers (1100 meters). A 0.7 mile radius would give a search area of 1.5 square miles. However, to locate 75% of missing persons with dementia the distance jumps out to 2.0 miles. In an urban environment, travel along roads is often easy. The search area has now grown to 12.5 square miles—six times larger than the 50%. The greatest challenge is posed by the maximum zone (95%), which is 7.8 miles. It is clear that persons with dementia can move considerable distances in an urban environment—a contrast to initial wilderness search reports of persons with dementia being found within 1.5 miles for the maximum zone. It should be noted that data for "distance from the IPP" does not include investigative cases. Those are cases in which the missing persons boarded a plane, train, bus, or automobile and were transported away from the search area.

The table below summarizes methods used to locate missing persons. Once again, example data is taken from dementia cases.

Search Outcomes	
SAR Find	43%
Investigative	9%
Self	7%
Other	35%
Suspension	5%

The data shows that the search effort was responsible for slightly less than half the finds. In other cases, the missing person simply walked back, or "self-rescued," (7%) or was located by the general public (35%). Clearly, the public plays a major role in search efforts. As discussed in Chapter 5, the public is typically alerted through media efforts, a helicopter circle overhead, using community word of mouth, flyers, or notification through an emergency notification system, such as Reverse 911® or TENS. People may take action because they notice someone who appears to need help. The data also indicates that 9% of cases were resolved through investigative means. These techniques are discussed in Chapter 7. Finally, 5% of the searches were suspended without finding the missing person. These cases potentially lead to legal issues and almost always end in loss of life. In many cases, the missing person was eventually found within the search area.

Find Location	
Structure	35%
Road	36%
Linear Feature	9%
Drainage	4%
Water	6%
Brush	1%
Scrub	
Woods/Forest	3%
Field	6%
Rock	

The find location table above gives the actual locations in or at which missing persons with dementia were found. A structure includes buildings, outbuildings, immediate yards, and vehicles. For such subjects in an urban environment, structure was second only to roads. A linear feature includes trails, power lines, railroads, pipeline right of ways, and other similar linear features. While roads and drainages are also linear, they were broken into separate categories since so many subjects are found along these two features. Water represents ocean, lake, river, pond, canal, irrigation ditch, or any other substantial body of water. Drainage is often more mountainous in nature and represents either a creek/stream or where an intermittent stream might be found during wet conditions. Brush refers to brush or briars or a generally overgrown area with ground vegetation. The other terms are self-explanatory. This data differs completely from data available for dementia subjects in the wilderness and thus, clearly shows the need for urban specific data.

| Survivability n=455 cases ||
Status	Percentage
Uninjured	80%
Injured	14%
Fatality	6%

Survivability statistics (see table above) help determine the probability of finding the missing person uninjured, injured, or deceased. While the data is general, every search is different. Incidents in the wintertime of northern states are quite different from incidents from the spring and fall of southern states. The data also does not reflect time, weather, or the unique personality and physical nature of the missing person. Nevertheless, they indicate overall urgency and likely outcome.

Track Offset (meters)	
25%	6
50%	15
75%	76
Max zone	298

Track offset is a term that originates from missing aircraft searches. In those searches, the question is asked: "How far off the plane's intended route was it eventually found?" In urban searches for subjects with often diminished cognitive ability, it is usually impossible to determine the intended route—if any even existed. However, it is possible to measure how far the missing person was found away from a potential route (road or trail). Therefore, the track offset represents—for those *not* found on a road or trail—the shortest possible distance they were away from the closest road or trail. In a city, it is not too surprising that half of all subjects not found on actual roads or trails are only 15 meters (16.7 yards) away.

Missing person statistics paint an important but incomplete picture. The next important component to building a complete picture of the missing person is a behavioral profile. The missing person behavioral profile describes how people within that particular category act, think, and have responded to being lost in the past. The more searchers understand about the missing person, the closer the team is to finding them. In most wilderness searches, the planner and teams often attempt to put themselves in the missing person's shoes. The idea is that by thinking like the missing person perhaps the searcher will be a few steps closer to finding them.

While most searchers have little difficulty thinking like a hunter, hiker, or even a child, many urban cases pose additional challenges: The world of someone with dementia, a mental illness, or someone who could conceive of abducting a child is foreign and beyond the ability of searchers. In order to overcome this challenge and be better prepared, the rest of this chapter provides a solid background on the more challenging behaviors of people in the following categories, which will be described in order of prevalence as listed below:

- Dementia (Alzheimer's disease)
- Missing and Abducted Children*
- Despondent
- Mental Retardation
- Mental Illness
- Autism
- Substance Abuse

*Missing children comprise the second most common type of missing person in the urban environment, while abducted children make up a much less prevalent category (seventh out of twelve categories; see bar graph on page 155). However, as described in the section on Missing and Abducted Children, the search tactics for all cases of missing children start out the same and remain similar throughout the search. Also, and perhaps more importantly, the two categories are combined in this section because of the risk factors and the need for urgency in searching for missing children.

Statistics similar to those described above are presented for each missing person behavior profile described in this chapter.

Dementia

In search and rescue, the term dementia is used generally to describe Alzheimer's disease as well as a large number of other conditions. Alzheimer's disease is the most common type of dementia; over half the number of people with dementia have Alzheimer's. Thus, for purpose of creating an understanding of the dementia profile, the following section describes Alzheimer's disease in detail, with the acknowledgement that although not all conditions of dementia are exactly alike, they do have similar characteristics that lead to behaviors encountered during a search incident.

> *"911 ... what is your emergency?"*
> *"My mother is gone! She has Alzheimer's disease and wandered away," the voice says frantically.*
> *"Please, send someone quickly!"*

Every day across the United States, as well as in countries throughout the world, this scenario is played and re-played by law enforcement officers who respond to missing persons with Alzheimer's and dementia who are at-risk. Yet, while this type of call has become more and more commonplace, many people underestimate the severity of danger that a missing person with Alzheimer's faces.

In urban settings, 44% of all missing persons that come to the attention of law enforcement and/or search and rescue personnel have Alzheimer's or dementia (ISRID data). In fact, while many search and rescue teams report a global decrease in the number of their missions, many teams also report that they are increasingly being called out on search missions for missing persons with Alzheimer's disease. As such, this section is devoted to providing search and rescue personnel with an understanding of Alzheimer's disease and suggested tactics necessary to locate persons with Alzheimer's and related dementias who have wandered and become lost.

What is Alzheimer's Disease?

Most people are familiar with the term "Alzheimer's disease" (AD), even if they do not fully understand the diagnosis. Pronounced "Alz-high-murz", it is named for the German neuropathologist Alois Alzheimer (1864-1915) who first recognized the disorder as a true disease in 1906. Most people in the United States, however, first heard about Alzheimer's disease when President Ronald Reagan first disclosed his own diagnosis in 1984.

Alzheimer's disease is one of nearly 70 diseases that fall into a category known as "dementia." Dementia, derived from Latin meaning "mind" and "away," is a term used to indicate a loss or reduction of mental capacity severe enough to interfere with daily functioning. It does not mean or signify stupidity, insanity or retardation.

Dementia refers to a variety of symptoms, but is not a disease in itself. Dementia symptoms include memory loss, confusion, a reduction in cognitive abilities, difficulty with language, perception, personality, judgment, coordination and changes in emotion and personality. There are four major types of dementia: Alzheimer's disease (AD); vascular dementia, which includes multi-infarct dementia and Binswanger's disease; frontotemporal dementia; and diffuse Lewy body dementia.

Alzheimer's disease is the most common type of dementia: approximately 60-70% of people who have dementia are diagnosed with Alzheimer's. Alzheimer's disease combined with vascular dementia accounts for another 20%.

It is important to note that because Alzheimer's is the most common type of dementia, the term Alzheimer's is used throughout this section. However, many families often will not disclose a diagnosis of Alzheimer's or any related dementia because of fear of stigma, embarrassment, supposed protection of the missing person, denial or simply because they may not know. Family members may play down a diagnosis of Alzheimer's, instead merely referring to "senility," or say that "Grandma's fine, she's just a little forgetful." It is far better to proceed with an assumed diagnosis of dementia, or Alzheimer's, than to ignore clear signs and symptoms in order to accommodate a family's embarrassment. In fact, doing so could condemn the entire search mission's success.

How is Alzheimer's Diagnosed?

Alzheimer's disease is distinguished from other forms of dementia by characteristic changes in the brain. These changes include a 50% reduction of acetylcholine, the primary brain chemical used in the retrieval of memory, and the formation of plaques and tangles. These plaques and tangles are abnormal growths or accumulation of certain proteins that build within and surrounding the brain cells. As a result of these changes, brain cells are damaged, and eventually destroyed, which results in the previously described symptoms of dementia.

AD is considered to be a disease of exclusion; this means that all other possible causes, such as infection, disease, alcohol/drug abuse, vitamin deficiency and mental illness must be ruled out before any probable diagnosis of Alzheimer's is given. This is accomplished by undergoing a complete physical, neurological and psychological examination. However, due to the very nature of the disease, a diagnosis of AD can only be confirmed by autopsy of brain tissue after death.

Understanding the progress of Alzheimer's and how it is diagnosed is critical to the Incident Commander, command staff, and search teams that are looking for a missing elder. Knowing the signs and symptoms can often lead search managers to the means, methods, tactics and utilization of resources.

Progression of the Disease

The American Psychiatric Association's *Diagnostic and Statistical Manual of Mental Disorders* (1987) characterizes Alzheimer's disease as a chronically "progressive, global, cognitive loss." The affected individual experiences a loss of thinking and learning capabilities of sufficient impairment to affect daily life, social or occupational functioning.

Changes are often slow to progress and thus difficult to detect in the early stages. These symptoms may include short-term memory loss, anxiety or irritability, difficulty in conversation or inability to complete involved processes, such as balancing a checkbook or map orientation.

> **Example:**   *Ms. Deborah Melvin reports an incident that occurred in January, approximately three days prior to her father John Melvin's disappearance. While at a bank's automated teller machine with her, Mr. Melvin forgot his personal identification number (PIN). He was adamant that the last four digits embossed on the card was the appropriate PIN. Deborah stated that Mr. Melvin became increasingly frustrated and repeatedly tried that incorrect number.*

Eventually, as the disease progresses, impairment becomes more severe and obvious. The person makes glaring mistakes in his or her work, repeats conversation or questions over and over, and loses more and more of the ability to remember persons, places or events. Short-term memory loss deteriorates into severe memory problems. Impaired judgment and radical personality changes may also become evident. The person's physical self remains in the present, but their memory may regress ten, twenty or more years in the past.

> **Example:**   *Christopher Allen states that his mother's "short-term memory is going." Christopher also reports changes in his mother's personality and abilities. He reports that she has become obsessed with a morning routine*

of waking, eating breakfast, and taking her medication. Once that routine is completed, however, Mrs. Allen apparently becomes without direction or purpose for the rest of the day.

Moderate stages include obvious functional declines. Traveling alone, even in familiar environments, is often difficult. Complicated tasks are more difficult. Memory of recent events is clearly impaired. Personality changes often begin to appear: flat affect and loss of inhibition, tact, social grace, and judgment. Changes in sense of time and place, as well as short- and beginning of long-term memory impairment also occur.

Severe stage begins generally when an individual can no longer care for himself, or survive without assistance. He begins to forget relevant facts such as current addresses, phone numbers, or close family members. Personality and emotional changes often become more pronounced, and he can become agitated, delusional, and/or paranoid in his behavior. Such losses of ability can lead to further problems, such as anxiety, paranoia, hallucinations, frustration or irritability, anger, aggression or violence, withdrawal, pacing, and wandering. More information on the stages and associated behaviors of Alzheimer's disease can be found on the Alzheimer's Association's Web site, www.alz.org.

In addition to the changes that occur to memory and cognitive abilities, Alzheimer's patients also experience significant impairment to visual, speech, and motor skills. Those skills and the resulting deficits (agnosia, aphasia, apraxia) are described below. It is important to note that for a diagnosis of Alzheimer's disease to occur, in addition to the presence of confusion and lack of cognition, at least one of these three conditions must be present. Most person's with Alzheimer's have some form of all three. Further, when someone with Alzheimer's becomes dehydrated, injured, ill, stressed or lost, signs and symptoms of agnosia, aphasia, and apraxia often become much more obvious and severe.

The "A" Triad

Because Alzheimer's disease can only be diagnosed by ruling out everything else, doctors often rely on the presence of related indicators. In addition to the changes that occur to memory and cognitive abilities, people with Alzheimer's also experience significant impairment to visual (agnosia), speech (aphasia), and motor skills (apraxia).

For the purpose of ease, these indicators can be referred to as the "A" triad. The "A" triad—agnosia, aphasia, and apraxia—is often the most accurate clue that a person with signs of dementia actually has Alzheimer's disease. The combined effect can lead to further emotional problems, such as anxiety, paranoia, hallucinations, frustration or irritability, anger, aggression or violence, withdrawal, pacing, restlessness and eventually to wandering. All of these behaviors are based on an unmet need or discomfort that is not being resolved.

Agnosia visual impairment

Aphasia   *Apraxia*
speech impairment   impairment of motor skills

Agnosia is the loss or reduction of the brain's ability to interpret images transmitted by the eyes. The eyes do not actually 'see'; they merely transmit images to the brain, which must then interpret those images into something familiar or known. It is quite common for someone with Alzheimer's to be able to clearly and accurately describe her home or a family member, but at the same time be unable to visually recognize her home or person in front of them.

Example: *Kayla Hardin recounts an incident, in regard to her grandfather, and provides an unmistakable example of agnosia: Grandpa Hardin was standing outside the house, on the back patio, and pointed to an object in the distance. Grandpa Hardin stated the "man in the boat" appeared to be having difficulty. After Kayla pressed as to "what man, where?", it was finally determined that Grandpa Hardin had misidentified one of his neighbor's wind socks, blowing in the breeze, as a man in a boat.*

With Alzheimer's disease, this interpretation process becomes altered. Even though the information being transmitted remains the same, and the eyes and optic nerve suffer no injury, the brain will no longer process that information in the same way. For instance, Grandma may mistake her grandchildren for her children, or Auntie may no longer recognize her home, car, spouse, children or beloved pet.

This is particularly important for a law enforcement officer or search and rescue personnel to know. Many times, a missing person with Alzheimer's has disappeared while on a routine errand, a customary walk, or from a familiar place. It is important to realize that as agnosia develops, a person will lose the ability to record or recognize change, even when it occurs slowly.

However, even with agnosia, it is typical and normal for people with Alzheimer's disease to be encouraged to walk, maintain their independence, and seek outdoor experiences. Walking and maintaining independence can be very therapeutic. The caregiver and person with Alzheimer's quite often agree to a pattern of travel or behavior, e.g., "don't leave the house," "always stay within the neighborhood," or "don't cross Fifth Street."

Additionally, family members will often tell the interviewer that the person will not cross a certain street. As a result, it is quite common for the search manager to set up boundaries along these given barriers. It is a dangerous fallacy to believe that a person who has agnosia, who does not recognize friends or family, will somehow recognize that they should not cross a certain street.

> **Example:**   *Mary always walks along Fifth and Vine; however, road construction has started, and she is forced to walk on the opposite side of the street. Even though Mary walks the same route every day, she now must view the street in an entirely different manner. Her route is no longer familiar and she wanders out of her normal area. People are used to seeing her walking, however, and no one stops to offer her assistance.*

Unfortunately, with such boundaries in place, caregivers often feel falsely secure. With this false sense of security, however, come dangerous assumptions that if followed by a search manager could lead to disastrous results. A missing person with Alzheimer's and agnosia will not see the same thing searchers see. They may not recognize a highway, road, train track, or environmental hazard such as blackberry patches, thick brush, cactus or bodies of water as dangerous. They may very well walk, fall, crawl, drive into or otherwise become trapped in such places. This is important for search managers to understand. Just as it is common for family members or nursing home staff to say "She will not ever cross the street," or "There is no way he could climb a fence," it is equally likely for searchers to declare "There is no way that guy went in there," or "No one would want to go into that …"

Search records and the accompanying mortality rates show that missing persons with Alzheimer's who get "stuck" in such dangerous hazards are most often unable to extricate themselves. Searchers much be cognizant of this and thoroughly search these areas.

Agnosia and Driving

A person with Alzheimer's who still drives may not recognize a red light and drive into the intersection, or may not recognize a highway off ramp as such and enter a highway into oncoming traffic.

Although a missing person may not have left in his own car, searchers should still be alert to driving history and vehicle availability. Are there other vehicles (garden tractors, golf carts, neighbors' cars) that can't be accounted for? Would, or could, the person take a bus? A taxi? Could he hail such a vehicle on his own? Would he get on a bus, or in a taxi, if someone else helped him? Lack of bus or taxi fare should not be considered a hindrance; it is all too common for a Good Samaritan to pay the person's way or a compassionate bus driver will just allow them on the bus without paying.

Interviewers must ask if there have been previous instances in which the missing person drove away or become lost while driving. Pay special attention to driving history and mechanical experience. Many times, family members will hide car keys or disable a vehicle (remove distributor caps, unhook batteries, remove tires) in order to prevent their loved one from driving. That has not always worked, as sometimes, persons with mechanical experience simply fix the disabling device and drive away.

Agnosia and Additional Concerns

A person with agnosia may interpret a person's body language, facial expression, law enforcement or SAR uniform, or other visual cue as a threat and react inappropriately, even violently. A person with agnosia may misinterpret searchers' actions and/or search dog behavior in the field.

Searchers must be aware of a missing person's likes, dislikes, attractions, and fears. Knowing the purpose of why the person went wandering can also help teams formulate search patterns, methods, equipment, and best approach to finding the missing subject.

> **Example:** *Peter K. is a 72-year-old man with Alzheimer's disease. He is a generally happy person, but can be very afraid of strangers. He walks with a pronounced limp and has severe arthritis. He has been missing for more than 14 hours, at which time local SAR is activated. Searchers quickly find his track and begin following sign. A helicopter unit with FLIR is brought in and a heat source believed to be Peter is located. As searchers move into the foothills in his direction, the helicopter turns its spotlight on and activates its public address (PA) system, calling for Peter. Searchers discover that Peter's track pattern has changed from walking to erratic running, in a direction away from search teams. They also discover sign that indicates he has fallen at least twice. When Peter's body is located the following day, searchers and management estimate he has run at least twelve miles from where he was originally spotted.*

Information later developed from in-depth interviews with family reveals that Peter K. had served in World War II; he was taken prisoner of war and was incarcerated in a Russian POW camp. It is assumed that Peter ran to his death, believing that the searchers who were there to rescue him, were in fact, trying to harm him.

Aphasia is the loss or reduction of the brain's ability to interpret and formulate language. Usually, the first evidence of language difficulty appears in naming objects or persons in normal speech or in naming tasks. A person may show significant pausing or strange word substitutions. Additionally, in the early stages, the person is aware of her worsening speech and may develop methods of hiding or compensating for the difficulty. She may ramble on or abruptly change the topic. A person with aphasia may drop words during the course of conversations such as "I go store with you?" She may substitute similar words for more common terms.

Example: *Instead of the more appropriate phrase "middle aged," they may say something like "light years" or "medium aged."*

Frequent usage of vague terms such as "thing," "there," "that," or nonspecific naming, such as "he," "she," or "it" may also demonstrate language deterioration.

Example: *Mary Ellen has Alzheimer's. She becomes increasingly frustrated when she is unable to name her needs: "I want that thing over there." Her caregiver says, "What thing? The watch? The book?" Mary Ellen says, "That thing!" Caregiver: "Where? On the dresser? On the table?" Mary Ellen: "THERE!"*

In moderate Alzheimer's disease, the person begins to show significant errors, both in speaking and comprehending conversation. She may not be able to appropriately answer questions, has difficulty in naming items or persons, and may answer nonsensically.

In the later stages of Alzheimer's, a person can be severely impaired in her naming abilities and expressing herself verbally; may use incoherent jargon; and may not be able to comprehend speech at all. In severe cases, all ability to use or understand verbal communication is lost.

Furthermore, persons with Alzheimer's may become responsive only to certain terms or phrases. Alzheimer's disease, and aphasia, can affect the way a person thinks of herself or responds. Nicknames from childhood, pet names, may begin appearing. A married woman may revert to her maiden name or a previous married name.

Examples: *Franklin will only respond to being told, "Mrs. Barnes wants to see you."*

Kathryn will only come when she hears "here, kitty, kitty, kitty!", an apparent nickname from her childhood.

Marjorie Simpson has been married to Joseph Simpson for 11 years. Prior to this marriage, Marjorie was married to Gordon Graham for 27 years until he passed away. Marjorie has Alzheimer's disease. She was reported to SAR and a search was initiated after she walked away from her residence. Unbeknownst to SAR teams and law enforcement, a Good Samaritan found her wandering an industrial district and took her to a local emergency room where Marjorie identified herself as Marjorie Graham. Hospital staff did receive a police notification about Marjorie Simpson, but they have nothing to connect Mrs. Simpson with the woman now sitting in their emergency department and thus, a fruitless search continues.

Aphasia can take many forms from minor (breaks in speech, forgetting obscure words) to severe (complete loss of language). Anomic aphasia—the misidentification or misnaming of two or more objects—can occur.

Example: *When told to get his jacket, Jim repeatedly gets a shirt.*

Aphasia can also manifest in the use of sexually explicit, profane, socially inappropriate language or communication that would be atypical of the person's past use of language.

Example: *An elderly white person with Alzheimer's encounters an officer of color. She is not likely, as her language regresses, to refer to the officer as a person of color, or an African American or black officer. Instead, she is more likely to use one of the several offensive terms more commonly used historically. By understanding that this may be part of her aphasia progression, the responding officer is less likely to react and escalate an already tenuous situation.*

Understanding this process is extremely important for the search team members and Incident Commander. Without a clear picture of how the missing person communicates verbally, searchers may miss important clues in the field. Searchers may miss the person entirely if they rely on him calling out or answering shouts for him.

> **Example:** *Border Patrol's Search, Trauma, and Rescue (BORSTAR) team is assisting local law enforcement in a search for David, a 67-year-old man with Alzheimer's disease. As Team 1 takes a hill as their* assignment and Team 2 *is deployed to a connecting ridge, all begin calling for David. As they shout for David, they hear what sounds like another searcher also calling for David. However, they know that no one else is deployed in their sector. Listening carefully, they begin moving toward the voice – and find David, trapped in a rocky area, calling his own name out, echoing the searchers. Had BORSTAR not been cognizant of this situation, David may not have been found in time, or at all.*

Some persons with Alzheimer's will lose all ability to use spoken language; however, there is nothing physically wrong with their vocal cords. They may not speak at all, but sing perfectly on key with the appropriate words. Even as they are normally silent, they still may sing, scream, moan, shriek, bark like a dog or make other sounds.

While a person who wanders is sometimes able to recognize and verbalize that he requires assistance, most are unable, or unwilling, to do so. A pioneering review of 46 search mission records from Virginia shows that in no case did a person with Alzheimer's ever call out for help nor answer to calls shouted by field personnel (Koester and Stooksbury 1992, 1995). Those records do not reflect, however, how many of those subjects suffered from aphasia, so it is difficult to know whether or not the subjects chose not to ask for help, or could not ask for help.

It is important to note here that persons who speak two or more languages may begin using words from the primary language when they forget the word in English (example, "pass me that, that, that naranja!"). As aphasia progresses, the speaker may use more and more of the primary language, combining a form of the two (or more) languages. Ultimately, the speaker may revert to the primary language totally, becoming completely non-responsive in English.

> **Example:** *Amparo de Gonzales, a resident of Nebraska, is by heritage Cuban. Her normal daily use language is English, however, her birth language is Cuban Spanish. Her husband reports that Ms. De Gonzales has begun using more Cuban phrases and words in her speech. Additionally, within the past few weeks, she told her husband that she has begun dreaming in Spanish. She does not speak, read or understand any other language.*

A multilingual person may not respond in any way to searchers calling in English, but may be completely coherent and responsive in Italian or German. The missing person report and interviews MUST address language issues. All languages the missing person is able to read, speak or understand must be detailed, even if that person has not used that language in years.

It is most important for the search and rescue personnel or law enforcement officer to recognize that symptoms may seem mild when at home, where the person is well fed, cared for, warm and comfortable. Under the stress of becoming lost or disoriented, dehydrated or injured, a person with aphasia will have more severe language difficulties, making verbal communication that much more difficult (or impossible). Thus, it is critical that field teams understand that the Alzheimer's subject may not be responsive to searchers or may not respond in a manner that a searcher would ordinarily expect.

Apraxia is the loss or reduction of the ability to coordinate fine and gross motor skills. A person with apraxia will have difficulty with basic life skills, such as dressing themselves, making a sandwich or eating, bathing, brushing their teeth or performing other basic hygiene. The person may look disheveled and unkempt and have the appearance of a homeless person. Coupled with aphasia and/or agnosia, apraxia may cause law enforcement to misinterpret a contact with the person as just another homeless encounter and actually transport the person with Alzheimer's to a shelter or public mental health facility. Historically, it was not uncommon for police to transport persons with Alzheimer's to jail, having failed to recognize the disease and its manifestations.

> **Example:** *A 75-year-old male comes to the attention of law enforcement for exposing himself to a woman in a park. The man comes out of a public bathroom with his pants unzipped and exposed. He approaches a woman, and makes grunting noises at her, gesticulating at his pants. Further investigation reveals the gentleman to have Alzheimer's disease, including moderate agnosia and apraxia, with severe aphasia. He had wandered away from his home. His primary caregiver is his daughter, whose hair coloring resembles that of the woman in the park. The gentleman can take himself to the bathroom, but cannot reassemble himself after urinating. It is habit, in his home, to toilet by himself, then come to his daughter for help in re-dressing.*

SAR interviewers should ask a variety of questions about the AD subject's abilities. Although it may seem inconsequential to ask how a person dresses, the responses can give much insight to the missing person's field capability. A person with Alzheimer's who can pick out his own clothing and be appropriate for the weather will have better ability to recognizing potential dangers in the field than a person who dresses in a sundress in winter or a heavy coat in summer. A person with Alzheimer's who must have her husband assist her dressing, and who must sit in order to place the pants over her feet, will have a harder time navigating difficult terrain. A person with Alzheimer's who must wear clothing that cannot be easily removed will have a very difficult time in public using a rest room facility or "finding a bush" in the field. A person with Alzheimer's who had an incontinence accident because he could not get his clothing removed in time may deliberately hide from searchers out of embarrassment.

Searchers should be aware that when a missing person is reported as "a strong walker," it is important to follow up with questions about what types of surfaces he usually walks on. If he usually walks on firm surfaces, walking on sand, river washes or hilly terrain will significantly tire him more so. The more an exhausted a person with Alzheimer's becomes, the worse his symptoms appear. For a missing person with Alzheimer's already experiencing fine motor deficits, it is logical to anticipate gross motor deficits early in the search. Searchers should be clue aware for worsening gross motor skills, worsening gait patterns, shuffling prints and foot dragging marks.

Cognitive Mapping

Cognitive mapping is the brain's ability to memorize patterns and locations. This is the ability that gives an individual the capability to locate the bathroom in the middle of the night, with the lights off, use the toilet, and return to bed without requiring conscious thought, turning on lights, or using a map.

People with Alzheimer's disease lose this ability. A person with Alzheimer's disease, who gets up in the middle of the night to use the bathroom, may find herself locked in a utility closet by accident. A man with AD who uses the elevator may instead find himself in a service elevator; without the proper codes to activate it, the elevator simply sits idle, with the person standing inside. A woman who habitually walks to the grocery every day becomes lost and confused as the route, once comforting and familiar, is no longer so.

Example: *Mr. Voight, a 72-year-old Canadian citizen with Alzheimer's disease, becomes lost while vacationing with his family in Arizona. While Mr. Voight appears to still be able to navigate his own home at this time, he has now twice become lost while on holiday. His inability to map his surroundings will significantly hamper his ability to find his way back to the vacation home.*

Searchers should be aware that it is quite common for people with Alzheimer's who wander to find a home, any home, and try to get in, particularly in developments in which most of the homes look alike or follow a similar design pattern. Searchers should not rule out other homes in the area, particularly vacant ones. Be alert for broken windows or locks, doors ajar, rifled gardens. Look for hoses that may have been left running; this may indicate that someone has made an attempt to drink. Law enforcement in the area should be notified and be alert for reports of returning homeowners who find something amiss or complaints of vandalism.

Sundowning

Sundowning, or sundown syndrome, is a pattern of delirious behavior, a condition that has been historically documented in Hippocrates' own medical writings. It affects many persons with dementia (all dementias, not only Alzheimer's disease) and manifests in the hours of sunset, hence its name. During the hours of sunset, a person with dementia often experiences a significant increase in confusion, agitation, aggression, paranoia, violence, obsessive behavior, and wandering. Significant decreases in physical capabilities, thinking and speech, as well as other sensory deficits can also occur.

In essence, a person with Alzheimer's disease and experiencing significant sundowning, lost in the field during the hours of sunset is more likely to be agitated and afraid, and less rational, less able to hear, see or maintain her balance. Persons in this state commonly will not bunk down for the night, and tend to push harder because of their altered perceptions. The result of this is often blindly barging into areas such as dense brush, thick vegetation or into hazardous terrain. They are less likely respond to searchers who shout, call or try to approach. They may often purposely evade or hide from search teams.

Example: *In a phone interview, Michaela Morey indicated that her mother seemed worse in the evenings, and that deterioration in her behavior and agitation began around 5:00 p.m. each day. Ms. Morey states that her mother's agitation and fearfulness becomes even more extreme when she misses her daily nap. Further, she states that the recent Daylight Savings Time switch seems to have made her mother's condition worse, and that she struck at Michaela out of frustration and fear last week for the first time.*

When a missing person with Alzheimer's is found, the risk of violence is usually highest during this period. Do not underestimate the capability of an elderly and apparently frail person with Alzheimer's. Search teams should be aware of and prepared for signs of a person lashing out.

Dysphagia

Dysphagia is the loss or reduction of the ability to swallow. This is an unfortunate progression of Alzheimer's disease and often leads to pneumonia, aspiration, choking, spitting, and/or difficulty eating or drinking.

Searchers need to be particularly aware of dysphagia combined with the missing person's lack of gross motor skills. Often when a person with Alzheimer's falls, whether in the field or in a home, the lack of ability to swallow and the inability to right oneself to his feet leads to aspiration pneumonia. It also inhibits the person's ability to call for assistance. Searchers must also be aware that even if a missing or wandering Alzheimer's subject has food or water with him, or has access to such, he may not be able to consume it.

It is important for the SAR interviewer to ask about the missing person's eating habits. A person who is regularly provided meals and fluid may not actually be able to swallow or ingest those foods. Do not assume that the missing person is always well nourished or well hydrated. Further, it is important for the SAR interviewer to ask whether or not the missing person wears dentures. Many do, and because of dysphagia swallowing issues, proper dental fit and usage can be difficult. It is important to know whether or not a person might remove his dentures for comfort.

> **Example:**   *Mary does not like wearing her dentures. She states that they are uncomfortable and rub. She has had repeated fittings and alterations, without success. No specific problem can be pinpointed, however Mary has dysphagia. Because her swallowing problems have progressed so, she now takes her dementia and other necessary medications in liquid and capsule form, so that they can be swallowed in applesauce or pudding for ease. Dry mouth is also a side effect of some of her prescription medication and contributes to her swallowing problems. Mary will wear her dentures when entertaining company, but otherwise, she will keep them in her sweater-coat pocket, wrapped in a paper napkin or Kleenex. As a result, she has often dropped her dentures, lost them in restaurant garbage or misplaced them in her residential nursing care facility. Mary will not answer nursing staff or see her family if she does not have her dentures in. As a result, it is logical to believe that Mary will hide from searchers in the field if she has dropped or does not have her dentures.*

Combine apraxia (loss or reduction of fine and gross motor skills) with dysphagia (loss or reduction of ability to swallow) and often the result is a person who falls and chokes or aspirates. Searchers must be aware that the missing person with Alzheimer's is at increased risk of aspiration and pneumonia, and even more so if they lay, fallen and prone, in the field. These subjects are even less likely to be able to call out for rescuers or aid.

Wandering

People with Alzheimer's often come to the attention of law enforcement officials and SAR because of wandering. As the person with Alzheimer's loses more and more of his memory, he will often go in search of a particular item, person, or place. These persons are not easily distracted idiots who have simply gotten lost. The brain changes in memory, thinking, personality, visual and other sensory impairments that occur in people with Alzheimer's cause an irrepressible urge to wander, walk, or seek something or someone in particular.

Wandering has proven such a common behavior that Alzheimer's experts predict that nearly 70% of all persons with Alzheimer's will wander away from safety at least once during the course of their illness. Many will wander an average of 6 to 8 times before they are placed into a residential facility or a qualified caregiver/nurse is brought into the home to help. Some, no matter how many times they wander, will never be placed into a secure facility because their caregiver(s) assume that since the person has always been found and returned before, there will always be a positive outcome.

> **One in eight persons aged 65 and over (13%)**
> **and nearly 50% of all persons aged 85 and over**
> **have Alzheimer's disease or related dementia.**
> Alzheimer's Association 2007

It would be easy, then, for a SAR IC to assume that thirteen percent of all searches for persons 65 and older are for persons with Alzheimer's (and along that same reasoning, half of all his searches for persons 85 and older). This is an incorrect and a dangerous assumption. *The reality is that a much higher percentage of call-outs for wandering or missing elderly are people with Alzheimer's. A person with normal cognition, even at age 85, is not likely to get up and wander at 2 a.m.*

Search records and anecdotal history from law enforcement officers show that even when wandering Alzheimer's subjects do encounter public citizens, they are often ignored, considered "homeless," or given aid, but are not reported to responsible agencies. In areas of high poverty or with a transitory or nomadic population, the likelihood of receiving aid is even less.

Additionally, MedicAlert®, Care Trak, Project Lifesaver or ID bracelets or necklaces such as those issued by the Alzheimer's Association's Safe Return® program, while certainly encouraged, are not a guarantee that the public will recognize or report people who are wandering.

Search team interviewers must be certain to ask whether the missing person is or has ever been enrolled in a wandering or medical alert program. If the person has been enrolled, it is vital to follow up with those organizations as they may hold crucial information or clues that prove helpful to the search operation.

It is also recommended best practice to notify Safe Return® or local Alzheimer's Association chapters of a missing person with Alzheimer's. If the person is found by a public citizen or the chapter/Safe Return® is familiar with her, reunification with her family will be that much swifter and easier. SAR teams should also as best practice notify those same organizations when the missing person is actually found, so that ongoing efforts are not made needlessly. Such effort continuing after the person is found is a waste of energy and resources, and leads to detrimental, negative feelings when future incidents arise.

Family Reporting Incidents of Past Wandering

In discussion and interviews with caregivers or family members, many initially report no previous history of the missing person "wandering" or becoming lost. Many become downright adamant: "He's never done this before!" However, when further queried or questioned by a skilled interviewer, many do then recall an incident or occasion when the person has become lost or disoriented.

Example: *Traditional Interview*

Interviewer: "Has this ever happened before?"

(The interviewer means, *"Has your loved one ever wandered away before?"*)

Reporting Family Member (looking at the deputies going down the hallway, the search dogs in the laundry room, the mounted SAR member combing the backyard, the helicopter with FLIR overhead, and the media in the driveway), responds honestly and truthfully: *"No, *THIS* has never happened before."*

It is essential for SAR interviewers to recognize and understand to understand the importance of the interview. Often, better answers come when the skilled interviewer opens dialogue that is both reassuring and non-blaming. Further, more detailed information comes when a family member or reporting party understands exactly what is being asked.

Example: *Better Interview*

Interviewer: *"I would like to talk to you about your father. I know how scary and confusing this can be, so I want to make sure that you are comfortable and understand what I am asking. No one is blaming you; wandering is a part of Alzheimer's disease and is often uncontrollable. I really need you to be as open and honest with me as possible so that we have the best shot at finding your father. No one will think badly or poorly of you or your dad. I'd like to ask you about previous wandering incidents. Has your dad ever turned up someplace you didn't expect him to be? Has he ever NOT been where you did expect him to be? I'd like to give you an example. Have you ever been in the store, talking to your Dad, and as you were talking, you realized he was no longer there? We would consider that wandering."*

Reporting Family Member: *"Okay, I understand. No, my dad's never wandered before, but this one time, we were in downtown San Francisco. He saw a man drop a gum wrapper on the ground. My dad went over, picked up the trash, and followed this man many blocks into Chinatown before catching up. He gave the man his wrapper and then didn't know where he was."*

The interviewer thought the family member was finished, however, the family member then continued on to provide several more incidents. It is important to note that none of these incidents had been considered "wandering" since the family had always found the person safely and within a reasonable time period. They "just didn't know where he was."

This real life example illustrates that quite often a missing person with Alzheimer's has a history of wandering—a history that may be extremely relevant to the current circumstance—and yet, the family will not recognize wandering for what it is. Many family members, caregivers or reporting parties feel that if a wandering person had found his way home, he wasn't really lost to begin with.

Using the above situation as an example, the skilled SAR interviewer can educate the reporting party that a missing person merely finding her way home, or discovering her location, doesn't negate being lost in the first place.

Example: A SAR Interviewer reports: *"Mrs. Ukrainetz continued to insist that her father had never wandered before, never been lost, that the few times she didn't know where he was, he always turned up. "See? He wasn't lost, he just wasn't where I thought he was." I then asked Mrs. Ukrainetz that if we were to find her father today, and found that he had been safely secured in an abandoned home, would that mean he hadn't been lost for the past ten days? She then understood, and was able to relate other several other instances in which her father became separated from her mother, walked away from home, or became disoriented, such as at the grocery store or in parking lots."*

Lost in the Labyrinth

People with AD who wander rarely find their own way home. When they are located in or near a home, the likelihood is greatest that they hadn't wandered far to begin with. Many become lost or disoriented from their own home or care facility, but an increasing number of people with AD are being reported missing from malls, parks, zoos, and other public arenas. These persons, already in an unfamiliar environment, are particularly unlikely to be able to navigate themselves to safety.

Search records and anecdotal history from law enforcement officers and SAR records often reflect, once a missing person has been found, he or she is unable to explain a number of different issues.

Example: *In a 1997 case in Escondido, California, Audrey, a 73-year-old woman, was last seen at her care facility wearing pink pajamas, slippers, and carrying her wig. When located nearly nine hours later, Audrey was found to have four separate canceled bus pass tickets on her person. As she left without money, it became obvious that Audrey—dressed in pajamas and carrying her wig—encountered persons who purchased bus fare for her. None of these people reported her missing, and no one called law enforcement or for medical aid. Audrey's case is not unusual.*

Additional Risk Factors

Law enforcement officers, search incident commanders and search teams need to be aware of how a person with Alzheimer's will react in a particular environment. Again, knowing the missing person's history and experience will help search managers define and determine a behavior profile. As the disease progresses, eventually the person with Alzheimer's will succumb to more devastating and debilitating brain dysfunction that will lead to eventual death. These include:

Catastrophic Reaction

Often described as a "super anxiety attack," a catastrophic reaction is generally a hyper-response to a stressful situation that may cause injury to self or others. The person with Alzheimer's will break objects, scream, cry, take off clothing, kick, bite, moan, rock, withdraw, lock themselves into a room or hide, etc. This could be the trigger that causes wandering or the behavior may be triggered because of wandering.

Example: *During the course of Ashley's third birthday, she fell off the trampoline and severely broke her arm. 911 was called, and both mother and father accompanied Ashley in the ambulance to the hospital. Carmela and Wilfred, Ashley's great-grandparents, both of whom have from Alzheimer's disease, were left behind. In the noise, confusion, ambulance sounds and lights, Carmela disappeared, and SAR was activated to look for her. Wilfred was found sitting alone at the kitchen table, rocking, and picking and eating the leaves off the fern centerpiece.*

Violence

When a person with Alzheimer's realizes that he cannot control his environment or that he is uncomfortable and has a need he cannot communicate, he may be resistant or even violent. These behaviors can be unpredictable. Once the person is found it is important to approach him calmly. When transporting a person with Alzheimer's disease, do not allow him to sit in the front seat where he could suddenly grab the steering wheel or hit the driver. Some persons with Alzheimer's have been known to open the door and step out of a moving vehicle.

Example: *John Allen Marble, 68, has been diagnosed with dementia. While driving back to his home of nine years, John became agitated. He did not recognize his home and insisted to his wife, Martha, that they were going the wrong way. John became so upset and frustrated with Martha that, in an effort to stop her from continuing, he grabbed her hair and pulled her head down below the dashboard. Martha was able to narrowly avoid an accident, but was unable to extricate herself from John's grip. The incident was brought to the attention of local police, who were forced to place John in a temporary 72-hour custody hold, where he was evaluated for being a risk to himself or others.*

Officer and SAR field team safety measures must be considered. A 1999 study found that 60.4% of all homes with a family member who has Alzheimer's disease or dementia have a firearm or gun present in the home; 44.6% of all those homes that have a firearm present reported that the weapon was kept loaded. Another 38% stated that they did not know if the weapon was kept loaded or not.

It is absolutely imperative for SAR interviewers to discover whether or not the missing person with Alzheimer's has, or previously has had, a gun in his home or available to him. Moreover, it is critical that the weapon be accounted for. If it, or any weapon, cannot be located or accounted for, then teams must assume that the missing person has it and proceed with due caution.

The skilled SAR interviewer needs to thoroughly explore any possibility or history that pertains to safety in the field, both that of the missing person and that of the team. Examine military experience and law enforcement history (as an officer or as an offender). Discover likes and dislikes, preferences and fears.

When teams discover a missing person, particularly one who may be hostile, it is often best to send forth one person. If the person is known to dislike women and dogs, it is clear that the contact person should not be a female dog handler. On the other hand, if the person is looking for his daughter, a male might not be the first choice.

Searchers must keep in mind the effects of agnosia (the loss or reduction of the brain's ability to interpret images) on the missing person's ability to perceive help in the field. A searcher approaching the subject may be perceived as a threat or a savior. If the person is known to be afraid of law enforcement or hostile to persons in uniform, a command decision to wear "subdued" clothing may be wisest.

> **Example:** *William has Alzheimer's disease. He lives at home and is cared for by his wife, Edith. When their daughter, Anne, had not been able to make contact for several days, she went to their home. The front door was barricaded and the family vehicle was gone. Edith's purse was spilled across the kitchen. William served in World War II and in Korea. He received several war injuries, including being shot in the leg and losing part of his left hand. As his Alzheimer's disease has progressed, his nightmares of war have returned. He believes "the enemy is coming for him." When Anne searched the house, she discovered than an antique .22 was missing. Law enforcement was notified, and a search began. William and Edith were later found deceased, both of gun shot wounds.*

Ultimately, if a missing person is known to be hostile and is reported to be armed, a decision must be made as to whether volunteer SAR teams are the best choice for searching.

Incontinence

As Alzheimer's disease progresses, it robs the person of bladder and bowel control. The bladder is essentially a large muscle and, as the person loses recognition of the urge to urinate, the bladder will fill until it spasms and voids. When this occurs often enough, the bladder muscle loses tension and control, which often leads to leakage. Because of the infectious waste associated with loss of bladder and bowel control, people with Alzheimer's often develop urinary tract and bladder infections. These infections only serve to further reduce bladder and bowel control as well as increase confusion and disorientation.

An undiagnosed, undetected or untreated bladder or urinary tract infection may cause or trigger a person to wander. This is of particular importance to the patrol officer, who is often called to transport a person with Alzheimer's who has been found. Many officers, in an effort to comfort this "nice old lady who was out wandering," will place the person in the front of a patrol car. This is unsafe for a variety of reasons, including the person's ability to open the door while in transit, reach the officer's weapon, radio or the steering wheel. The wandering subject is most often best placed securely, safely, and respectfully in the back of a patrol car.

Incontinence is yet another reason to safely place the person with Alzheimer's in the back of the patrol car, because the seats are often an easy to clean, one-piece plastic bench. Loss of bowel and bladder control can produce what is considered a hazardous material spill incident (HAZMAT), which will require special clean-up services.

Cleaning of such a spill on a fabric seat can take considerable time and often ends up with that patrol car out of service for the rest of its shift. If there is no other alternative and incontinence is an issue, the person may be transported sitting on or with a plastic garbage bag tied around their waist.

Treatment

While there is no cure for Alzheimer's there are several medications that delay the effects of the disease for a short time. When investigating the medical history of the missing person it is important to recognize what medications they use, what they look like and the side effects. As mentioned before, families will sometimes not reveal to search and rescue or law enforcement interviewers that the missing person has Alzheimer's or dementia, either because they don't know or because they are ashamed or in denial. If asked whether the missing person takes any medications, they may list one of the following Alzheimer medications. That will give search managers essential information about the missing person and interviewers can follow up with more detailed questions about behaviors to help focus the search effort.

Alzheimer Medications
Donepezile hydrochloride (*Aricept*, pronounced AIR-ih-sept) • Taken in the early to moderate stages of Alzheimer's • Can aggravate asthma and other breathing problems
Memantine (*Namenda*) • For the moderate to severe stages of Alzheimer's • Often prescribed with Aricept
Rivastigmine tartrate (*Exelon*, pronounced ECKS-ell-on)
Galantamine (*Razadyne*), pronounced (RAZ-ah-dine)

Dealing with the Family (Caregivers)

Question: "How many family members will know about the medications or even the medical history?" The answer will be "not many." This answer may sound cruel. But when looked at objectively it is found that this is due to low frequency of regular contract with family member who has Alzheimer's. There is a certain amount of denial that the person has a "problem." The person with AD on the other hand may be embarrassed to admit he or she has the disease. They fear the loss of freedoms and privileges being taken away, for instance driving a car.

Seven out of ten people who have AD live at home by themselves or with family members. The daughter or daughter-in-law usually ends up being the caregiver. As the disease progresses the family caregivers become more frustrated with outbursts of violence and other reactions. The caregivers may have given up many things: work, their homes, sleep, vacations and other sacrifices. There may be signs of elder abuse (e.g., burns, malnutrition, bed sores). It is important to be aware of the signs and symptoms and how the missing person will react to being back in this environment.

SAR Resource Considerations

Dog and Scent

People with Alzheimer's, especially in care facilities, will put on several layers of clothes sometimes due to a thermal regulation problem or obsessive-compulsive behavior. This leads to borrowing clothing from others. Trailing dogs will have a problem with distinguishing the right scent and may not follow the right person. The interview of the caregiver should determine if person exhibits this behavior.

Man-tracking

Searchers need to get started early. The person who wanders can keep going and going. They exhibit what is called the Pinball Effect. They will walk a straight line until they hit an obstacle like a fence, turn and continue on until the next obstacle, and so on. Eventually they will keep going until they get stuck.

Water Hazards

Drowning is one of the major causes of death to people with Alzheimer's who wander. Because of the Pinball Effect described above and the inability to perceive danger they will walk into lakes, ponds, rivers, and canals. All these potential hazards need to be checked with dive teams and water dogs. Also searchers need to be made aware of the possible biohazards.

Media

In an urban environment, the average missing person will encounter up to several people who have no idea the person is lost. In several documented cases, the person who wandered got on public transportation and the drivers did not bother to take a fare. The person will ride all day, may even talk to other riders who offer help and who will take them to a requested destination. In one case in San Diego, California, a Latino person who got lost trying to get home received help and transportation all the way back to Mexico and was left in the middle of a city he did not know. Thus, the need to get the word out with pictures and descriptions is critical. Flyers are effective.

When you find the person with Alzheimer's who has wandered

The most important thing to remember when approaching the person who has been found is to *show you care. Treat him or her with respect. Use his or her last name*, e.g., Mr. Smith, Mrs. Jones. Other approaches include:

✓ Approach from the front—one person only—so as not to startle the person;

✓ Speak slowly so he or she can understand;

✓ Touch when appropriate;

✓ Be consistent in your directions and use simple terms; and

✓ Give the person something to hold and focus on, such as a child's teddy bear; it may help to calm him or her down.

In some cases, the person may be in a room or automobile and refuse to leave. At this point it may be acceptable (and depending on your comfort level) to tell a lie, for example: "Your wife is waiting for you to come to dinner."

Be aware that a uniform may cause the person to think they have done something wrong. This will increase their stress. On the other hand, a uniform may gain a person's trust and cooperation.

A Death March

In order to understand how the missing at-risk person with Alzheimer's may behave or react to his environment, search managers must understand Alzheimer's disease. Without understanding the impairments in thinking, logic, emotion, vision, and other critical areas of the brain, searchers may be less likely to attach a significance of risk to these persons. The result, quite often, is that searchers overlook important clues, thus reducing the likelihood of finding the missing person.

It is therefore extremely important and helpful to get a complete detailed life history of the person. This information will provide insight into the missing person and his or her behavior. This oftentimes can help searchers develop a possible intent or destination for the missing person. An effective way to set a benchmark is to use an evaluation form specific to missing persons with dementia, such as one by Robert Koester in Appendix I.

Because of the nature of Alzheimer's disease, the person may not be aware and therefore unable to ask for help. Because of the impairment to judgment and logical thinking, many persons with Alzheimer's are unable to recognize danger. They may wander across roads or highways, fall into bodies of water or become entrapped in heavy brush.

This is extraordinarily important to realize, since many law enforcement agencies do not consider a missing person with Alzheimer's to be at- risk. Some departments do not consider a person over the age of eighteen to be missing until after twenty-four hours. Some departments still require a mandatory 48 hours, or worse, 72 hours since last seen. A missing person with Alzheimer's does not have the luxury of time.

Studies by Robert Koester and David Stooksbury (1992, 1995) show that wandering persons with Alzheimer's lost in Virginia faced a 46% mortality rate if not found within 24 hours. Information provided by the Emergency Services Council of Nova Scotia reported death incidents of 70% for Alzheimer's subjects not found within 24 hours. Records by the Rim of the World Search and Rescue team (California) from 1968 to 1994 showed 100% mortality rates for persons over the age of 60 who were not found within 24 hours (No distinction was made for person's with Alzheimer's versus elder persons.)

Unfortunately, many persons with Alzheimer's disease who wander will succumb to personal or environmental hazards. In the urban environment, the three leading causes of death are drowning, hypothermia, and dehydration/heat related disorders, in that order.

"That Others May Live…"

Originally the creed of the United States Air Force Pararescue Airmen—"This We Do, So That Others May Live" or more simply "That Others May Live"—the motto, and attitude, have been adopted by many SAR teams throughout the world. While many people think the slogan only really belongs to teams who go after injured climbers on Mt. Hood or trekkers in Nepal, the reality is that, for a missing at-risk person with Alzheimer's, searchers are often the difference between living and dying.

In SAR, there are certain situations in which search management can rely on past history to inform current search planning. For example, planes typically get caught in swirling winter wind patterns and usually crash in a fairly predictable pattern or area. Or people often walk a particular hiking trail in a certain pattern, following a map in a local guide book which SAR teams know to be misleading; thus hikers are often found lost in the same area of the trail.

In searching for or managing the search for missing at-risk persons with Alzheimer's, methods that work so well in other types of searches are simply not reliable. Missing persons from a plane crash do not generally deliberately hide from search teams. Overdue hunters do not call their own names back to searchers. And injured or stuck climbers do not only respond to assistance if they are told, "Mrs. Barnes wants to see you."

It is critical that field searchers and managers alike understand Alzheimer's disease and its affect on each particular missing person with the disease. SAR personnel must understand agnosia, aphasia, apraxia, and how those changes affect a person's behavior in the field.

As our society ages and as people with Alzheimer's disease continue to wander, our law enforcement and SAR teams will only continue to have increasing demands made on them. No one person or single team alone will be able to solve the problem of missing Alzheimer's subjects. By educating the public, the Alzheimer's family and caregiver, the SAR member, SAR team, SAR manager, responding law enforcement officer, and other first responders, we can together reduce the number of repeat searches, the time and resources required for searching, the injuries the missing person incurs, and most importantly, the lives lost.

Summary

The box below provides a review of essential tips for planning a searching for a person with Alzheimer's who has wandered.

Tips for searching for a person with Alzheimer's

✓ Alzheimer's is a progressive disease that effects the brain.

✓ Understand the medical problems of agnosia, aphasia and apraxia; they are associated with the disease and the loss of cognitive mapping.

✓ Be aware of some of the behaviors that people with Alzheimer's may exhibit, such as wandering and violence.

✓ Understand the concept of sundowning, or getting tired and disoriented toward the end of the day.

✓ Search everywhere.

✓ Get flyers out early.

✓ Get the media involved early.

✓ Once the person is found, be aware of catastrophic reactions.

✓ Approach slowly, speak calmly and treat the person with respect.

Dementia Profile

They go until they get "stuck."

Appear to lack ability to turn around.

Oriented to the past, the more severe the disease the further in the past they exist.

In urban environment, typically found in structures (includes yards) or walking along roads. Often found behind shrubbery, out buildings.

Leaves own residence or nursing home, often with a sighting on a road.

May cross or depart from roads.

Attracted to water features.

May attempt to travel to former residence or favorite place.

Will not leave many verifiable clues.

Will not cry out for "help" or respond to shouts (only 1% respond).

Succumb to the environment (hypothermia, drowning, dehydration).

Urban Statistics—Dementia

Distance from IPP

n=336 cases	Miles	Km
25%	0.2	0.4
50%	0.7	1.1
75%	2.0	3.2
Max zone	7.8	12.6

Search Outcomes

SAR Find	43%
Investigative	9%
Self	7%
Other	35%
Suspension	5%

Find Location

Structure	35%
Road	36%
Linear Feature	9%
Drainage	4%
Water	6%
Brush	1%
Scrub	
Woods/Forest	3%
Field	6%
Rock	

Survivability
n=455 cases

Status	Percentage
Uninjured	80%
Injured	14%
Fatality	6%

Track Offset

n=92 cases	Meters
25%	6
50%	15
75%	76
Max zone	298

Initial Reflex Tasks—Dementia

Highly systematic search of residence/care facility and grounds. Conduct search out to 300 meters from IPP as thoroughly as possible.

Begin investigation.

Secure the IPP.

Investigate areas the person has been previously located.

Canvass neighborhood.

Patrol roads within the theoretical search area.

Activate emergency telephone notification system (e.g., TENS, Reverse 911®) for theoretical search area if early in the search, or max zone radius if later.

Establish containment.

Use trackers early at IPP and cut for sign along roads.

Use tracking dogs early at IPP, along roads, and at clues.

Deploy air-scent dogs into drainages and streams, starting at nearest IPP.

Use ground sweep teams and dogs (in separate segments) expanding from IPP.

Ensure heavy briars/brush are searched.

Task air-scent dogs and ground sweep teams to search 100 meters parallel to roads.

Search nearby previous homes and area between home sites.

Repeat searches of residence/nursing home grounds at least twice daily.

Post flyers in appropriate locations.

Expand search outward from IPP after initial tasks.

Missing and Abducted Children

Each year in the United States many women and children become the victims of abduction, sexual assault and homicide. Dozens of cases each year result in a massive search for the victim and the killer. Searching for clues and the victim of an abduction is difficult at best and many are found months later and sometimes not recovered. In order to succeed in finding clues of an abduction with a sexual assault and homicide more often, we must change how we respond to abduction searches. This section focuses primarily on children, articulating how to respond more efficiently and effectively to missing children and possible abduction incidents. Behavior profiles of children in three age categories and current urban data are included at the end of this section.

On a late afternoon in June 1998, a twelve-year-old girl named Christina Williams was reported missing by her parents after she was overdue from a short walk with her dog. She lived on the Fort Ord Military Base in Monterey County, California, a mostly abandoned installation at that time. The Presidio Police filed a missing person report and conducted a hasty search. Two days later the local search and rescue team was requested to do a search of the area, and later additional teams from the military assisted in the search. After several days, the FBI became involved when they began to suspect that she was the victim of an abduction.

The search for Christina became a focus in the media as the FBI launched a massive investigation and utilized numerous search dog teams over several weeks to search the hundreds of abandoned buildings and sites on the old base. Several sightings of suspicious people in the area during the time she was out walking were the only significant clues. Weeks later, the search came to an end, and the investigation was frustrated by few leads. Seven months later, a surveying crew found Christina's severely decomposed body about three miles away from her home, adjacent to a road. Her body and the crime scene had deteriorated to the point that few useful clues remained to find her abductor.

Newly developed abduction search strategies may have helped find her body and crime scene sooner, potentially in time to find useful clues that would lead to her abductor and killer.

This entire incident shares many things in common with other abductions with sexual assault that result in a homicide and search for the victim. The Washington State Attorney General's Office, under a grant from the U. S. Department of Justice, completed a comprehensive study in 1997, updated in 2006, entitled, "Investigative Case Management for Missing Children Homicides." The study evaluated 735 cases from 1968 to 2002, all of which included victims under the age of 18 years old whose bodies were recovered or, if not recovered, whose killer was identified, tried and convicted. Drawing upon this study and nearly a dozen cases he has researched over the last twenty years, Michael St. John (the author of this section) has made the following conclusions.

Including the Possibility of Abduction Early in the Incident

One of the significant challenges in abductions comes in the early hours of an incident. Since the majority of abduction incidents ending with a homicide are not reported as a witnessed abduction, the reason the child is missing is unclear. According to the Washington study, 60.2% of stranger child abductions are initially reported as simply a missing person, with no foul play obvious. While the frequency of abductions that include homicide is low—less than 0.5% of all reported homicides—it is important to consider the possibility of abduction whenever a child is missing. A chilling finding in the study showed that 76.2% of murdered abduction victims were killed within 3 hours, and 88.5% were dead within 24 hours. However, only about half of the victims were reported missing to law enforcement in the first three hours. These statistics indicate that by the time a search begins, the victim is often dead.

In California, statistics provided by the California Department of Justice shows that an average of 100,000 children are reported missing each year. The vast majority—nearly 90,000—are classified as runaways. Fifty children on average each year are reported to be victims of a stranger abduction. Of these, several cases will result in a homicide with a large search effort to recover the victim and locate the killer.

Discriminating among Scenarios

Unless clear evidence of abduction exists, a thorough investigation and search must occur before choosing an abduction search strategy, as search strategies vary greatly by type of incident. The search strategy of looking for the victim of abduction-with-a-homicide is very different from that of a missing person in either a wilderness or urban area, for instance. The abduction search strategy will not likely locate a victim who is lost or down in the woods.

Therefore, when a child is missing, it is critical to quickly order sufficient resources to do a comprehensive search of the likely area and a thorough investigation. With small children, water hazards account for numerous deaths each year and should be one of the early focuses of search efforts. As the search and investigation begin, officers should consider each of the following scenarios:

Possible Scenarios

- ✓ Child is late or distracted
- ✓ Miscommunication among adult guardians
- ✓ Lost child (unaware he is lost)
- ✓ Lost child (attempting to self-rescue)
- ✓ Injured child (unable to self-rescue)
- ✓ Runaway child
- ✓ Family abduction
- ✓ Staged abduction to conceal emotional family homicide

    (This is when the parent or caregiver intentionally or accidentally kills the child and stages the incident to appear like a stranger abduction.)
- ✓ Stranger abduction

The older the child, the more challenging it is to determine the best course of action. With a missing teenage girl, many experienced police officers quickly assume a runaway scenario, and in most cases they are correct. However, immediately conducting a thorough investigation often yields accurate, timely information that allows a more appropriate course of action to quickly be initiated in the event that it is abduction.

Considering each of the above scenarios as a possibility while conducting an immediate, thorough investigation allows those responsible for the search to more carefully discern which search strategies to employ.

> *It is vitally important that agencies only start an abduction search after obtaining leads that point to a likely abduction or after they have done an extensive missing person search and investigation and have ruled out each of the other scenarios.*

It is likely that an abduction search may be one of several scenarios to which the investigation will assign resources.

Preplanning for an Abduction Search

In many abduction incidents that result in a large search effort, lead law enforcement agencies have put little time or effort in training or preparing for the possibility of an event. This results in significant delays, friction, and missteps in the investigation and search. By training and developing a preplan, agencies will be able to better and more quickly respond to and manage an abduction incident. Below are considerations in relationship building, training and preplanning for an abduction search and investigation.

Preplanning considerations

- Relationship building between search and rescue organizations and local law enforcement agencies. Many jurisdictions and law enforcement agencies are unaware of the local search and rescue resources and capabilities. Below are some examples of preplanning to consider in developing closer working relationships with your local law enforcement agencies.

    ✓ Share resource lists and preplans

    ✓ Conduct joint training exercises

    ✓ Maintain professionalism and confidentiality

- Training of management teams

    ✓ Use of the Incident Command System (ICS)

    ✓ To use specific abduction with homicide search strategies

    ✓ Where to obtain and how to properly deploy the large number of resources often needed to do an effective neighborhood canvass (door to door interviewing), crime scene and search for the victim

- Training of the field searchers

    ✓ Specific training in recognizing crime scenes

    ✓ Recognition of the most common clues in abduction searches: hair, blood, weapons, and fibers

    ✓ How to conduct a neighborhood canvass and field interviews

Continued on next page ...

- Create a preplan for a missing child or abduction investigation and search. It should include:
  - ✓ Agency and position that will manage the search
  - ✓ The Incident Command System (ICS)
  - ✓ The information for issuing an AMBER Alert
  - ✓ "The F.B.I. Child Abduction Response Plan, an Investigative Guide"
  - ✓ The National Center for Missing and Exploited Children® manual entitled "A Law Enforcement Guide to Case Investigation and Program Management"
  - ✓ An Emergency Response Directory (ERD) with lists of search and rescue teams, K-9 teams, and other appropriate resources including mutual aid
  - ✓ Resource sharing agreement with other local law enforcement agencies
  - ✓ Initial search strategies
  - ✓ Management forms
  - ✓ The sources of appropriate maps
  - ✓ A plan for managing the media
  - ✓ Family liaison plan

With the above considerations as a foundation, initial law enforcement units should secure the point last seen (PLS) and the victim's house, including computers, phones, journals and PDAs as a potential crime scene and clues. Even though the house may not be an abduction site, many items provide scent for search dogs. Additionally, the victim's DNA and other valuable clues, such as computer records, e-mail, and stored cell phone numbers, may be present in the home. Some predators contact children through the Internet.

Investigators should obtain scent articles, shoe print and size, recent photographs, and a description of personal items likely being carried or worn by the child, such as clothing or a backpack. This information should be passed on to ground search and K-9 teams.

In addition to laying the foundation for an effective search, such preplans and training are of tremendous value from a financial perspective. In jurisdictions where a large, protracted search to locate the victim of an abduction has occurred, the investigation and search efforts have often exceeded the costs of other major local disasters. Some law enforcement agencies have spent hundreds of thousands of dollars in overtime and other associated costs on abduction cases. The emotional impacts and fear generated by an unresolved abduction case cast a large shadow over the entire community that is hard to measure.

Use of Volunteers for Searching

A missing child or adult who is suspected to be the victim of an abduction will often attract non-profit search centers and many concerned citizens who will search individually or in coordination with volunteer search/center efforts. In many parts of the country with limited search and rescue resources, law enforcement may need to rely on volunteers to carry out a search.

Challenges posed by working with volunteers

- Minimal or no background investigation screening
- Little or no training in search operations
- Inability to provide accurate probability of detection (POD) of assigned search area
- Lack of Worker's Compensation Insurance
- Limited ability to share sensitive case information that would help with the search as it could be leaked to the media

---

According to the Washington study, in 10% of cases, the suspect injected himself into the investigation in a volunteer capacity. However, volunteer search efforts may be valuable in that they often can deploy more people for a longer period of time than law enforcement search efforts. Volunteer search centers are generally eager to cooperate with law enforcement, so law enforcement agencies need to evaluate how best to work with volunteer agencies based on the circumstances of the case and resource needs. Whenever possible, the use of trained search and rescue teams for ground search efforts is encouraged.

Commonalities in Abductions with a Sexual Assault and Homicide

The modus operandi among abductors who sexually assault and kill their victims is often similar. Because of this predictability in how the crime is commonly executed, the search strategy can begin with the similarities, adding whatever specific clues or evidence exists in each case. According to the Washington study, all child abductions involving homicide include four critical sites that should be the focus of the search and investigation:

1. The initial contact site
2. The abduction site
3. The assault and murder site
4. The body dump location

The study revealed that in cases where the initial contact site could not be determined, the likelihood of resolving the case dropped 23.9% below the average clearance of other cases where the initial contact site was known. Therefore, finding a witness who may have unknowingly observed the victim and/or killer near the time of the abduction significantly increases the chance of identifying the initial contact site. The best strategy for uncovering this witness is to canvas the neighborhood within a ¼ mile radius (300 meters) of the likely abduction site. Because stranger abduction is most often a crime of opportunity, a good questioning strategy focuses on "What did you see that was normal?" instead of "What did you see that was out of the ordinary?" According to the study, the perpetrators most often happened to be in the same area as the victim because of: residence (26.3%), social circumstances (13.9%), occupation (10.2%), or it was a common transportation corridor.

Another commonality among abductions with a homicide is the discovery of the body dump location. According to the Washington study, 55.3% of victims are located by a chance passerby. Only 25.4% were located by law enforcement search efforts. Often by the time a chance passerby stumbles upon the victim and crime scene, many valuable clues have deteriorated. Increasing the amount of law enforcement finds and locating victims more rapidly, when there may be tangible clues, is a major priority of the abduction search strategy and tactics.

Adult Abductions

The information from the Washington study is limited in that it contains no specific profile for where to locate adult victims and little information on how to search. Although the study only looks at cases involving children under 18 years old, the author speculates much of the information may be relevant to incidents involving adults. Also, search strategies and tactics vary greatly based on incident circumstances and the geographic area in which the abduction occurred.

Many cases the author has reviewed in the past two decades suggest numerous similarities between adult and child abductions with a sexual assault and homicide. As with children, each of the four critical sites listed above warrant focused attention in investigation and search related to an adult abduction. The primary difference in cases involving adults versus children is that often more force is used to subdue an adult victim and a longer delay in the person being reported missing to authorities. The abduction search strategy has been utilized successfully for several adult female victims of an abduction with a sexual assault and murder that involved a significant search to locate the victim and crime scene.

The Abduction Search Strategy

The abduction search strategy assumes that the victim has been murdered and that the victim's body was dumped, generally in an isolated area where a vehicle can make access. Specific information about suspects or clues such as credit card receipts, witness and surveillance camera sightings can be important in developing search areas. If available, the timeline from when the abduction occurred and when the suspect surfaces again may also assist in developing a search area.

In searches where there is no suspect information or clues, the abduction search strategy can be focused on searching areas along remote roads several square miles or more from where the abduction occurred. Many of the profile areas may be locations local law enforcement knows well. If the abduction occurred at night, areas such as industrial parks or large urban parks should be considered for searching profile areas as few people are in the area at night.

When developing an assignment, teams should search profile areas up to 300 feet from where a vehicle can be driven. Little effort should be made to search trails or open space lands that are not accessible to vehicles; in the author's experience, the vast majority of victims are located near a remote road. The search effort will most often focus on pullouts or very remote roads where a suspect could have little chance of being discovered while discarding the body. In many cases, the body dump site is very near the location where the victim was assaulted and murdered.

Search teams need to be aware of "critical spacing" for clues based on terrain. The most common clues at a crime scene of a child abduction and homicide are hair, followed by semen, finger and shoe prints, weapons and fibers. Searchers need to have specific information on what they are looking for to be effective and not miss valuable clues.

Search for the Concealed Body

According to the Washington study, 55.4% of child victims of a sexual assault and homicide were concealed. This compares with an average of 14% for all other homicides. Searchers need to be trained to search for the concealed body. Generally, the suspect makes due with whatever materials are available in the body dump location. This may include vegetation, trash, debris, rocks or ground cover. Searchers can often detect attempts to conceal a body if they are made aware this is a common scenario for abduction searches. While the Washington study does not have concealment statistics for adult victims, in the author's experience, many adult victims were concealed in order to hide discovery of the body.

Other Search Considerations

In some cases, the body was dumped into the garbage system. When a law enforcement agency has a missing person who may be a possible abduction victim, it is important to know when garbage collection occurs for that community and where it is taken. If needed, the garbage for an area for that week may be isolated at the landfill or transfer station until it can be ruled out or searched. Often the possibility of the body being in the garbage system is considered very late into the investigation. If a body is suspected to be buried in a landfill, a very challenging and prolonged search effort may be involved.

Other victims have been dumped into the water. Locations of remote road access adjacent to creeks, flood channels, lakes and bays need to be cleared. This is most often done using water certified cadaver search dog teams. If one dog has an alert, request a second water certified K-9 team to check the area. If both dogs alert, divers can be deployed to search the water in that area.

Conclusion

The abduction search strategy and tactics have been utilized successfully in Maine and California since 2001. While the abduction search strategy will not locate all victims of abductions, the goal is to increase the number of victims found quickly by law enforcement so that the perpetrators are much more likely to be brought to justice and closure is afforded to grieving families.

In addition, the following Children Profiles will assist search managers in determining how to approach the search for a missing child, based on the missing child's age.

More Missing and Abducted Children Information

FBI Manual—available by contacting the local FBI field office

Missing child law enforcement check list:
http://www.marinsar.org/PrePlan/index.htm

NCMEC Manual: http://www.missingkids.com/

For more information about predator abduction search courses for law enforcement and search and rescue teams, contact

Michael St. John
C/O Marin County Sheriff's SAR Unit
RM 145, 3501 Civic Center Drive
San Rafael, CA 94903
Tel 415-499-7437 Ext. 2
E-mail saintsar@aol.com

Children Age 1–3 Profile (Toddlers and Early Preschoolers)

Concept of being "lost" does not develop until age 3.

Lack any true navigational skills and sense of direction is almost non-existent.

Aimless wandering the general rule. May be attracted to animals and water.

Tend not to respond to whistles or calls. Prior training may alter this, but preventative programs at this age uncommon.

Rarely walk out by themselves.

Difficult to detect due to small size and ability to squeeze into small spaces. Often hiding or sleeping in a structure. Structures include yards and outbuildings.

Good survivability due to tendency to find shelter and typically urgent aggressive response.

Even in urban environment will sometimes find brush to penetrate to sleep or hide. More typically in building, under table, inside vehicles, boxes or any small space.

Urban Statistics—Children Age 1–3

Distance from IPP

n=17 cases	Miles	Km
25%	0.1	0.2
50%	0.3	0.5
75%	0.5	0.8
Max zone	0.7	1.2

Search Outcomes

SAR Find	52%
Investigative	4%
Self	9%
Other	34%
Suspension	

Find Location*

Structure	56%
Road	12%
Linear Feature	7%
Drainage	4%
Water	3%
Brush	
Scrub	3%
Woods/Forest	8%
Field	8%
Rock	

*Statistics are combined for all Children profiles.

Survivability
n=21

Status	Percentage
Uninjured	95%
Injured	
Fatality	5%

Track Offset**

n=130 cases	Meters
25%	8
50%	15
75%	50
Max zone	279

**Statistics are combined for Children, Despondent, and Substance Abuse profiles.

Initial Reflex Tasks—Children Age 1–3

Highly systematic search of residence/care facility and grounds. Any neighbor's yard where children have a tendency to play also require a thorough search.

Begin investigation. Initial strategy should center around a missing person incident until evidence indicates an abduction.

Secure the IPP as a potential crime scene.

Investigate areas the child has been previously located.

Canvass neighborhood with thorough search techniques close to the IPP.

Patrol roads within the theoretical search area.

Activate emergency telephone notification system (e.g., TENS, Reverse 911®) for theoretical search area if early in the search, or max zone radius if later.

Contact media early in the search process.

Establish containment.

Use trackers early at IPP and cut for sign along roads.

Use tracking dogs early at IPP, along roads, and at clues.

Deploy air-scent dogs into drainages and streams, starting nearest IPP.

Check for sign or hasty search nearby water sources.

Use ground sweep teams and dogs (in separate segments) expanding from IPP.

Ensure small spaces a child could hide are searched, including heavy briars/brush.

Make sure any appliances and trunks or other spaces in vehicles are checked.

Repeat searches of residence/care facility grounds at least twice daily.

Post flyers in appropriate locations.

Expand search outward from IPP after initial tasks.

Children Age 4–6 Profile (Preschool to Young School Age)

Often follow tracks, trails, plus short cuts that do not easily appear or make sense to adults.

In urban settings, hiding in structures and in yards still accounts for over 50% of finds.

Difficult to detect due to small size and ability to squeeze into small spaces. Often hiding or sleeping in a structure. Structures include yards and outbuildings.

Often have been instructed to avoid strangers. May hide or not respond to searchers.

Urban Statistics—Children Age 4–6

Distance from IPP

n=25 cases	Miles	Km
25%	0.06	0.1
50%	0.3	0.5
75%	0.6	1.0
Max zone	2.1	3.4

Search Outcomes

SAR Find	46%
Investigative	14%
Self	16%
Other	24%
Suspension	

Find Location*

Structure	56%
Road	12%
Linear Feature	7%
Drainage	4%
Water	3%
Brush	
Scrub	3%
Woods/Forest	8%
Field	8%
Rock	

*Statistics are combined for all Children categories.

Survivability
n=42

Status	Percentage
Uninjured	98%
Injured	
Fatality	2%

Track Offset**

n=130 cases	Meters
25%	8
50%	15
75%	50
Max zone	279

**Statistics are combined for Children, Despondent, and Substance Abuse profiles.

Initial Reflex Tasks—Children Age 4–6

Highly systematic search of residence/care facility and grounds. Any neighbor's yard where children have a tendency to play also requires a thorough search.

Begin investigation. Initial strategy should center around a missing person incident until evidence indicates an abduction.

Secure the IPP as a potential crime scene.

Investigate areas the child has been previously located.

Canvass neighborhood with thorough search techniques close into the IPP.

Patrol roads within the theoretical search area.

Activate emergency telephone notification system (e.g., TENS, Reverse 911®) for theoretical search area if early in the search, or max zone radius if later.

More mobile and capable than those in the 1-3 year old category.

Understand being lost and attempts to return home, familiar place, or the caregiver.

Have definite interests and may attempt to travel to specific locations. May easily be drawn by animals (including following pets), water, finding a playmate, exploring, following older children, or imaginative play.

May not understand the concept of a return trip when engaged in imaginative play.

Contact media early in the search process.

Establish containment.

Continued on next page ...

Initial Reflex Tasks—Children Age 4–6

Use trackers early at IPP and cut for sign along roads.

Use tracking dogs early at IPP, along roads, and at clues.

Deploy air-scent dogs into drainages and streams, starting at nearest IPP.

Check for sign or hasty search nearby water sources.

Use ground sweep teams and dogs (in separate segments) expanding from IPP.

Ensure small spaces a child could hide are searched, including heavy briars/brush.

Make sure any appliances and trunks or other spaces in vehicles are checked.

Repeat searches of residence/care facility grounds at least twice daily.

Post flyers in appropriate locations.

Expand search outward from IPP after initial tasks.

Children Age 7–12 Profile

Visual-spatial (directional) skills much more developed than in children under six. Have a mental map of local area but it is often distorted or wrong. Common to become lost in a new setting.

Frequently become lost due to short cuts (which may represent a longer route).

Commonly involved in fantasy play, exploring, or adventuring.

When lost use trail/road following strategy. This accounts for those who travel considerable distances.

More than half found in structures, vehicles, and/or yards. May be intentionally hiding to avoid punishment, gain attention, or sulking.

Drawn to wilderness areas within an urban area, social places, commercial places, and isolated places.

Age group has many of the same fears and concerns as adults but with greater emotion.

Urban Statistics—Children Age 7–12

Distance from IPP

n=39 cases	Miles	Km
25%	0.1	0.2
50%	0.3	0.5
75%	1.5	2.4
Max zone	3.5	5.6

Search Outcomes

SAR Find	43%
Investigative	29%
Self	18%
Other	11%
Suspension	

Find Location*

Structure	56%
Road	12%
Linear Feature	7%
Drainage	4%
Water	3%
Brush	
Scrub	3%
Woods/Forest	8%
Field	8%
Rock	

*Statistics are combined for all Children profiles.

Survivability
n=84

Status	Percentage
Uninjured	81%
Injured	2
Fatality	1%

Track Offset**

n=130 cases	Meters
25%	8
50%	15
75%	50
Max zone	279

**Statistics are combined for Children, Despondent, and Substance Abuse profiles.

Initial Reflex Tasks—Children Age 7–12

Highly systematic search of residence/care facility and grounds. Any neighbor's yard where children have a tendency to play also requires a thorough search.

Begin investigation. Initial strategy should center around a missing person until evidence indicates an abduction.

Secure the IPP as a potential crime scene.

Investigate areas the child has been previously located.

Canvass neighborhood with thorough search techniques close to the IPP.

Patrol roads within the theoretical search area.

Activate emergency telephone notification system (e.g., TENS, Reverse 911®) for theoretical search area if early in the search, or max zone radius if later.

Contact media early in the search process.

Establish containment.

Use trackers early at IPP and cut for sign along roads.

Use tracking dogs early at IPP, along roads, and at clues.

Deploy air-scent dogs into drainages and streams, starting nearest IPP.

Check for sign or hasty search nearby water sources.

Continued on next page ...

Initial Reflex Tasks—Children Age 7–12

Use ground sweep teams and dogs (in separate segments) expanding from IPP.

Ensure small spaces a child could hide are searched, including heavy briars/brush.

Make sure any appliances and trunks or other spaces in vehicles are checked.

Repeat searches of residence/home grounds at least twice daily.

Post flyers in appropriate locations.

Expand search outward from IPP after initial tasks.

Despondent

A lost person who is described as "despondent" can present a set of difficult challenges. Generally, this means a person shows signs of depression and may be suicidal. Thus, lost despondent persons are difficult to find because they do not want to be found and, once found, they may pose a threat to law enforcement and SAR personnel as well as to themselves. Understanding and recognizing signs and symptoms of depression and suicide is important for SAR personnel to be able to effectively and safely respond to a search for a lost despondent person.

What is Depression?

Depression is a mood disorder in which a person strongly feels sadness, despair and discouragement. Depression can cause a significant and enduring disruption in an older person's emotional well-being and overall functioning. Left untreated, it can cause serious health problems or even death. Depression is bio-chemical in nature. Three major neurotransmitters in the brain (serotonin, dopamine and norepinephrine) need to be in the correct balance for a person to have a positive, stable self image and optimistic mood. If these chemicals are not in balance, the person can become depressed. In general, when serotonin levels drop, depression can quickly settle in; when serotonin levels rise, a contented mood generally results. Personal and genetic factors can pre-dispose some people to depression.

Depression in later life is not the same as when an older person temporarily feels "blue" or experiences grief immediately following death of a spouse, other people or things that may be important to him. Depression lasts much longer and does not go away by itself. The person often describes the condition of being depressed as feeling very different than his former self.

Suicide

Myths and facts about suicide

- *"People who talk about suicide won't commit suicide."* "Eighty percent of people who committed suicide previously either threatened suicide or made a suicide gesture.

- *"Suicides happen without warning."* Most often the person clearly warns of his intentions. Less than 50% of suicides are a result of panic type behavior.

- *"Improvement after a suicidal crisis means that the suicide risk is over."* Over one-half of suicides follow within 90 days after an emotional crisis. Increased activity, perhaps even reflecting a new "cheerfulness" may mean that the person has finally "decided" to end his/her life, hence the acute anxiety diminishes.

- *"Suicide and depression are synonymous."* Depression, though common, is only one of many symptoms that a person may experience before committing suicide.

- *"Suicide is a disease."* It is not a disease, but a form of behavior that occurs at all ages and economic levels and has different meanings and motivations.

- *"Suicide is immoral."* Judgment about suicide is cultural and based on circumstances. The Greeks (Socrates), the Orientals (Hari-kari), and certain groups in the South Seas accept suicide.

- *"Suicide can be controlled by legislation."* England has a law against suicide, Scotland does not; yet the suicide rate is twice as high in England. Potential punitive action may encourage lethal behavior.

- *"The tendency toward suicide is inherited."* Children learn from their teachers (i.e., parents). This principle accounts for most behavior that is said to be hereditary.

- *"All suicidal persons are insane."* Faberow, et al., report, "The majority of persons who commit suicide are tormented and ambivalent: i.e., they are neurotic or have a character disorder, but are not insane."

- *"Suicide is the 'curse of the poor' or 'disease of the rich'."* Suicide does not correlate with economic status.

Suicidal Tendencies

Drastic behavior changes

- ✓ Insomnia
- ✓ Weight loss, appetite loss, self-imposed starvation
- ✓ Withdrawal from usual activities
- ✓ Decrease in sex
- ✓ Sadness/crying
- ✓ Mood variations
- ✓ Lethargy
- ✓ Excessive risk taking
- ✓ Unreasonable high expectation for success in job or business, academics/athletics

Verbal cues

- ✓ Feeling hopeless/helpless
- ✓ Talking only about the past
- ✓ Saying "I'm going to kill myself"

Prior history

Prior attempts or family history of suicide

History of mental illness

Indirect cues

- ✓ Makes will/changes will
- ✓ Give away prized personal possessions
- ✓ Makes funeral plans

Job history

- ✓ Loss of employment
- ✓ Business reversals

Continued on next page ...

Medical history

- ✓ Recent/chronic illness
- ✓ Hypochondria
- ✓ Refusing to follow doctor's orders or take medication

Marital difficulties

- ✓ Recent marital problems
- ✓ Loss of family member, death, or rejection

Financial difficulties

Alcoholism

Psychosis

Marking the anniversary date of a catastrophic change or event in his life, for example, the death of a spouse

Demographics

Age

1—9	Rare
15—19	Third leading cause of death
18—21	8-12% of deaths; second most frequent cause of death; college students
>45	66% of suicides are by males over 45; more than 50% of females who commit suicide are over 45
70—80	Peak at-risk age group

Sex

- ✓ Attempted suicide—women outnumber men 3 to 1
- ✓ Completed suicide—men outnumber women 70% to 30%

Time of Year

- ✓ Most occur in spring or around holidays, e.g., Christmas.

Ethnic Variances

✓ Whites are twice as likely to commit suicide as African Americans.

✓ Native Americans have highest rate in the U.S.; Eskimos have the highest rate in the world.

Police Suicide

• Suicide rates are higher among professions with high stress potential, e.g., law enforcement.

• Police Officers are eight times more likely to die by their own hand than by homicide.

• Highest suicide rate occurs among officers with marital problems, i.e., problems are not directly related to the job.

• Watch for warning signs among fellow officers; know how to get help within the department and how to refer to a special assistance program.

Methods of Suicide

• Sleeping pills and other pharmaceuticals—12%

• Hanging and strangulation—15%

• Firearms and explosives—48%
  ° Use of pistol versus shotgun is more frequent
  ° Usually shoot in temple, face or heart

• Males
  ° Most common attempts involve barbiturates
  ° Committed suicides usually involve guns, hanging, and carbon monoxide

• Females
  ° Most attempts and committed suicides involve barbiturates

Continued on next page ...

- "Suicide by cop" is a method used by an individual to compel officers to use deadly force against him.

  For example: An incident is initiated by an individual (subject) with a prior history of mental and chronic physical illness as well as alcohol/substance abuse or a third party to ensure police response. The subject forces confrontation by using aggressive action toward police officers, indicates presence of a deadly weapon, threatens the officers, and advances toward officers even if they are retreating.

Talking with the Suicidal Person

- If it is a telephone contact, the person's location should be identified if possible.

- If a person appears suicidal, the officer need not be reluctant to confront him/her with a question about it.

- The officer should try to be aware of his or her own feelings and how the suicidal person is feeling. Hopelessness can mean the person has exhausted his or her resources. If the person is angry and it is directed toward someone else, it can be easier to handle the situation.

- Reflect the person's feelings. Allow the person to vent his or her feelings. Orient the conversation toward the immediate future, its alternatives, and possible resources.

- Try not to be trapped into condoning or rejecting an expressed wish to die.

- Crisis intervention can fail and injury or death may be the result. Although it is easy to feel responsible, do not accept responsibility for another person's decision to harm himself or others. The officer responding to a suicide often will need to talk to someone after a serious crisis or during the intervention offer support to another officer. Ongoing support may also be needed.

- Use caution! Remember that a suicide attempt can often turn into a homicide attempt.

Signs of Depression in Older Adults

Older adults may exhibit signs of depression that families and caregivers are likely to misinterpret as symptoms of dementia or Alzheimer's disease. If the signs are mistaken for dementia, relatives and caregivers may overlook the possibility that their loved one is depressed and/or suicidal. In some cases an elderly caregiver for someone with dementia may be the one who is depressed and possibly suicidal. The following signs are most frequently misunderstood:

Signs of depression

- Depressed affect and mood

- Neuro-vegetative signs (e.g., insomnia, weight loss, and decreased appetite, energy and sexual drive)

- Slow, monotonous speech, doesn't say things to people voluntarily

- Gap in time between your question and their answer

- Frequent "I don't know" responses

- Quick to give up, but persists with encouragement

- Disoriented

- Impaired attention/distraction

- Incomplete responses

- Forgetfulness—particular deficits in learning new information, although memory may be patchy

- Poor abstract thinking

- Typically makes errors of omission (leaving things out) rather than errors of commission (filling things in)

- Aware of his or her cognitive difficulties

- May have concern over memory deficits— "Do I have Alzheimer's? See, I can't remember anything!"

- If there is psychosis, delusions are typically nihilistic, self-deprecatory, paranoid

- No signs of not being able to speak (aphasia), apraxia, or not knowing people (agnosia)

- Greater similarity to subcortical dementias, such as Parkinson's disease.

Summary

People who are despondent and/or contemplating suicide should be taken seriously. A good investigation and profile needs to be created to confirm the possibility of suicide. It is necessary to find evidence that the lost person may attempt to take his or her own life, especially if there is a means and/or method to carry out the act. To find such evidence, a thorough search of the residence should be completed to look for missing weapons or medications. If the use of weapons is suspected, those searching for the lost person should be briefed on the dangers or the search should be conducted by law enforcement rather than volunteer searchers.

Information on Depression and Suicide

Information for this section was adapted from the following sources:

Center for Mental Health in Schools at UCLA (2003). A technical assistance sampler on school interventions to prevent youth suicide. Los Angeles, CA: Author.

CDC – National Center for Injury Prevention and Control

American Foundation for Suicide Prevention

Despondent Profile

Two distinct patterns emerge for distances traveled from the IPP:

1. Most despondents are seeking to get just out of sight (50% within 0.2 miles of the IPP). This is particularly true in an urban environment

2. Despondents seek out a specific location, often scenic or significant in their life history. Location may be method of suicide (e.g., cliffs, bridge, water).

Those seeking scenic (often in a city park or greenbelt area) or significant location are willing to travel (max zone 95% = 8.1 miles).

No subjects really "lost." Many survivors walked out of their environment on their own.

Typically (47%) located in structures. This usually represents investigative, self, and other finds.

May hang themselves (especially in countries with limited access to firearms).

Age or sex does not predict "just out of sight" pattern.

High mortality rate (31%).

Often found at the interface of two different types of terrain. Rare to be found in thick brush or briars.

Rarely respond to searchers.

Urban Statistics—Despondent

Distance from IPP

n=96 cases	Miles	Km
25%	0.06	0.1
50%	0.3	0.5
75%	0.9	1.5
Max zone	8.1	13

Search Outcomes

SAR Find	34%
Investigative	12%
Self	15%
Other	25%
Suspension	15%

Find Location

Structure	47%
Road	11%
Linear Feature	10%
Drainage	2%
Water	19%
Brush	
Scrub	
Woods/Forest	6%
Field	5%
Rock	

Survivability
n=145

Status	Percentage
Uninjured	54%
Injured	15%
Fatality	31%

Track Offset*

n=130 cases	Meters
25%	8
50%	15
75%	50
Max zone	279

*Statistics are combined for Children, Despondent, and Substance Abuse profiles.

Initial Reflex Tasks—Despondent

Investigate any potential danger to searchers. Under most circumstances exclude minors from field operations.

Begin investigation. Focus on potential methods the person may use to commit suicide, buildings, significant locations, etc.

Secure the IPP.

Investigate areas the person has been previously located.

Use trackers early at IPP and cut for sign along roads.

Use tracking dogs early at IPP, along roads, and at clues.

Deploy air-scent dogs into drainages and streams, starting nearest IPP.

Canvass neighborhood.

Hasty search all scenic/significant locations.

Check segments within 0.3 miles (0.5 km) with air-scent dogs, sweeps, and grids.

Patrol roads within the theoretical search area.

Consider establishing containment; passive search tactics are not usually successful.

Repeat searches of residence/nursing home grounds at least twice daily.

Post flyers in appropriate locations.

Expand search outward from IPP after initial tasks.

Response should be urgent, especially for subjects who might have taken overdoses.

Mental Retardation

> *Critical Missing Person: Kevin Jackson—Updated*
>
> *Original Release: Friday, May 31, 2002*
>
> *Source: Government of the District of Columbia*
>
> *The Metropolitan Police Department is seeking the public's assistance in locating a missing person who was last seen at about 10:35 this morning. The missing person is identified as 38-year-old Kevin Jackson of the 1200 block of Lawrence Street NE. Mr. Jackson reportedly walked away from a group while participating in a field trip to Union Station, located at 50 Massachusetts Avenue NE. He was reportedly last seen outside of Union Station before wandering away.*
>
> *Mr. Jackson is mentally retarded and is unable to verbally communicate. He appears to react to the name "Rico" when it is spoken to him. He is described as a light-brown complexioned black male, 5'6" tall, weighing 140 pounds, with brown eyes and black hair. He is further described as having scars on his forehead and a light growth of facial hair. He was last seen wearing gray colored pants and an orange shirt and hat.*
>
> *Update: 6/2/02*
>
> *Mr. Jackson was located this morning at an area <u>Metrorail</u> station. He was unharmed.*

This news release is an example of a search for a lost person who is mentally retarded. In order to plan and execute operational directions in a missing person incident involving a person who is mentally retarded, it is important to understand the disability.

Some people are uncomfortable in the presence of perceived abnormal behavior of people who are mentally retarded. They may respond by looking away, turning in the opposite direction or calling the police to come take them away. A mentally retarded person may be described as "looking normal" but not "acting normal." He may have the physical body appropriate for his age, for instance a 26-year-old may look 26 years old, but have the mental capacity of a young child. Stories that poke fun at the trials, tribulations, clumsiness and slow nature of these citizens are undeserved and misleading. Most people with mental retardation are self-sufficient and productive contributors to our society. Occasionally, a person with mental retardation may become confused and wander off. He usually will be reported to authorities as a missing person at risk. This section is a summary of mental retardation to help search managers and emergency responders better understand the disability and how to interact with persons who are affected by it.

What is Mental Retardation?

The term mental retardation (MR) is the accepted medical definition of a person with specific limitations in mental functioning and skills, such as communication, self-care and social skills. These limitations affect learning and development seen early in childhood. Children with MR take longer to learn to walk, talk and dress themselves. They are likely to have trouble learning in school and therefore are placed in special learning environments.

What Causes Mental Retardation?

Mental retardation is not a disease and it is not contagious. Mental retardation is also not a type of mental illness, like depression. There is no cure for MR. However, most children with MR can learn to do many things. It just takes them more time and effort than other children. Doctors have found many causes of mental retardation.

Common causes of mental retardation

- *Genetic conditions.* Sometimes MR is caused by abnormal genes inherited from parents, errors when genes combine, or other reasons. Examples of genetic conditions are Down syndrome, fragile X syndrome, and phenylketonuria (PKU).

- *Problems during pregnancy.* MR can result when the baby does not develop inside the mother properly. For example, there may be a problem with the way the baby's cells divide as it grows. A woman who drinks alcohol or gets an infection like rubella during pregnancy may be likely to have a baby with MR.

- *Problems at birth.* If a baby has problems during labor and birth, such as not getting enough oxygen, he or she may have MR.

Continued on next page ...

- *Health problems.* Diseases like whooping cough, the measles, or meningitis can cause mental retardation. MR can also be caused by extreme malnutrition (not eating right), not getting enough medical care, or by being exposed to poisons like lead or mercury.

How is Mental Retardation Diagnosed?

Mental retardation is diagnosed by looking at two main things:

1. The ability of a person's brain to learn, think, solve problems, and make sense of the world (called IQ or intellectual functioning)

2. Whether the person has the skills he or she needs to live independently (called adaptive behavior, or adaptive functioning)

Intellectual functioning, or IQ, is usually measured by a test called an IQ test. The average score is 100. People scoring below 70 to 75 are thought to have mental retardation. To measure adaptive behavior, professionals look at what a child can do in comparison to other children of his or her age. Certain skills are important to adaptive behavior:

Adaptive functioning

✓ Daily living skills, such as getting dressed, going to the bathroom, and feeding one's self

✓ Communication skills, such as understanding what is said and being able to answer

✓ Social skills with peers, family members, adults, and others

---

Our nation's special education law, the Individuals with Disabilities Education Act (IDEA), is the federal law that guides how schools provide early intervention and special education and related services to children with disabilities. IDEA defines mental retardation as:

> ". . . *significantly subaverage general intellectual functioning, existing concurrently with deficits in adaptive behavior and manifested during the developmental period, that adversely affects a child's educational performance.*" 34 Code of Federal Regulations §300.7(c)(6)

Providing services to help individuals with mental retardation has led to a new understanding of how we define MR. After the initial diagnosis of MR is made, we look at a person's strengths and weaknesses. We also look at how much support or help the person needs to get along at home, in school, and in the community. This approach paints a realistic picture of each individual. It also recognizes that the "picture" can change. As the person grows and learns, his or her ability to get along in the world grows as well.

How Common is Mental Retardation?

As many as 3 out of every 100 people in the United States have MR (The Arc, 2001). Nearly 613,000 children ages 6 to 21 have some level of MR and need special education in school (Twenty-fourth Annual Report to Congress, U.S. Department of Education, 2002). In fact, one out of every ten children who need special education has some form of MR.

Signs of mental retardation

   ✓   Sit up, crawl, or walk later than other children;

   ✓   Learn to talk later, or have trouble speaking;

   ✓   Find it hard to remember things;

   ✓   Not understand how to pay for things;

   ✓   Have trouble understanding social rules;

   ✓   Have trouble seeing the consequences of their actions;

   ✓   Have trouble solving problems; and/or

   ✓   Have trouble thinking logically.

About 87% of people with MR are only a little slower than average in learning new information and skills. When they are children, their limitations may not be obvious. They may not even be diagnosed as having MR until they get to school. As they become adults, many people with MR can live independently. Other people may not even consider them as having MR.

The remaining 13% of people with MR score below 50 on IQ tests. These people will have more difficulty in school, at home, and in the community. A person with severe retardation will need more intensive support his or her entire life. Every child with MR is able to learn, develop and grow. With help, all children with MR can live a satisfying life.

Dealing with Persons Who Have Mental Retardation

Law enforcement and search personnel must understand the following aspects of MR:

Psychological profile elements

✓ May be unable to formulate thoughts and answer questions readily

✓ May have speech impediments

✓ May appear interested in children as they can better understand what children are doing

✓ May have slow responses similar to alcohol or drug abuse

✓ Often have poor judgment

✓ Often unable to foresee the consequences of an act

✓ Easily influenced by an authority figure

✓ Often inadequate in their personal relationships

✓ Socially immature

✓ Resent unkind nicknames/teasing and may do something foolish because of it

✓ May be quite sensitive and very aware that they are different

✓ To compensate for feeling different, may become aggressive in order to feel "important"

✓ Awareness of being different may be responsible for feelings of inferiority, frustration, and resentments; and as a result, less tolerant to stress

✓ Fear may be the major characteristic in a confrontation with an authority figure or emergency personnel

✓ Potential for violence or aggression exists since the appropriate outlet channels may never have been learned

---

Additionally, search personnel should also know how to best approach someone with MR, specifically one who has gotten lost and is wandering aimlessly.

How to interact with a person who has MR

✓ *GO SLOWLY.* Rapid questions during an interview or confrontation may confuse or frighten the person.

✓ *Patience* is needed to overcome a communication barrier and alleviate any exaggerated fears.

✓ *Rephrase questions into simpler language* if it appears the person does not comprehend.

✓ *Minimize unnecessary sensory input*—noises, crowds—as they may confuse the person.

✓ *Identification of and information about parents/guardians must be established immediately.* Many persons with MR carry cards with important contact information.

✓ If any doubts, *ask if they go to a special school.*

✓ *Understand how your actions may be misinterpreted.*
   For example:

   • The person may quickly reach into his pocket to get the contact card with information about a parent, doctor, or employee name and number.

   • The person may flee if he has fear of authority or emergency personnel.

✓ Contact one of the following organizations that provides services for people with MR:

   • Association for Retarded Citizens (The Arc)

   • Mental Health, Mental Retardation, and Substance Abuse Services

   • Special Education Department of the local school system

   • Vocational Rehabilitation Office

Summary

An understanding of mental retardation, its causes and characteristics, and the communication and behavior challenges it presents gives law enforcement and SAR personnel clearer insight into how to manage lost persons in this category. Most people with MR function quite well in their local and everyday environments, however, similar to young children, they will become confused and disoriented in unfamiliar surroundings. It is therefore critical to list these lost persons as "at-risk" and initiate the appropriate actions. It is also critical to understand that there may not be physical limitations to impair mobility and the person may travel great distances. When found and approaching a person with MR be aware he may react in an unexpected manner.

Information on Mental Retardation

Information for this section was adapted from the following sources:

National Dissemination Center for Children with Disabilities: Disability Fact Sheet, No. 8 January 2004

Individuals With Mental Illness or Mental Retardation. North Carolina Justice Academy (1998). Http://www.jus.state.nc.us/ NCJA/mental.pdf.

Mental Retardation Profile

MR Profile is a blend of both children and dementia profiles.

Elderly MR persons are more similar to dementia; MR children are more similar to age-adjusted range.

Unlike child profile, no MR subjects got lost taking a short cut.

Almost all will not respond to their name (97%).

Will not travel to identifiable target.

Many found in structures, including yards and vehicles, or along roads.

Will travel into brush or structures to seek shelter.

Attracted to water features.

Good survivability due to urgent response.

Urban Statistics—Mental Retardation

Distance from IPP

n=44 cases	Miles	Km
25%	0.2	0.3
50%	0.5	0.8
75%	2.3	3.7
Max zone	6.14	9.9

Search Outcomes

SAR Find	44%
Investigative	14%
Self	6%
Other	33%
Suspension	3%

Find Location

Structure	57%
Road	23%
Linear Feature	3%
Drainage	7%
Water	3%
Brush	3%
Scrub	
Woods/Forest	3%
Field	
Rock	

Survivability
n=65

Status	Percentage
Uninjured	92%
Injured	5%
Fatality	3%

Track Offset

n=12 cases	Meters
25%	10
50%	13
75%	16
Max zone	93

Initial Reflex Tasks—Mental Retardation

Highly systematic search of residence/care facility and grounds.

Begin investigation.

Secure the IPP.

Investigate areas the person has been previously located.

Canvass neighborhood.

Patrol roads within the theoretical search area.

Activate emergency telephone notification system (e.g., TENS, Reverse 911®) for theoretical search area if early in the search, or max zone radius if later.

Establish containment.

Use trackers early at IPP and cut for sign along roads.

Use tracking dogs early at IPP, along roads, and at clues.

Deploy air-scent dogs into drainages and streams, starting at nearest IPP.

Use ground sweep teams and dogs (in separate segments) expanding from IPP.

Ensure heavy briars/brush are searched.

Task air-scent dogs and ground sweep teams to search 100 meters parallel to roads.

Consider having the family shout names of the person (best done after tracking/trailing dogs have been deployed and retrieved).

Repeat searches of residence/nursing home grounds at least twice daily.

Person may flee or move; areas will need to be re-searched with continual importance of clue/sign conscious teams.

Post flyers in appropriate locations.

Expand search outward from IPP after initial tasks.

Mental Illness

Although seldom thought of, mental illness is a serious health problem second only to heart disease as the most disabling disease. According to the World Health Organization (WHO) and other sources, mental illness accounts for nearly 11% of the total worldwide disease burden. Everyone probably knows someone who has some sort of mental illness or has it him or herself. Mental illness knows no boundaries for economic or social status, age, sex, occupation, or educational level. It is unfortunate that when you say "mental illness" many people think of insane asylums with comatose patients and the evil Nurse Ratched from "One Flew Over the Cuckoo's Nest." Others will think of homeless and discarded persons who wander the streets of the cities.

Facts about mental illness

- Mental illness and mental retardation are not the same thing. Mental illness can be treated; mental retardation cannot.

- Those with mental illness are not dangerous. Generally, they are only dangerous when they are psychotic, off medication and/or under the influence of drugs or alcohol.

- Persons with mental illness are not lazy and can live productive lives, with treatment.

- Mental illness can be treated successfully with medications, some for a short period of time; others many require lifelong medication and treatment.

- Mental illness is not caused by a moral failing, a divine punishment, or demonic possession. There is no one specific cause for mental illness; however, it is caused by a combination of biological, psychological, and environmental factors.

- Those with mental illness cannot get better by applying will power. Will power cannot overcome the psychological, biological, and environmental factors associated with the disease.

It is important to learn these truths and obtain accurate information from professionals as needed in order to have a better understanding of persons with a mental illness who may go missing. This approach ensures that proper decisions are made in the management of the lost subject. As those involved with searching for missing persons are associated with law enforcement in one form or another, the probability of searching for an individual with some sort of mental illness is high.

Causes of Mental Illness

Mental health practitioners will cite publications and texts that list as many as 400 classifications of mental illness. While there is no exact known cause for mental illness, what is known is that the brain mediates all human behavior. The brain is shaped by a variety of genetics, environments and life experiences all mixed together to produce infinite mental results for individuals. The brain is a delicate balance of electrical and chemical activity that can change under circumstances both known and unknown. The brain is always changing. Every time a person learns something new, whether it's conscious or unconscious, that experience alters the structure of the brain.

Biological, physical, social, and/or psychological risk factors that may trigger mental illness in vulnerable people are listed below.

Risk factors for mental illness
• Stress (anxiety or depression)
• Genes
• Infections (HIV, measles, chronic meningitis)
• Physical trauma
• Nutrition
• Hormones
• Toxins
• Gender
• Drugs
• Stressful life events and social influences
• Breakup of intimate romantic relationship
• Death of a family member or friend
• Economic hardships
• Racism and discrimination
• Poor physical health
• Accidental and intentional assaults on physical safety
• Inadequate health care
• Cumulative adversity (more potent than stressful events as a predictor of psychological distress and mental disorders)

Certain types of people have been shown statistically to be at higher risk of developing a mental illness.

People at higher risk for mental illness

✓ Women

- Single mothers face twice the risk of depression as do married mothers
- Twice as likely than men to experience post traumatic stress disorder (PTSD) after exposure to life-threatening trauma

✓ Young and unmarried

✓ African Americans

✓ Individuals with lower socioeconomic status

✓ People with relationship problems (at least double the risk)

✓ Victims of child abuse (one of the most common stressors)

- 15-33% of females
- 13-16% of males

✓ Domestic violence survivors

Types of Disorders

Of the many different types of persons reported missing, those with mental illness often present challenges from a planning and strategy point of view. Psychological disorders can be broken down into three types: mood, psychotic and personality.

Mood disorders

Mood disorders include ***depression and bipolar disorder*** (also known as manic depression). *Major depression* interferes with thoughts, behavior, physical activity, as well as physical health. If left untreated, symptoms can last from six months to a year and eventually lead to suicide.

Symptoms may occur spontaneously or be caused by stressful life events, such as the death of a loved one, chronic stress, loss of a job, alcohol and/or drug abuse, illness, medications, or a combination of successive tragic life events.

Other symptoms include:

> **Symptoms of depression**
> - A profound sad or irritable mood
> - A change in sleeping habits (more or less than usual)
> - A change in appetite (eating more or less than usual)
> - A change in sexual habits
> - A change in energy level, memory loss
> - Difficulty in thinking and concentrating
> - Diminished physical activity
> - A lack of interest in or pleasure from activities that were once enjoyed
> - May express feelings of guilt, worthlessness, hopelessness, emptiness
> - Have recurrent thoughts of death or suicide
> - Problems with physical symptoms that do not respond to medical treatment (e.g., headaches, digestive problems, chronic pain)

Bipolar disorder includes some of the symptoms of depression, but there is also the additional stage of the illness called "mania," a state of mind in which individuals appear elated and happy or irritable, angry and unpleasant.

> **Symptoms of manic depression**
> - Activity and energy levels increase
> - Accelerated flow of thought
> - Rapid speech
> - Decreased sleep
> - An increased interest and participation in sexual activities
> - Grandiose plans are often developed
> - May believe he or she is a celebrity, the President of the United States or Jesus
>
> Continued on next page ...

- May withdraw large sums of money, gamble, go on spend-
  ing sprees or decide to travel across the country on the spur
  of the moment
- May experience "mixed states" of the illness in which symptoms of mania and depression occur at the same time
- If alternating periods of mania and depression occur within
  a 12-month period, the individual is said to be bipolar with
  "rapid cycling."

Medication is focused on mood stabilizers: lithium, depakote, anticonvulsants, and antipsychotics.

It should be noted that the person's energy level will increase before her mood improves, but watch for other symptoms when decisions are made easily and the depression is still high as this puts her at risk for suicide.

Psychotic disorders

Psychotic disorders include *schizophrenia*, typically seen in people beginning in the teens into the twenties when the pressures to succeed in school are extremely high. Contrary to popular belief, people with schizophrenia do not have a "split personality" and are not dangerous or violent while receiving treatment. Symptoms include profound disruption in perceptions, thoughts, sense of self, language, and feelings. There are also symptoms known as positive (or psychotic) and negative (or disorganized).

Positive symptoms include delusions or hallucinations. Delusions are erroneous beliefs resulting from distorted or exaggerated reasoning. Symptoms manifest in such things as claims that the person is being directed by secret radio waves or that files are being kept on him or her by law enforcement. Hallucinations are distorted or exaggerated perceptions from the five senses and are often manifested in "hearing voices."

Negative symptoms include emotional flatness, lack of expression, inability to follow or start activities, brief and confused speech patterns, and a lack of pleasure or interest in life. Disorganized symptoms include confused thinking or speech, and behavior that does not match (e.g., slow movements, repetition of rhythmic gestures, walking in circles, pacing). During these episodes, individuals with schizophrenia cannot make sense of everyday sights, sounds or feelings.

Although schizophrenia can be treated with medication, sadly many people with the illness do not get help; families are often unable to cope with the person and choose not to give support. The person can eventually end up on the street or homeless and self-medicate with alcohol or drugs.

Personality disorders

Personality disorders (anti-social personality) are sometimes called emotional retardation, referring to deficiencies in emotional growth. Unfortunately, personality disorders are not usually treatable with medication. Psychotherapy can modify unwanted behaviors, however individuals with personality disorders do not generally display the same feelings that "normal" people do and probably never will. Law enforcement recognizes these "psychopathic" individuals as serial killers, child molesters, rapists, gang members, etc.

The continued behavior of juveniles who fight in school or cut school, who engage in frequent drug abuse, and have brushes with the law may lead to an anti-social personality. Such persons are incapable of significant loyalty to individuals or group, or of adopting social values. As well, they can be grossly selfish, callous, irresponsible, impulsive and unable to feel guilt or remorse, or learn from experience or punishment.

Borderline personality disorder is seen as a coping mechanism in children to deal with abuse, neglect, inconsistent parenting or abandonment. Persons with borderline personality disorder are often more dangerous to themselves than others; the illness manifests in self-damaging themes including gambling, shopping, binge eating, substance abuse, unsafe sex, self-harm including suicidal behavior or threats as well as self-mutilation. Such persons are often easily bored, have an inability to express or control anger, are characterized by impulsivity and instability in mood, have a poor self-image, and have a very difficult time with personal relationships. Because of fear of the pain of rejection, they may cause others to reject them in order to avoid the stress they endure while waiting for acceptance. A craving for closeness to others is seen along with the fear of disappointment. Persons with borderline personality disorder will sometimes act out suicidal gestures to win the affections of others, especially loved ones.

Schizoid personality disorder creates an indifference to social relationships. Such persons are seen as 'loners' who choose solitary activities, lack relationships (even with family), lack sexual desire, and have a restricted range of emotional experience and expression. They may appear aloof, self-absorbed, and indifferent to praise or criticism from others.

Schizotypal personality disorder is seen as a pattern of peculiar ideation, appearance, and behavior. Such persons often experience paranoia, odd beliefs, bizarre fantasies or preoccupations, and inappropriate feelings towards others. They may be anxious in social situations, prefer unusual perceptual material, and present off-speech patterns and unusual mannerisms.

> ### *Safety of everyone is of paramount importance!*

Dealing with the Mentally Ill in Crisis

When a mentally ill person is in crisis, he or she is usually terrified by the loss of control over his or her thoughts and feelings. Strange thoughts are not uncommon. However, someone in a psychotic state will often act on what he or she is thinking or experiencing in his or her own reality. Voices or messages from inanimate objects may be making life-threatening commands. The environment may appear unsafe and dangerous.

For search personnel, talking and one's own attitude are the best ways to resolve a crisis. A calm and slowed-down approach will help defuse the situation. Make no sudden moves, decrease the environmental stimulus such as loud noises (shut off TVs and radios), and remove unnecessary personnel from the area. A mentally ill person may have a greater need for space and it may be necessary to back off to adapt to his or her comfort zone. Show a willingness to listen and take an interest in the person's situation. By showing concern a rapport is built. The person may select someone he or she trusts as a favorite person with whom to talk. Listen to the person's story but do not accept his or her reality by acknowledging the voices he or she hears. A good response to the person's claim that he or she hears voices is "No, I don't hear the voices, but I can understand that you do. I understand you are very frightened by what you hear/see." People in a uniform may increase or decrease the crisis based on the mentally ill person's perceptions because of his or her altered state of reality. The responder's body language may need to be adjusted to avoid problems. Some suggestions include:

Body language

- Do not block the door, but place yourself between the person in crisis and the door.
- Avoid staring.
- Keep hands open and visible (in front of the body around the mid section).
- Avoid calling attention to your equipment, including weapons if visible.
- Stand with feet at an angle that protects your equipment.
- If the mentally ill person is seated, make sure you sit, squat, or kneel to be on his level.
- Do not stand over him with a commanding or threatening posture.

If the need arises, do not touch the individual or make any contact without prior warning. Inform the person of your intent and explain that you are there to help and not harm him or her.

When speaking, avoid doing so loudly or shouting, rather speak softly and in short, simple sentences. To evaluate the circumstances that precipitated the crisis some suggested questions to ask the mentally ill person as well as family and friends include:

- "What is your name?"
- "Do you take medication?"
- "When was the last time you slept?"
- "Tell me why you're so upset?"

If it becomes necessary for discussions with the person on a course of action (e.g., self-commit to go to the hospital or seek other psychiatric help), keep in mind the following suggestions:

- Be prepared to talk forever.
- Have one person make the connection.
- Use a "touchy feely" talker, an individual who can remain calm.
- Negotiators can't be afraid or shocked at the negatives they will hear.

If the person in crisis is suicidal, make a contract for time to talk or ask him or her to put off suicide. Talking about suicide doesn't cause it. The person already has the idea to commit suicide or he or she does not. The person should be asked about a plan—when, where, how, and why.

Additional Challenges and Safety Issues

A mentally ill person who is conscious but unresponsive can pose a challenge to communication. Do not assume he or she cannot hear the questions being asked. Make an effort to obtain a response and look for subtle body movement like a nod or other body posturing or emotional changes. Do not discuss or make strategies on what to do with the person while within ear shot as this may cause an adverse reaction.

A very serious problem is paranoia or delusions. A mentally ill person with these symptoms will be suspicious and tense, and perceive those around him or her as threatening. The goal is to become as non-threatening as possible. Explain all actions beforehand and avoid any physical contact until absolutely necessary; give the person as much space as he or she needs. Delusional statements can trap the people who are there to help the person. Agreeing with the person's statement "Someone is out to get me" can reinforce his or her fears. However, disagreeing may breakdown any rapport that has been built so far. The suggestion is to neither agree nor disagree, but simply acknowledge the person's view of the world and assure him or her that search personnel are there to help.

As noted earlier, persons with mood disorders such as depression or bipolar disorder are considered to be at high risk for suicide. These individuals may go so far as to take a family member hostage or commit a homicide. Sometimes these acts are done with the intent of forcing a confrontation with law enforcement to provoke a response sometimes referred to as "suicide by cop." These confrontations are best dealt with by law enforcement personnel trained to handle these situations. Search personnel should not try to intervene alone.

Information on Mental Illness
Information for this section was adapted from the following sources:

Criminal Justice Institute, University of Arkansas System – CJI Management Quarterly Volume VIII, Issue I Spring 2003, Issue II Summer 2003 and Issue III Fall 2003

www.cji.net/cji/Publications/mq/MQ2003Spring.pdf

www.cji.net/cji/Publications/mq/MQ2003Summer.pdf

www.cji.net/cji/Publications/mq/MQ 2003Fall.pdf

Mental Illness (Psychotic) Profile

Most common disorders are schizophrenia or bipolar.

Lack of medication or stopping medications caused most searches.

No one in this category was "lost" in the traditional sense.

Some persons with MI may evade searchers.

Subjects did not travel to identifiable destinations.

Subjects are often found in structures or along roads. They are also attracted to water features.

Tend not to penetrate into thick brush/briars.

Search efforts accounted for 50% of finds.

Many travel considerable distances without ever being "far" from the IPP.

Urban Statistics—Mental Illness

Distance from IPP

n=38 cases	Miles	Km
25%	0.2	0.3
50%	0.4	0.6
75%	0.9	1.5
Max zone	7.7	12.4

Search Outcomes

SAR Find	50%
Investigative	5%
Self	15%
Other	20%
Suspension	10%

Find Location

Structure	65%
Road	8%
Linear Feature	
Drainage	8%
Water	8%
Brush	
Scrub	
Woods/Forest	8%
Field	4%
Rock	

Survivability
n=44 cases

Status	Percentage
Uninjured	64%
Injured	20%
Fatality	16%

Track Offset

n=8 cases	Meters
25%	10
50%	23
75%	27
Max zone	31

Initial Reflex Tasks—Mental Illness

Law enforcement agency should provide for safety of searchers.

Limit field use of minors due to potential safety issues.

Highly systematic search of residence/care facility/structure and grounds.

Repeat thorough systematic search of residence and local yards frequently.

Begin investigation. Thorough investigation is critical.

Secure the IPP.

Use trackers early at IPP and cut for sign along roads.

Use tracking dogs early at IPP, along roads, and at clues.

Deploy air-scent dogs into drainages and streams, starting at nearest IPP.

Searchers should stop and listen before shouting name, if not contra-indicated.

Person is not likely to respond to shouted name.

Investigate areas the subject has been previously located.

Patrol roads within the theoretical search area.

Subject may flee or move; areas will need to be re-searched with continual importance of clues. Use clue/sign conscious teams.

Subject may have a fear of authority; consider not wearing uniforms.

Develop a contingency plan if subject is actively evasive.

Post flyers in appropriate locations.

Expand search outward from IPP after initial tasks.

Autism

A group of persons with disabilities now seen more frequently in the community is persons with autism. It is a lifelong developmental disability, which seriously impairs the way the brain processes information sent from the senses. It is sometimes confused with mental retardation.

Autism is not the same as mental retardation.
It is a severe disorder of communication and behavior.

> **Primary characteristics of autism**
> ✓ Withdrawal from contact with others
> ✓ Very inadequate social relationships
> ✓ Language disturbances
> ✓ Monotonous repetitive body movement
> ✓ Behavior problems in terms of resistance to change and emotional responses

Theses characteristics can make communication nearly impossible and search personnel should approach autistic persons with caution.

Autism Profile

Vast spectrum of ability, from awkward Ph.D. to complete inability to communicate.

Hallmarks of autism include:

1. Slowed development of physical, social, and language skills.

2. Abnormal response to sensations.

3. Difficulty relating to people, objects, or events.

Easily over stimulated, cannot filter out normal distractions.

Prefer being alone. Will often leave group or group setting.

No real fears of danger. May have under-sensitivity to pain.

Nonresponsive to verbal cues; acts as if deaf. Subject expected to be unresponsive to searcher's shouts.

In urban environment, hiding in structures, including yards and vehicles, is most common. Also, typically found walking on roads or near water.

Good survivability largely due to rapid and urgent response.

Urban Statistics—Autism

Distance from IPP

n=16 cases	Miles	Km
25%	0.2	0.3
50%	0.4	0.6
75%	0.9	1.5
Max zone	7.7	12.4

Search Outcomes

SAR Find	50%
Investigative	5%
Self	15%
Other	20%
Suspension	10%

Find Location

Structure	65%
Road	8%
Linear Feature	
Drainage	8%
Water	8%
Brush	
Scrub	
Woods/Forest	8%
Field	4%
Rock	

Survivability
n=26 cases

Status	Percentage
Uninjured	96%
Injured	4%
Fatality	

Track Offset

n=8 cases	Meters
25%	9
50%	15
75%	22
Max zone	335

Initial Reflex Tasks—Autism

> Highly systematic search of residence/care facility and grounds.
>
> Begin investigation.
>
> Secure the IPP
>
> Investigate areas the subject has been previously located.
>
> Canvass neighborhood.
>
> Patrol roads within the theoretical search area.
>
> Activate emergency telephone notification system (e.g., TENS, Reverse 911®) for theoretical search area if early in the search, or max zone radius if later.
>
> Establish containment.
>
> Use trackers early at IPP and cut for sign along roads.
>
> Use tracking dogs early at IPP, along roads, and at clues.
>
> Deploy air-scent dogs into drainages and streams, starting at nearest IPP.
>
> Use ground sweep teams and dogs (in separate segments) expanding from IPP.
>
> Ensure heavy briars/brush are searched.
>
> Task air-scent dogs and ground sweep teams to search 100 meters parallel to roads.
>
> Search nearby previous homes and area between home sites.
>
> Repeat searches of residence/care facility grounds at least twice daily.
>
> Post flyers in appropriate locations.
>
> Expand search outward from IPP after initial tasks.

Substance Abuse

Occasionally, the missing person may be under the influence of drugs or alcohol. This section outlines the basic physical and behavioral effects of various substances that searchers should be aware of when looking for a missing person. It also addresses techniques for approaching a person under the influence of a substance and how to handle the situation with the safety of the searchers in the forefront.

There are various consequences from the abuse of drugs. The interaction of a combination of drugs may cause severe and dangerous health problems. A person with a serious mental problem may have his disorder exacerbated by using alcohol and drugs. If he is on medication for the problem and have mixed this medication with other drugs, the person should be evaluated by a psychiatrist or by health professionals in a substance abuse treatment facility.

Affects of substance abuse

✓ Sedation, depressed respiration, a semi-hypnotic state, contracted pupils, depressed reflexes, and intoxication

✓ Lack of pain or fatigue

✓ Lack of coordination, restlessness, excitement, disorientation, confusion, and delirium

✓ Hallucination, pupil dilation, increased blood pressure and body temperature, depressed appetite, and on occasion, nausea and chills

---

Affects of substance withdrawal

✓ Sweaty, fearful, and tremulous

✓ Restless, agitated, and having convulsions

✓ Hallucinations or delusions

✓ Hot and cold flashes, vomiting, diarrhea

Once the missing person has been found he may need to be committed to a hospital, mental health or detoxification facility if it is felt he has the potential to harm himself or others. A person may be committed for 24 to 72 hours in order to give a health care professional an opportunity to observe the person and set an appropriate rehabilitation plan. It is recommended to consult local protocols and legal requirements (codes) and to know who has the authority to commit a person. A person also may commit himself voluntarily.

Procedures upon finding a person under the influence

✓ Law enforcement and emergency medical personnel should be dispatched to the search scene to provide safe transportation.

✓ Some institutions are reluctant to accept people who abuse substances. Voluntary commitment should be directed to the appropriate facility, e.g., alcohol or drug treatment facility.

✓ Longer commitment periods may be dictated by the courts depending on the following: the circumstances of the substance abuse, presenting mental health issues, and if laws have been broken. Search personnel do not need to be concerned with discussing and determining the length of a commitment.

Precautionary advice and techniques for handling a person who is abusing substances, particularly if there is potential for violent behavior:

Advice and techniques when violent behavior is possible

✓ A person abusing substance(s), stimulants in particular, may be impervious to pain and exhibit extraordinary strength.

✓ While a mentally disturbed person can often be calmed down, people who abuse substances, especially stimulants, usually cannot be calmed down easily. The search manager should request back up. It may be necessary to assign more than two searchers to prevent injury.

✓ The person is likely to be unpredictable. This is a key factor for searchers to keep in mind.

When there is probable cause that a criminal offense has been committed law enforcement may need to take the person into custody or place them under arrest. While this may seem dramatic, it is important to understand the following aspects of such an outcome:

Understanding an arrest

✓ It may actually help the person realize that he or she has a problem.

✓ Alcoholism and drug addiction are serious illnesses that require treatment.

✓ The person may not be aware that they are being arrested.

✓ The person's reaction to officer confrontation varies depending upon:

- whether the person is under the influence of a drug or just in possession of it, and

- the type of drug taken and the effect it is having on the person.

✓ Jails may have a policy that does not allow a person under the influence of drugs to be admitted. The person must first be transported to a hospital. Consult local protocols for jail policy and hospital admission procedures.

Searcher safety is of paramount importance. Search managers must also understand that additional briefing on potential problems may be required in certain circumstances in which a missing person is under the influence of drugs or alcohol.

Information on Substance Abuse

Information in this section was adapted from the following source:

"Older Adults, Alcohol and Depression" © May, 2003, Seeking Solutions: Canadian Community Action on Seniors and Alcohol Issues.

Substance Abuse Profile

Most cases related to excessive alcohol. Cases may also involve other drugs or mushrooms.

Subject typically leaving party/bar en route on foot to another destination.

Investigative finds (29%) often involve subject going to a friend's house without notifying the reporting party.

Subjects typically poorly dressed or equipped for weather.

Many intoxicated individuals drawn to water. They may attempt to swim or enter into the water.

Many individuals in an argument or fight prior to being last seen.

High fatality rate (42%) suggesting an urgent need to search after basic investigation is started.

Subjects also tend to lie down to "sleep off" affects, often in severe weather.

Urban Statistics—Substance Abuse

Distance from IPP

n=6 cases	Miles	Km
25%		
50%	1.2	2.0
75%		
Max zone		

Search Outcomes

SAR Find	29%
Investigative	29%
Self	
Other	14%
Suspension	29%

Find Location

Structure	63%
Road	
Linear Feature	
Drainage	
Water	25%
Brush	
Scrub	
Woods/Forest	13%
Field	
Rock	

Survivability
n=12

Status	Percentage
Uninjured	50%
Injured	8%
Fatality	42%

Track Offset*

n=130 cases	Meters
25%	8
50%	15
75%	50
Max zone	279

*Statistics are combined for Children, Despondent and Substance Abuse profiles.

Initial Reflex Tasks—Substance Abuse

Begin investigation. Concentrate on other bars/pubs and friend's residences.

Secure the IPP.

Patrol roads within the theoretical search area.

Containment generally not an effective tactic for urban substance abusers.

Use trackers early at IPP and cut for sign along roads.

Use tracking dogs early at IPP, along roads, and at clues.

Direction of travel still relevant for substance abusers.

Deploy air-scent dogs into drainages and streams, starting nearest IPP.

Search any water source located between the IPP and any possible destination the subject any have been attempting to reach.

Use ground sweep teams and dogs (in separate segments) expanding from IPP.

Ensure wooded areas and water features are searched. Attempt to search structures.

Search nearby previous homes and area between home sites or possible destinations.

Post flyers in appropriate locations.

Expand search outward from IPP after initial tasks.

Electronic Tracking Systems

Commercially available mobile locators such as Care Trak and equipment used under the name "Project Lifesaver" are now on the market. These devices use the same technology that is used to track wild animals for scientific research. These devices are helpful for families, care givers; managers of care homes with people with Alzheimer's who have the potential to wander. Tamper-proof transmitters in the form of a large wristwatch can be placed on the wrist, ankle or sewn into the clothing of the person who is likely to wander. The transmitters can be detected by receivers up to a mile on the ground and 10 to 15 miles from the air. The receivers can discriminate up to 200 frequencies, making it ideal for multiple care homes within close proximity to each other in an urban setting. The cost is in the receiving equipment. The transmitters can be purchased or rented at a nominal fee. Project Lifesaver programs are established in local communities, usually by law enforcement agencies. As with ELT locators, training on the use of the devices is essential.

Community Awareness Programs

Many communities have developed community awareness programs for the elderly and very young. Safety fairs are a good opportunity for search and rescue teams to participate in child fingerprinting and photo programs, demonstrate skills, show off search gear and toys and have the children pet the dogs. Moreover, fairs make excellent recruiting pools. Some communities have developed brochures, such as Missing Persons Guides for Caregivers of the Elderly, which describe how to deal with older adults and the possibility of wandering. Such brochures include intensification and history forms to be filled out, along with a recent photograph to be kept on file with the caregivers in case the elderly person goes missing. The Alzheimer's Association's Safe Return® program can be accessed throughout the United States through 81 local chapters. Safe Return® provides identification bracelets and pendants (similar to MedicAlert® tags) to enable citizens and law enforcement officials to identify a confused, disoriented or lost elderly person and help them return home safely.

Chapter 13. Management Training

Managing urban searches, as with management in general, requires training and practicing the principle discussed in this chapter. There are many search management courses available through national, state and local agencies. These courses are anywhere from 20 to over 40 hours over several days, covering the following topics:

Management training topics

   ✓ An introduction to the Incident Command System

   ✓ How to properly manage a search

   ✓ How to develop a preplan and its importance to a successful search mission

   ✓ Search theories and statistics

   ✓ The types of search and rescue resources and how to use them

   ✓ Search tactics and investigation

   ✓ Clue detection and management

   ✓ Factors involved in deciding to suspend a mission

   ✓ How to manage outside influences on search and rescue incidents

   ✓ Preventative search and rescue programs

   ✓ "Table-top" map problem exercises to demonstrate the ability to use the learned skills

---

The map exercises are usually based on well-documented actual searches and focus on one or two principles such as investigation and use of specialized resources. A new approach to traditional map problems is to have one continuous problem broken up over the several days of instruction. This approach is designed to lead the students through a series of exercises that will take them from the first notice of a potential search, through major planning and operational periods of the search, to finally finishing the mission.

Example Training Outline (Two Missing Persons)

Once a scenario is established, the training is divided into the following instructional goals, actions and deliverables.

Exercise #1A　First Notice

Instructional Goals
(What the group is to learn)

Combined Plans/Operations Function

Start an investigation

Determine if this is an actual SAR mission

Determine search urgency

Determine initial resources to be called

Determine time of response and staging area

Initiate a call-out for SAR resources

What to do with your reporting party

Actions
(What the overhead team needs to do)

Investigate the report

Decide if it is a valid SAR mission and if so, how urgent it is

Call-out for the local SAR resources

Deliverables
(What the overhead team must produce on paper)

Initial Missing Person Report

Search Urgency Determination form or Notes

Identify a preliminary PLS on a map of the area

Short call-out messages for dispatching local resources

    1.　Alpha pager message, 150 characters or less

    2.　Voice mail message, 3 minutes or less

Instructions for the reporting party

Top 10 questions to ask the reporting party

Exercise 1A continues on next page ...

Materials Provided
(Given to the group)

SAR preplan for jurisdiction

Maps

First response incident management kit with forms

Resources Provided
(People to talk to)

Deputy who responded to the call and spoke to the reporting party

---

Exercise #1B   First Operational Period
(Combined Plans/Operations)

Instructional Goals

Continued investigation

Define rough search boundary

Containment and hasty search assignments

Focus on small overhead and quick action to resolve the incident

Actions
(Taken by combined Plans/Operations Sections)

Investigate

1. Interview the reporting party

2. Talk with park ranger to get info about the area

Develop a small ICS structure for your overhead team

Plan hasty search assignments

Deploy resources quickly

Keep track of what's going on

Exercise 1B continues on next page ...

Deliverables

    General Briefing Form

    201 Form for this operational period

    List of Assignments

    Map Showing IPP and Initial Assignments

    Missing Person Flyer

Materials Provided

    Park maps

    List of responding resources

Resources Provided

    Reporting party (not simulated by an instructor)

        Instructions: Find small office for the "interview." Interviewer is allowed to read the interview notes first, and then make a summary to the group (without the notes).

    Park Ranger

    Team leaders for arriving search resources (last 15 minutes)

Exercise #2
Transition from hasty to full scale SAR operation

Introduction

This exercise builds on the previous exercises. The group should locate the existing incident documentation and familiarize themselves with prior search plans. While the search teams are out in the field completing their initial assignments, the overhead team will prepare for a full scale search operation to be conducted the following day. They will make plans, request resources and arrange logistics in order for the next day's operation to function smoothly.

Exercise 2 continues on next page ...

Instructional Goals/Action

Scenario development

Search assignments

1. Continued use of hasty techniques and confinement
2. Use of efficient techniques
3. Use of specialized resources

Requesting additional resources, local or mutual aid

Adjust the ICS structure to meet changing needs

Identify logistical issues

Written Incident Action Plans including:

1. Section organizational structure and staffing requirements
2. Short list of functions to be performed by each section during next operational period
3. Note ongoing functions or assignments (e.g., teams in the field, resources in route)
4. Note items requiring special attention

Transition to the incoming overhead team

Deliverables

Plans

1. Map showing planned search assignments
2. List of all planned search assignments (including special resources)
3. Team assignment forms (prepare at least one for each type of search assignment)
4. Briefing materials for next operational period
5. Short written Incident Action Plan for Plans Section (what the Plans Section will do during the daytime operation)

Deliverables continues on next page ...

Logistics

1. Identify resource needs including:

   a. Staging areas, parking, feeding, water, command post

   b. Communications, transportation, helicopter landing zones

   c. Equestrian staging

   d. Overnight camping and/or lodging, fuel for vehicles and aircraft

2. Short (written) Incident Action Plan for Logistics Section (what Logistics Section will do during the daytime operation)

Operations

1. Incident safety and medical plan

2. Written press release for the media

3. Short written Incident Action Plan for Operations Section (what the Operations Section will do during the daytime operation)

All ICS sections as a group

1. ICS 201 for next operational period

2. Written local and/or mutual aid resource request, including ground searchers, specialized resources, overhead support, logistical supplies

3. Call the State SAR Coordination Office and make a mutual aid resource request

4. Overhead team transition briefing to one of the other groups)

Materials Provided

List of assignments completed during First Operational Period

1. Resources Provided

   a. State SAR Coordination Office (via telephone)

Exercise #3   Beginning Second (Multi) Operational Period (Check-in, Briefing, Deployment, Teams in the field)

Instructional Goals

Overhead Team Transition
(Pick up where class left off last week)

Check-in procedures

How teams are formed and briefed

Issues in deploying teams

Maintaining situation status

Communications

Clue management

Dealing with on-site media presence

Dealing with the family on-site

The rescue/recovery function

Actions

Plans

1. Collect Check-in information.
2. Keep resource status updated for Operations Section (tools include T-cards, magnet board, post-it notes).
3. Provide briefers for outgoing teams.
4. Keep situation status map updated with resource locations, clues, etc. (work with Operations Section).
5. Collect and file incident documentation.

Actions continues on next page ....

Operations

1. Assemble resources into teams.

2. Match teams with assignments and hand off to Plans Section for briefing.

3. Keep situation status map updated with resource locations, clues, etc. (work with Plans Section).

4. Provide briefings to officials, the media and the family as required.

5. Coordinate teams in the field.

6. Make changes or create new assignments as the situation requires.

7. Receive, track and act on incoming "clues," changing situations and new information.

8. Coordinate the rescue or recovery of the missing person(s) or SAR personnel as necessary.

Logistics

1. Incident Communications (All phone and radio traffic comes through you. Log it!)

2. Since the searchers are all fictional, issues of transporting and caring for them are ignored.

Exercise 3 continues on next page ...

Deliverables

Plans

1. Situation status map

2. Resource status summary (total number of searchers by resource type and agency)

Operations

1. List of assignments that were deployed

2. Notes on clues, new information or changes to the situation

3. Team Assignment forms for new or modified assignments

Logistics

1. Communications Logs (phone and radio)

Materials Provided

Check-in information as teams check in

Messages from teams and other external participants

Resources Provided

Team Liaisons to assist Operations Section with team assignments

Team Leaders to get briefings from Plans Section

Team Leaders reporting clues over the radio

Team Leader with injured searcher

Family member who wants to know what's going on and wants to help, bringing outside non-SAR resources

Team leader reporting finding one of the missing persons

Exercise #4A   End Second (Multi) Operational Period

Instructional Goals

Debriefing

Night search operations

Check-out / releasing resources

1. Are they available for the next operational period?

2. Are they "safe" to travel?

Changing tactics, expanding the search area

Actions

Plans

1. Debrief returning team.

    a. Do at least one debriefing for the following types of teams:

        ✓ Trail or Route of Travel Search
        ✓ Area Search
        ✓ Area Dog

2. Possibly brief the instructor/simulator on what the assignment was, so that they can make up reasonable debriefing information.

3. Determine and track release status of the team members to debrief.

4. Revisit the scenarios and apply the new information and clues.

5. Determine if they will search at night and if so, what the assignments would be.

6. Search assignments for the next operational period:

    a. Discuss tactics and types of resources to use

    b. Prepare a map marked with desired assignments

    c. Determine resource needs

Actions continues on next page ...

Operations & Logistics

There are still many things for these sections to do; however, since this portion of the exercise focuses on Plans, tasks for Operations and Logistics Sections are covered later in the training.

Deliverables

Plans

1. Debriefing forms for several types of search resources

2. List of planned night search activities

3. Estimation of resources that will stay for the next operational period

4. Request for additional Mutual Aid resources

5. Planning map showing assignments for next operational period

6. List of assignments for next operational period

Materials Provided

First missing person found and interviewed

Resources Provided

Team leaders for debriefing

Exercise #4B   Finishing the Mission

Instructor's Notes

Bring the teams back into the main room. The remainder of the exercise will be in the large group. The goal is to have a directed discussion about what to do after several more days of searching and no additional information on missing person's location has been revealed. Following the discussion, instructors conduct a short presentation on what happened in the actual missing person search, including how and where the person was found.

Scenario

The search operation is now in its fifth day. No additional clues or other information have been found. Volunteer participation is dwindling and resources are being requested from distant counties. Daytime temperatures have been over/below _____ degrees every day of the search.

Instructional Goals

Considering mission suspension or scale down

Demobilization

Deliverables

How to proceed

What to tell the missing person's family

What to tell the media?

What to tell the law enforcement agency

How to pack up all of the documentation for future use

Materials Provided

None

Chapter 14. Conclusion

The goal of this book is to provide a basic knowledge for those who will be or are involved in the search for missing persons in an urban environment. While 90% or more of missing persons cases are resolved within a short period of time by good investigative skills and looking in the obvious locations, there are times when more in-depth and thorough skills are required.

Take time to understand the urban environment and develop a pre-plan accordingly.

   ✓ Look at the history of missing persons in your area.

   ✓ What are the more common locations in which they are found?

   ✓ Develop a cache of maps and equipment.

   ✓ Develop lists of personnel and resources that can be tapped at a moment's notice.

Be extremely thorough in the investigation and interviewing.

   ✓ Develop trained personnel who can conduct in-depth interviews.

   ✓ Use and/or develop lists of questions to be better prepared to gather the necessary information.

   ✓ Determine the missing person's health and mental status.

   ✓ Determine the missing person's intent: What is their goal? Where are they trying to go?

   ✓ Determine the missing person's ability to survive in the environment.

   ✓ Determine the missing person's ability to travel.

   ✓ Determine the missing person's ability to respond.

Develop an accurate profile of the missing person.

   ✓ "Paint a mental picture" of the missing person from the information gathered during the investigation and interviews.

Use the investigation, information and scenario analysis to prevent wasted effort on a non-search.
- ✓ Look at the possible reasons for why the person is missing.
- ✓ Is the person voluntarily missing or truly lost and disoriented?
- ✓ What are the possible outcomes—the missing person could be found alive or dead.

Take advantage of the media, which is an effective source of clues.
- ✓ The more eyes that are looking for the missing person increase the chances the person will be found in a short time.
- ✓ Be prepared to handle the increased number of clues that will be generated; more personnel will be needed to answer phones and sift through information.

Consider that the missing person may have used public transportation and left the area.
- ✓ Know the public transportation available in your area and whom to contact for information.

Trailing dogs are an effective resource.
- ✓ Identify local, state and federal sources of trained search and rescue trailing dogs. Consider training your own dogs.
- ✓ Use trailing dogs to get a direction of travel from the point last seen (PLS).

Call in mutual aid search team resources early in the search mission.
- ✓ Identify and train with the local search and rescue teams in your area.
- ✓ Call on them early!

Train personnel to implement the labor intensive and time-consuming tasks of investigation and door-to-door canvassing.
- ✓ Establish protocols to use auxiliary volunteers from law enforcement and allied agencies.
- ✓ Develop a procedure to use spontaneous volunteers.

Thoughts for the Future

While this book is meant to be comprehensive it is by no means able to cover or include all that is known about missing person searches in the urban environment. Many readers of this book will have experiences and skills that have been successful in finding missing persons. We would like to hear about readers' experiences. To that end, the Web site www.urbansearchbook.com has been established. Readers' thoughts and stories may be posted on the Web site for all to share and learn from.

Appendix A. Incident Command System (ICS)

Introduction

What follows is an overview of the Incident Command System (ICS). It does not give a comprehensive description of the total workings of the system. Homeland Security Presidential Directives 5 and 8 require that all jurisdictions within the United States adopt the National Incident Management System (NIMS) and use ICS as a standard management scheme. It is recommended that in order to understand how the system works, readers should complete at minimum the I-100 course (offered online at www.training.fema.gov/EMIWeb/IS/is100.asp). It is also advisable that search personnel pursue higher levels of training in ICS appropriate to their level of responsibility.

History of Incident Command System

The Incident Command System was the result of observations and critiques of managing fast moving wildfires in California during the 1970s. The main concerns revolved around the organizational structure and the supervision of large numbers of equipment and personnel resources from multiple jurisdictions.

Observations uncovered the following problems:

- One supervisor responsible for too many personnel
- Different organizational structures for emergency response
- Lack of reliable, up-to-date incident information
- Disjointed structure for coordinated planning between agencies
- Unclear lines of authority
- Poor and incompatible radio communications
- Terminology differences between agencies
- Vague or indeterminate incident objectives

A management system was needed that would satisfy the following requirements:

1. The system must be organizationally flexible to meet the needs of incidents of any kind and size.

2. Agencies must be able to use the system on a day-to-day basis for routine situations as well as for major emergencies.

3. The system must be sufficiently standard to allow personnel from a variety of agencies and diverse geographic locations to rapidly meld into a common management structure.

4. The system must be cost effective.

Out of the assessment of these problems, local state and federal agencies in a cooperative effort developed the Incident Command System which was incorporated into FIRESCOPE (Firefighting Resources of California Organized for Potential Emergencies).

Originally ICS was developed and used exclusively in fighting wildfires. Over the years it has been adapted for use by many law enforcement and emergency situations large and small. As well, ICS has proven successful in various events, such as:

Unplanned events

- Fires
- HAZMAT
- Air, rail, water, or ground transportation accidents and disasters
- Multi-casualty incidents
- Terrorist incidents
- Multi-jurisdictional and multi-agency disasters
- Search and rescue missions
- Single and multi-agency law enforcement incidents

Planned events

- Concerts
- Celebrations
- Parades

Many federal, state and local authorities have adopted ICS as the on-scene management structure, including the following agencies:

- ✓ Federal Emergency Management Agency (FEMA)
- ✓ FEMA's National Fire Academy (NFA)

✓ FEMA's Urban Search and Rescue Response System (USAR)

✓ The Occupational Safety and Health Administration (OSHA)

✓ Environmental Protection Agency (EPA)

✓ California Governor's Office of Emergency Services (OES)

What makes ICS so desirable for use in managing emergency incidents?

✓ ICS provides for the following types of operations:

- Single jurisdiction/single agency
- Single jurisdiction with multi-agency involvement
- Multi-jurisdiction/multi-agency involvement

✓ ICS is able to adapt to any type of incident to which emergency service personnel would be expected to respond.

✓ ICS is applicable and accepted throughout the country.

✓ ICS is readily adaptable to new technology (e.g., computers, GPS).

✓ ICS expands in a logical manner from an initial response to a complex incident.

✓ By design, ICS has common elements in organization, terminology and procedures.

Because or the flexibility of the Incident Command System it can grow or shrink to meet dynamic needs of the incident. This makes ICS a very efficient as well as cost effective management system.

ICS Organization in Search and Rescue Incidents

In a search and rescue incident the goal is to locate the lost person in the shortest period time with the most efficient use of resources. Good management and the use of ICS will greatly increase the chances of success. This requires good leadership and leadership skill, and a clear understanding of the organizational structure. Everyone that participates in the incident must also have an understanding of ICS in order to work within the system.

Every incident or event will have specific major management activities or functions that must be performed. Even if the incident is small, and only one or two people are involved, these functions will still need to be addressed.

The organization of the Incident Command System is built around five major management functions.

1. COMMAND
   - Has overall responsibility at the incident or event
   - Sets objectives and priorities

2. PLANNING
   - Develops the action plan to accomplish the objectives
   - Collects and evaluates information through investigation and interviewing
   - Ensures appropriate briefing and debriefing
   - Maintains resource status

3. OPERATIONS
   - Conducts tactical operations to carry out the plan
   - Develops the tactical objectives
   - Directs all resources

4. LOGISTICS
   - Provides support to meet incident needs
   - Provides resources and all other services needed to support the incident

5. FINANCE/ADMINISTRATION
   - Monitors costs related to incident
   - Provides accounting of procurement time recording cost analyses

These five major management functions are the foundation upon which the ICS organization develops. They apply whether one is handling a routine emergency, organizing for a major event, or managing a major response to a disaster. On small incidents, these major activities may be managed by one person—the Incident Commander (IC). Large incidents usually require that they be set up as separate Sections within the organization. (See organization chart on p. 280.)

The specific organizational structure established for a search and rescue mission is based on the management needs of the incident. Initially, one individual can simultaneously manage all major functions. If the search and rescue incident is resolved quickly there may be no further organization required. As more trained management personnel arrive and the incident expands, then the functional tasks are assigned. The overall person in charge of the incident is the Incident Commander (IC). The persons assigned to oversee the remaining major functions are called the Section Chiefs (e.g., Plans Section Chief). The IC and Section Chiefs, along with certain staff positions (e.g., Public Information, Liaison, and Safety Officers) which support the management functions, make up the Overhead Team. Each Section function also can be broken down and delegation assigned further to Assistant (Deputy) Section Chief, Branch Director, Division Supervisor and Unit Leader. Anyone assigned as an Assistant (Deputy) must have the same qualifications as the person he is assigned to assist and may act as a relief manager in extended operations.

When considering the expansion of ICS as an incident unfolds, keep in mind the manageable span of control. ICS recognizes the optimal ratio of resources to supervisor to be between three and seven to one. Safety as well as management planning will influence and dictate span of control considerations.

Multi-jurisdictional and Unified Command Structure

In a multi-agency or multi-jurisdictional incident there is one Incident Commander mutually agreeable to all agencies involved. The incident still follows ICS. When the search incident requires a search effort, allowing all agencies with responsibility for the incident—geographical or functional—to manage an incident by establishing a common set of incident objectives and strategies, then a unified command structure is established. It is essential to understand that searches are managed with no regard to boundaries since most incidents are not confined to one jurisdiction. The selection of participants to work in the unified command should be made with regard to the location of the incident (e.g., jurisdictional) and the type of incident (e.g., plane crash vs. law enforcement issue). A Memorandum of Understanding (MOU) can be established prior to an incident, which would predetermine who will be in charge of particular functions or activities on specific types of emergencies.

Action Plan

In order to manage an incident under ICS management there is a need for an action plan. Every incident, no matter how short in duration or small in size, needs to have a plan. In larger incidents when resources from many agencies or jurisdictions are being used the action plan should be written. Written action plans are also necessary when the incident moves into multiple operational periods and there is a turnover of management personnel.

Resource Management

Resources are managed depending upon the needs of the incident. They are broken down as follows:

- **Single Resource.** The smallest unit that can operate independently. This can be a helicopter, a search dog with handler, an ambulance, etc., each of which can be assigned as a primary tactical unit. A single resource also includes its equipment (e.g., food, water, backpack)

- **Task Force.** A task force is any combination of resources that can be temporarily assembled for a specific mission. All resource elements within a task force will have common communications and each task force will have a leader. A task force is established to meet a specific tactical need and subsequently demobilized into single resources or reorganized into another task force configuration as required.

- **Strike Team.** A strike team is a set number of resources of the same kind and type that have an established minimum number of personnel. A strike team will have a leader and will have common communications. Strike teams can be made up of four wheel drive vehicles, ground searchers, search dogs and handlers, aid vehicles, or any other kind of resource where the combination of single resources of the same kind becomes a useful tactical unit.

Strike teams and task forces are used, whenever possible, to maximize the use of resources, increase the management control of a large number of single resources, and reduce the communications load.

Keeping track of resources under the Operations function requires a resource status board. One system uses "T-cards." Under this system, a card is filled out for each resource (personnel, equipment, and dogs). The cards are then placed in a "T-card" holder that is divided into the following sections:

- Available (ready to go on assignment)
- Assigned (already assigned to a team or in the field)

- Out of service (too tired to go out, sleeping, injured, but still at search, re-supplying pack, etc).
- Resources en route
- Transport units

As the resource's status changes the "T-card" is moved to the appropriate slot.

References

Incident Command System—Overview. Search and Rescue Society of British Columbia.

Standardized Emergency Management System (SEMS) State of California Governor's Office of Emergency Services

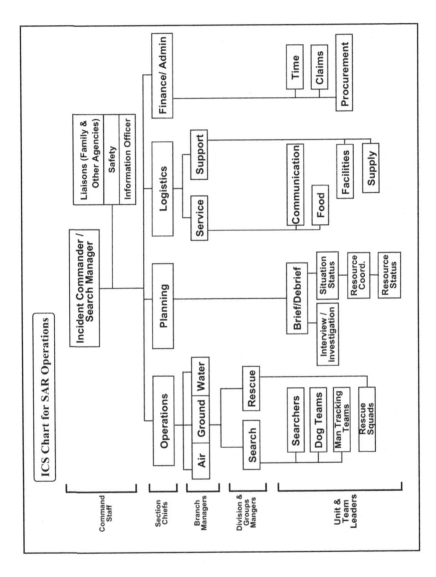

ICS organization chart

Appendix B. Glossary of ICS Terms

National Incident Management System (NIMS) was established as a comprehensive, integrated national mutual aid and resource management system that provides the basis to type, order, and track all (Federal, State, and local) response assets. NIMS also dictates the use of ICS on all incidents. ICS mandates that terminology be standardized. That is, a term such as "Incident Commander" should mean the same thing to everyone.

This Glossary of ICS Terms is a compilation of those found in NIMS and other ICS documents developed over the years and used during missing person incidents.

Agency Executive or Administrator. Chief executive officer (or designee) of the agency or jurisdiction that has responsibility for the incident (e.g., sheriff, police chief, fire chief).

Agency Representative. A person assigned by a primary, assisting or cooperating Federal, State, local or tribal government agency or private entity that has been delegated authority to make decisions affecting that agency's or organization's participation in incident management activities following appropriate consultation with the leadership of that agency. Agency Representatives report to the incident Liaison Officer.

Allocated resources. Resources dispatched to an incident that have not yet checked in with the command post or base of operations.

Area Command (Unified Area Command). An organization established (1) to oversee the management of multiple incidents that are each being handled by an ICS organization or (2) to oversee the management of large or multiple incidents to which several Incident Management Teams have been assigned. Area Command has the responsibility to set overall strategy and priorities, allocate critical resources according to priorities, ensure that incidents are properly managed, and ensure that objectives are met and strategies followed. Area Command becomes Unified Area Command when incidents are multi-jurisdictional. Area Command may be established at an emergency operations center facility or at some location other than an incident command post.

Assigned resources. Resources checked in and assigned tasks on a search or rescue incident.

Assignments. Tasks given to resources to perform within a given operational period based on operational objectives defined in the Incident Action Plan (IAP).

Available resources. Resources assigned to an incident, checked in, and available for a mission assignment; normally located in the Staging Area.

Branch. The organizational level having functional or geographical responsibility for major aspects of incident operations. A branch is organizationally situated between the section and the division or group in the Operations Section, and between the section and units in the Logistics Section. In SAR, it is the organizational level under a major section that has responsibility for a specific functional task, e.g., air operations branch, ground operations branch, water operations branch. Branches are identified using Roman numerals or by functional area.

Camp. A geographical site within the general incident area, separate from the base, equipped and staffed to provide food, water and sanitary services to incident personnel.

Chain of command. A series of command, control, executive, or management positions in hierarchical order of authority.

Check-in. The process through which resources first report to an incident. Check-in locations include the incident command post, resources unit, incident base, camps, staging areas, or directly on the site.

Chief. The ICS title for individuals responsible for management of functional sections: Operations, Planning, Logistics, Finance/Administration, and Intelligence (if established as a separate section).

Command. The act of directing, ordering, or controlling by virtue of explicit statutory, regulatory, or delegated authority.

Command Post (CP). The location at which the primary command and control functions are executed, usually co-located with the search base.

Command staff. In an incident management organization, the command staff consists of the Incident Commander and the special staff positions of Public Information Officer, Safety Officer, Liaison Officer, and other positions as required, who report directly to the Incident Commander. They may have an assistant or assistants, as needed.

Deputy. A fully qualified individual who, in the absence of a superior, can be delegated the authority to manage a functional operation or perform a specific task. In some cases, a deputy can act as relief for a superior and, therefore, must be fully qualified in the position. Deputies can be assigned to the Incident Commander, General Staff, and Branch Directors.

Dispatch. The ordered movement of a resource or resources to an assigned operational mission or an administrative move from one location to another.

Division. The partition of an incident into geographical areas of operation. Divisions are established when the number of resources exceeds the manageable span of control of the Operations Chief. A division is located within the ICS organization between the branch and resources in the Operations Section.

Emergency Operations Center (EOC). The physical location at which the coordination of information and resources to support domestic incident management activities normally takes place. An EOC may be a temporary facility or located in a more central or permanently established facility, perhaps at a higher level of organization within a jurisdiction. EOCs may be organized by major functional disciplines (e.g., fire, law enforcement, and medical services), by jurisdiction (e.g., Federal, State, regional, county, city, tribal), or some combination thereof.

Facilities. Buildings and sections in and around the incident area that are used during the course of the search mission, e.g., command post, heliport, staging area.

Function. Refers to the five major activities in ICS: Command, Operations, Planning, Logistics, and Finance/Administration. The term function is also used when describing the activity involved, e.g., the planning function. A sixth function—Intelligence—may be established, if required, to meet incident management needs.

General staff. A group of incident management personnel organized according to function and reporting to the Incident Commander. The General Staff normally consists of the Operations Section Chief, Planning Section Chief, Logistics Section Chief, and Finance/Administration Section Chief.

Group. Established to divide the incident management structure into functional areas of operation. Groups are composed of resources assembled to perform a special function not necessarily within a single geographic division. When activated, groups are located between branches and resources in the Operations

Section. (See Division.) In SAR, it is a functional division, e.g., air support, search group, rescue group.

Hazard. Something that is potentially dangerous or harmful, often the root cause of an unwanted outcome.

Incident. An occurrence or event, natural or human-caused, that requires an emergency response to protect life or property. Incidents can, for example, include major disasters, emergencies, terrorist attacks, terrorist threats, wildland and urban fires, floods, hazardous materials spills, nuclear accidents, aircraft accidents, earthquakes, hurricanes, tornadoes, tropical storms, war-related disasters, public health and medical emergencies, missing person searches and other occurrences requiring an emergency response.

Incident Action Plan (IAP). An oral or written plan containing general objectives reflecting the overall strategy for managing an incident. It may include the identification of operational resources and assignments. It may also include attachments that provide direction and important information for management of the incident during one or more operational periods. The search and rescue action plan, which is initially prepared when the mission is confirmed, contains general control objectives that reflect overall strategy and specific plans for the first operational period.

Incident Base (SAR Base). The location at which the primary logistical functions are coordinated and administered. (The search name or other designator will be added to the "Base.") The command post may be co-located with the base. There is usually only one base per incident.

Incident Command System (ICS). A standardized on-scene emergency management construct specifically designed to provide for the adoption of an integrated organizational structure that reflects the complexity and demands of single or multiple incidents without being hindered by jurisdictional boundaries. ICS is the combination of facilities, equipment, personnel, procedures, and communications operating within a common organizational structure, designed to aid in the management of resources during incidents. It is used for all kinds of emergencies and is applicable to small as well as large and complex incidents. ICS is used by various jurisdictions and functional agencies, both public and private, to organize field-level incident management operations.

Incident Commander (IC). The individual responsible for all incident activities, including the development of strategies and tactics and the ordering and the release of resources. The IC has overall authority and responsibility for conducting incident operations and is responsible for the management of all incident operations at the incident site.

Incident Objectives. Statements of guidance and direction necessary for selecting the appropriate strategy, or strategies, and the tactical direction of resources. Incident objectives are based on realistic expectations of what can be accomplished. Incident objectives must be achievable and measurable, yet flexible enough to allow strategic and tactical alternatives.

Initial (Reflex) Action. The actions taken by those responders first to arrive at an incident site.

Initial Response. Resources initially committed to an incident.

Intelligence Officer. The intelligence officer is responsible for managing internal information, intelligence, and operational security requirements supporting incident management activities. These may include information security and operational security activities, as well as the complex task of ensuring that sensitive information of all types (e.g., classified information, law enforcement sensitive information, proprietary information, or export-controlled information) is handled in a way that not only safeguards the information, but also ensures that it gets to those who need access to it to perform their missions effectively and safely.

Jurisdiction. A range or sphere of authority. Public agencies have jurisdiction at an incident related to their legal responsibilities and authority. Jurisdictional authority at an incident can be political or geographical (e.g., city, county, tribal, State, or Federal boundary lines) or functional (e.g., law enforcement, public health).

Liaison. A form of communication for establishing and maintaining mutual understanding and cooperation.

Liaison Officer. A member of the command staff responsible for coordinating with representatives from cooperating and assisting agencies.

Logistics. Providing resources and other services to support incident management.

Logistics Section. The section responsible for providing facilities, services, and material support for the incident.

Multi-jurisdictional Incident. An incident requiring action from multiple agencies that each have jurisdiction to manage certain aspects of an incident. In ICS, there is one appointed Incident Commander.

Mutual Aid Agreement. Written agreement between agencies and/or jurisdictions that they will assist one another on request, by furnishing personnel, equipment, and/or expertise in a specified manner.

Operational Period. The time scheduled for executing a given set of operation actions or tactics, as specified in the Incident Action Plan (IAP). Operational periods can be of various lengths, although usually not more than 24 hours.

Operations Section. The section responsible for all tactical incident operations. In ICS, it normally includes subordinate branches, divisions, and/or groups. Also known as Operations or Ops.

Organizational Functions. A standard set of major functions and functional units must be established and named. Terminology for the organizational elements should be standard and consistent.

Planning Meeting. A meeting held as needed prior to and throughout the duration of an incident to select specific strategies and tactics for incident control operations and for service and support planning. For larger incidents, the planning meeting is a major element in the development of the Incident Action Plan.

Planning Section. Responsible for the collection, evaluation, and dissemination of operational information related to the incident, and for the preparation and documentation of the IAP. This section also maintains information on the current and forecasted situation and on the status of resources assigned to the incident. Also known as Plans Section or Plans.

Public Information Officer (PIO). A member of the command staff responsible for interfacing with the public and media or with other agencies with incident-related information requirements.

Qualification and Certification. This subsystem provides recommended qualification and certification standards for emergency responder and incident management personnel. It also allows the development of minimum standards for resources expected to have an interstate application. Standards typically include training, currency, experience, and physical and medical fitness.

Resource Management. Efficient incident management requires a system for identifying available resources at all jurisdictional levels to enable timely and unimpeded access to resources needed to prepare for, respond to, or recover from an incident. Resource management under the NIMS includes mutual aid agreements; the use of special Federal, State, local, and tribal teams; and resource mobilization protocols.

Resources. Personnel and major items of equipment, supplies, and facilities available or potentially available for assignment to incident operations and for which status is maintained. A key element in effective management of emergency resources is to establish common names for all primary and support personnel and equipment. Resources are described by kind and type and may be used in operational support or supervisory capacities at an incident or at an EOC. Search and Rescue resources are clearly categorized by capability, e.g., trackers and hasty teams, area dogs, trailing dogs, and equestrian teams. These teams are initial deployment resources.

Resources Unit. Functional unit within the Planning Section responsible for recording the status of resources committed to the incident. This unit also evaluates resources currently committed to the incident, the effects additional responding resources will have on the incident, and anticipated resource needs.

Safety Officer. A member of the command staff responsible for monitoring and assessing safety hazards or unsafe situations and for developing measures for ensuring personnel safety.

Section. The organizational level having responsibility for a major functional area of incident management, e.g., Operations, Planning, Logistics, Finance/Administration, and Intelligence (if established). The section is organizationally situated between the branch and the Incident Commander (and command staff).

Span of control. The number of individuals a supervisor is responsible for, usually expressed as the ratio of supervisors to individuals. (Under NIMS, an appropriate span of control is a ratio between 1:3 and 1:7.)

Staging Area. Location established where resources can be placed while awaiting a tactical assignment. The Operations Section manages Staging Areas. Usually from this location resources can be immediately committed to the field.

Status Condition. Three status conditions are given to tactical resources at the search base:

1. ASSIGNED - performing an active assignment.
2. AVAILABLE - ready for assignment. All resources in staging areas should be available.
3. OUT OF SERVICE - not ready for "available" or "assigned" status.

Strategy. The general direction selected to accomplish incident objectives set by the IC.

Strike Team. Specific combinations of the same type of resource, with common communication and a leader (e.g., a hasty team, two trackers; two dogs and their handlers).

Task Force. A group of various resources with common communication and a leader temporarily assembled for a specific mission (e.g., two trackers with two sign cutters each; a tracking team and a dog and its handler; a tracker).

Type. A classification of resources in the ICS that refers to capability. Type 1 is generally considered to be more capable than Types 2, 3, or 4, respectively, because of size; power; capacity; or, in the case of incident management teams, experience and qualifications.

Unified Command (UC). A unified team effort, which allows all agencies with responsibility for the incident, either geographical or functional, to manage the incident by establishing a common set of incident objectives and strategies in a single Incident Action Plan (IAP). Participants are comprised of the senior person from each agency and/or discipline.

Unit. The organizational element having functional responsibility for a specific SAR planning, logistics or finance activity.

Appendix C.

Urban Preplan Surveys & Hazard Risk Chart

CITY PLAN

City: _____

1. Responsible Law Enforcement Agency: _____

2. Agency Offices: _____
   _____

3. Contacts: _____

4. Phone Numbers: _____
   _____

5. People who are very familiar with this city: _____
   _____

6. Large assembly areas available (churches, schoolyards etc.) for CP
   considering elevation for communications: _____
   _____
   _____

7. Location of 24-hour gas stations: _____
   _____

8. Location of 24-hour food stores or restaurants: _____
   _____

9. Helicopter landing available? YES/NO
   If YES, location and coordinates:_____
   _____

10. Local hazardous, attractive nuisances or crime areas:_____
    _____
    _____

11. Locations where other lost subjects have been found missing from
    here: _____
    _____

12. Other: _____

13. Date of Last Update: _____

14. Update Done By Whom? _____

PARKS/OPEN SPACE/REGIONS PLAN

Area: _____

1. Responsible Law Enforcement Agency: _____

2. Agency Offices: _____
   _____

3. Contacts: _____

4. Phone Numbers: _____
   _____

5. People who are very familiar with this area: _____
   _____

6. Names and phone #'s of neighboring property owners: _____
   _____

7. Location of 24-hour gas/food resources (see nearest City Plan): ___
   _____
   _____

8. Large assembly areas available for CP considering elevation for
   communications site: _____
   _____
   _____

9. Location of 24-hour food stores or restaurants: _____
   _____
   _____

9. Helicopter landing available? YES/NO
   If YES, location and coordinates:_____
   _____

10. Local hazardous or attractive nuisances:_____
    _____
    _____

11. Locations where other lost subjects have been found missing from
    here: _____
    _____

12. Other: _____

13. Date of Last Update: _____

14. Update Done By Whom? _____

BUSINESS/SHOPPING CENTER PLAN

Business/Shopping Center: _____

1. Responsible Security/Law Enforcement Agency: _____

2. Agency Offices: _____

3. Contacts: _____

4. Phone Numbers: _____

5. People who are very familiar with this Business/Shopping Center: _

6. Local hazardous or attractive nuisances: _____

7. Locations where other lost subjects have been found missing from here: _____

8. Other: _____

9. Date Of Last Update: _____
10. Update Done By Whom? _____

TRANSIT SYSTEM PLAN

Transit System: _____

1. Type of Transit System (Rail; Road; Air; Maritime): _____
    _____

2. Responsible Security/Law Enforcement Agency: _____
    _____

3. Agency Offices: _____
    _____
    _____

4. Contacts: _____
    _____

5. Phone Numbers: _____
    _____

6. People that are very familiar with this Transit System: _____
    _____

7. Other Connected Transit Systems or Hubs (see their Transit System Plan): _____

8. Hazardous or attractive nuisances: _____
    _____
    _____
    _____

9. Locations where other lost subjects have been found missing from here: _____
    _____
    _____

10. Other: _____
    _____
    _____

11. Date Of Last Update: _____

12. Update Done By Whom? _____

INSTITUTION PLAN

Institution: _____

1. Type of Institution (School; Hospital; Jail; Other): _____
   _____

2. Location of Institution: _____
   _____

3. Responsible Security/Law Enforcement Agency: _____
   _____

4. Agency Offices: _____
   _____

5. Contacts: _____
   _____

6. Phone Numbers: _____
   _____
   _____

7. People who are very familiar with this Institution: _____
   _____
   _____

8. Local hazardous or attractive nuisances: _____
   _____
   _____

9. Locations where other lost subjects have been found missing
   from here:_____
   _____
   _____

10. Other: _____
    _____

11. Date Of Last Update: _____

12. Update Done By Whom? _____

ELDERLY/CHILD CARE FACILITIES PLAN

Facility Name:_____

1. Type of Facility (Day Care; Assisted Living; Continuous Care; Skilled Nursing Care; Memory/Lock-down (wander restriction)):____
   _____

2. Location of Facility (See also City Plan): _____
   _____

3. Contacts: _____
   _____

4. Phone Numbers: _____
   _____

5. People who are very familiar with this Facility: _____
   _____

6. Adjacent or close Open Space/Parks (See Parks/Open Space/Regions Plan): _____
   _____

7. Adjacent or close Business/Shopping Centers (See Business/Shopping Center Plan):_____
   _____
   _____

8. Local Transit System(s) (See Transit System Plan):_____
   _____

9. Large assembly areas available for CP considering elevation for communications site:_____
   _____

10. Local hazardous or attractive nuisances: _____
    _____

11. Locations where other lost subjects have been found missing from here:_____
    _____

12. Other: _____
    _____

13. Date Of Last Update: _____

14. Update Done By Whom? _____

Hazard Risk Chart

**Contra Costa County Sheriff
Search And Rescue Team**

HAZARD AND RISK ANALYSIS

INCIDENT NAME	DATE PREPARED	TIME PREPARED	APPLICABLE

1. **Cross Country Travel Hazards:** River & Stream crossings, high water, slippery rocks, NO ROCK HOPPING, footing hazards, rotten logs, undercut ledges, areas of dense vegetation and difficulty in finding routes, etc.

2. **Steep, Unstable Slopes:** Many steep & unstable slopes that cause rock fall. Stop & use caution. Be especially careful during rescue operations, stokes lowering, dislodging material, persons up slope dislodging material, ropes and lines and tripping hazards. Use of helmets and goggles suggested.

3. **Ticks:** Wear long sleeves and leggings, use tick repellent at arm and leg cuffs. Tape or rubber band at cuffs (just snug, not tight). Check WHOLE body daily. If bitten, remove properly and promptly. Lyme disease is active in this area.

4. **Rattlesnakes:** Keep alert, take snake bite kit, don't put hands or feet in blind places. If bitten, follow current first aid, stay calm, send or radio for help.

5. **Poison Oak:** Know all forms of plant, avoid contact. Apply protection, wash thoroughly and promptly all exposed skin with soap and cool water, avoid exposure from clothing & equipment.

6. **Stinging Nettles:** Be aware of stinging nettles in areas of dense vegetation.

7. **Mountain Lions:** Known to be present in the area. Be aware of encounter precautions.

8. **Giardia:** Filter water through one micron filter or rolling boil for three minutes

9. **Wet Weather:** Inclement weather present or predicted. Be properly equipped for rain & wind conditions. Avoid cotton garments. Take precautions from hypothermia.

10. **Heavy Fog:** Dense fog present or predicted. Reduced vision, disorientation with direction, use caution when traveling cross country and on steep slopes. Be properly equipped for rain and wind conditions.

11. **Cold Weather:** Temperatures currently or expected to be under 40 degrees. Take extreme caution. Threat of hypothermia and frostbite. Wear insulated gloves and multiple layers.

12. **Hot, Dry Weather:** Heat exhaustion, heat stroke, dehydration, exhaustion, sunburn, potential fire hazards. Keep hydrated. Don't park vehicles on or near dry grass or brush, no smoking or fires.

13. **Lightning:** Keep alert, avoid projecting above the surrounding landscape, stay away from water, wire fences, metal railings, solitary trees, ridges, rock outcrops, open meadows, etc.

14. **Night Work:** Reduced vision, disorientation with direction, use caution when traveling cross country and on steep slopes. Use of helmets and goggles suggested.

15. **Wilderness Night Out:** Your assignment has a high probability for an extended night out under primitive conditions. Make sure you have provisions, and safeguard food from animals.

16. **Urban Search Area:** Heavy vehicle traffic, abandoned buildings, homeless camps, aggressive dogs. Stay alert, maintain an escape route, always know your location, maintain communication with CP.

17. **Physical Capacity:** Ability to carry 35+ pounds over difficult terrain, aggravation of prior back, knee, ankle or foot injuries very likely, exhaustion.

18. **Aircraft Operations:** Exiting and boarding hazards, pay close attention to heli-crew instructions. Secure gear & equipment. Flying dust & debris hazards on takeoff & landing. Keep search dogs on leash and quick release harness.

19. **Possibly Dangerous / Emotionally Unstable Victim:** Keep alert, officer safety is a priority.

20. **Victim Possibly Armed:** Keep alert, officer safety is a priority, do not approach – call in sightings.

21. **Transportation One hour Plus:** Plan ahead for pickup

22. **Communications:** Assignment involves areas where communications can be difficult & sometimes impossible. Be aware of high points & lines of site to be more accessible.

23. **Other Hazards / Risks:** List...

PREPARED BY:	APPROVED BY:
(SAFETY OFFICER)	(IC / SEARCH MANAGER)

Appendix D. Law Enforcement Protocol

The following policies and procedures for law enforcement are taken from the Contra Costa County Sheriff-Coroner Patrol Division Manual – Investigations Policies and Procedures, dated 2/5/01. These serve as an example only. Each county, district or local law enforcement agency will have its own set of policies and procedures for missing persons, which may be similar to those listed here.

Policies and Procedures for Missing Persons

Policy   In recognition of the intent and spirit of State laws, deputies will accept and investigate any missing person report with sensitivity toward the family of the missing person(s).

Reference   PC 14205, 14210, AB 2512 SB 391

Procedure 1   Accepting Reports

Patrol deputy will accept, without delay, any missing person report, including runaways, regardless of where the missing person resides or was last seen.

Procedure 2   Searches

A search will be instituted immediately whenever the following circumstances are present:

- All juveniles under twelve years of age.
- Juveniles missing under suspicious or special circumstances (e.g., foul play suspected, juvenile is suicidal, juvenile is mentally retarded).
- For missing juveniles under sixteen years of age but over twelve the Field Supervisor will make an assessment of the reasonable steps to be taken to locate the person.
- The assigned deputy will contact the area supervisor and advise him/her of the circumstances. The supervisor may then authorize/request assistance of special units (search and rescue).

Procedure 3   Notifications

A Be On the Look Out (BOLO) bulletin will be broadcast without delay within the Sheriff's jurisdiction if the missing person is under sixteen years of age, or there is evidence that the person is at risk (per 14205 PC). The deputy initially taking a missing person report of persons at risk (including runaways of juveniles sixteen years or under will ensure the missing person information is entered into National Crime Information Center (NCIC) within four hours of receiving the report. The NCIC number will be included in the report.

- Entries into NCIC of missing persons under eighteen years of age but over sixteen will be made no later the end of the deputy's shift.

- Entries into NCIC of missing persons over eighteen will be based on the following circumstances:
  - Age
  - Mental condition, medical condition or immediate needs
  - Possible foul play
  - Media interest

- The NCIC number will be included in the MO report in any case

- The Deputies will contact dispatch who will make all entries into NCIC and furnish the deputy with the NCIC number for his/her report.

- A copy of the NCIC entry will be affixed to a "C" page and included with the original report.

- Supervisors will review the NCIC entry and the original report to verify the accuracy of the information entered into NCIC and the entry information is supported in the original report.

Procedure 4   Reporting Requirements

A separate report will be written for each missing person/runaway even if they are together or suspected of being together. Patrol sergeants will route two copies of missing person report to Investigation Division for follow-up investigation.

Procedure 5   Located Missing/Runaway Persons

When located by Contra Costa County Sheriff's Office patrol, the patrol deputy will:

- Write a supplemental report requesting Investigations to remove the juvenile from the system;
- Ensure any special units (search and rescue) which have been summoned are canceled.

When advised by an outside agency that a missing person/runaway has been located, the patrol deputy will:

- Contact the agency and confirm the identification and status of the missing person/runaway;
- Write a supplemental report;
- Confirm or change NCIC status via the appropriate dispatch center;
- Cancel any special units (search and rescue) summoned, if applicable.

In addition, if the original report was an outside assist for another agency, the patrol deputy will:

- Contact the agency and advise them of the person's status;
- If requested, have the appropriate dispatch center send a confirmation tele-type to the agency.

Procedure 6   Crime Involvement

When the missing person/runaway person is the victim or suspect in any crime in the county, patrol deputy will:

- Advise the area sergeant of the circumstance;
- Follow procedures in "Stranger Abduction Protocol," if applicable;
- Request any assistance needed;
- Write the appropriate report;
- Make arrests or issue a citation, as needed.

Appendix E.
California Penal Code Section 14205

14205.   (a) All local police and sheriffs' departments shall accept any report, including any telephonic report, of a missing person, including runaways, without delay and shall give priority to the handling of these reports over the handling of reports relating to crimes involving property.   In cases where the person making a report of a missing person or runaway, contacts, including by telephone, the California Highway Patrol, the California Highway Patrol may take the report, and shall immediately advise the person making the report of the name and telephone number of the police or sheriff's department having jurisdiction of the residence address of the missing person and of the name and telephone number of the police or sheriff's department having jurisdiction of the place where the person was last seen.   In cases of reports involving missing persons, including, but not limited to, runaways, the local police or sheriff's department shall immediately take the report and make an assessment of reasonable steps to be taken to locate the person.

(a) If the missing person is under 16 years of age, or there is evidence that the person is at risk, the department shall broadcast a "Be on the Look-Out" bulletin, without delay, within its jurisdiction.

(b) If the person reported missing is under 16 years of age, or if there is evidence that the person is at risk, the local police, sheriff's department, or the California Highway Patrol shall submit the report to the Attorney General's office within four hours after accepting the report.   After the California Law Enforcement Telecommunications System online missing person registry becomes operational, the reports shall be submitted, within four hours after accepting the report, to the Attorney General's office through the use of the California Telecommunications System.

(c) In cases where the report is taken by a department, other than that of the city or county of residence of the missing person or runaway, the department, or division of the California Highway Patrol taking the report shall, without delay, and, in the case of children under 16 years of age or where there was evidence that the missing person was at risk, within no more than 24 hours, notify, and forward a copy of the report to the police or sheriff's department or departments having jurisdiction of the residence address of the missing person or runaway and of the place where the person was last seen.

The report shall also be submitted by the department or division of the California Highway Patrol which took the report to the center.

(d) The requirements imposed by this section on local police and sheriff's departments shall not be operative if the governing body of that local agency, by a majority vote of the members of that body, adopts a resolution expressly making those requirements inoperative.

Appendix F.
Emergency Telephone Notification System

Sample Protocol
Telephone Emergency Notification System (TENS)
Contra Costa County, California Department of the Sheriff
Office of Emergency Services (OES) Division

Policy

The TENS should be used to alert households and businesses of imminent or active threats in their area. In order to earn and preserve the public's trust, confidence and support, the TENS is used only in emergency incidents that may affect life safety. TENS will not be activated by anyone not trained in its uses.

Definitions

A. **TENS.** An automated telephone calling system that delivers recorded warnings and instructions to businesses and households.

B. **Life Safety Incident.** TBD by responsible agency.

C. **Imminent or Active Incident.** An active incident is one that currently impacts the lives, property and safety of the public. An imminent incident is one expected by the emergency manager or incident commander to become active.

D. **Required Activation.** Several hazards exist in the county, which can cause an immediate life safety impact on the public. TENS activation is required for these hazards.

E. **Optional Activation.** Hazards exist in the county, which may have a life safety impact on the public. TENS activation may be beneficial or become necessary for these hazards.

General

A. **Community impact of TENS.** TENS is an intrusive and fairly expensive way to disseminate information to the community. TENS is an integral part of a county's community warning system.

Procedure 1

The following events *require TENS activation:*

- ✓ Terrorism level 3 active
- ✓ Dam failure active
- ✓ Dam failure imminent
- ✓ Levee failure active
- ✓ Wildfire active
- ✓ Flash flood active

A. Consider:

1. Is the planned area for notification appropriate?
2. Is evacuation imminent?
3. Will additional notification be needed?

B. Activation Process

1. Identify area to be notified using Thomas Bros. Maps™ grids.
2. Notify the officer-of-the-day, COMM1, the CWS manager or the OES manager to activate TENS.

Procedure 2

For the following events, *TENS activation is optional:*

- ✓ Hazardous materials—level 3
- ✓ Airplane crash, terrorism—level 2
- ✓ Missing person, AMBER Alert, levee failure—imminent

A. Consider:

1. Time of day (if calling between 10 p.m. and 7 a.m.): Is this a life safety issue?
2. Is the planned area for notification appropriate?
3. Is evacuation imminent?
4. Will additional notification be needed?

B. Activation Process

1. Identify area to be notified using Thomas Bros. Maps™ grids.
2. Notify the officer-of-the-day, COMM1, the CWS manager or the OES manager to activate TENS.
3. Get approval from the Emergency Services division, Homeland Security Lieutenant for selecting the time of day to make calls.

Pre-Approved for TENS Activation

The following county staff is pre-approved to activate TENS for Procedure 1 or Procedure 2 events:

1. OES Manager
2. CWS Manager
3. COMM1 Dispatch Supervisor
4. Health Services Risk Manager

Approved for TENS Activation Request

The following county staff can request to activate TENS for Procedure 1 or Procedure 2 events:

1. Search and Rescue Sergeant
2. Officer-of-the-day Lieutenant
3. Emergency Services Division Captain
4. Homeland Security Unit Lieutenant
5. Health Services Hazards Manager
6. Incident Commander
7. OES Manager
8. Fire Dispatch Manager
9. COMM1 Dispatch Supervisor
10. Health Services Risk Manager
11. Health Services HAZMAT Mobile Response Unit

Approved Chain for TENS Activation Request

The following may approve TENS activation for Procedure 2 events:

1. Emergency Services Division Captain
2. Homeland Security Unit Lieutenant
3. Health Services Hazards Manager

Appendix G.

Mutual Aid Request Form—SAR 141

SAR **MUTUAL AID REQUEST**	1. INCIDENT NAME	2. DATE/TIME
4. REQUEST TYPE ☐ NEW MUTUAL AID REQUEST ☐ ADDITIONAL RESOURCES FOR ONGOING MUTUAL AID OPERATION		4. OES MISSION #

REQUESTOR

NAME/TITLE	4. CONTACT INFORMATION
AGENCY	

OES LAW DUTY OFFICER

NAME	4. CONTACT INFORMATION

SITUATION SUMMARY

4. MISSING SUBJECT(S) INFORMATION

NAME	AGE	CITY/COUNTY/STATE OF RESIDENCE

4. NARATIVE DESCRIPTION OF SITUATION

4. URGENCY FACTORS

4. PAST AND CURRENT SEARCH EFFORTS AND RESOURCES COMMITTED

4. TERRAIN

4. CURRENT AND PREDICTED WEATHER

COMMAND POST INFORMATION

4. NAME OF IC AND/OR PLANS CHEIF	4. CONTACT INFORMATION

4. LOCATION

SAR 141
PAGE 1
BASARC 2/05

NOTES

Appendix H. Interview and Clue Forms

Urban Interview Log

URBAN INTERVIEW LOG | 1. INCIDENT NAME | 2. DATE/TIME | 3. TEAM IDENTIFIER

STREET ADDRESS	RESIDENT CONTACTED	RESIDENT'S NAME	OTHER'S AT HOME	PHONE #	HOW LONG HOME	RESIDENT TO CHECK HOME AND YARD	SAR CHECKED YARD	PLACES TO HIDE IN AREA	COMMENTS	SUGGEST FOLLOW UP VISIT
	Y N		Y N			Y N	Y N			Y N
	Y N		Y N			Y N	Y N			Y N
	Y N		Y N			Y N	Y N			Y N
	Y N		Y N			Y N	Y N			Y N
	Y N		Y N			Y N	Y N			Y N
	Y N		Y N			Y N	Y N			Y N
	Y N		Y N			Y N	Y N			Y N
	Y N		Y N			Y N	Y N			Y N
	Y N		Y N			Y N	Y N			Y N
	Y N		Y N			Y N	Y N			Y N
	Y N		Y N			Y N	Y N			Y N
	Y N		Y N			Y N	Y N			Y N
	Y N		Y N			Y N	Y N			Y N
	Y N		Y N			Y N	Y N			Y N
	Y N		Y N			Y N	Y N			Y N

SAR 132 BASARC 3/98 | 5. PREPARED BY

Clue Log

CLUE LOG	1. INCIDENT NAME		2. DATE	3. INCIDENT NUMBER	
CLUE #	ITEM FOUND	TEAM	DATE/TIME	LOCATION OF FIND	INITIALS

SAR 134
BASARC 3/98

Clue Report

CLUE REPORT	1. INCIDENT NAME		2. DATE	3. INCIDENT NUMBER
4 CLUE NUMBER	5.DATE/TIME LOCATED		6. TEAM THAT LOCATED CLUE	

7. NAME OF INDIVIDUAL THAT LOCATED CLUE

8. DESCRIPTION OF CLUE

9. LOCATION FOUND

10. TO INVESTIGATIONS

☐ **URGENT REPLY NEEDED**, TEAM STANDING BY TIME _____

☐ INFORMATION ONLY

11. INSTRUCTIONS TO TEAM

☐ COLLECT

☐ MARK AND LEAVE

☐ DISREGARD

☐ OTHER _____

CLUE & SEGMENT PROBABILITIES TO BE COMPLETED BY PLANS

12. CLUE PROBABILITY	13. SEGMENT PROBABILITY	LIST SEGMENTS
☐ VERY LIKELY A GOOD CLUE	VIRTUALLY 100% CERTAIN CLUE MEANS SUBJECT IS IN THESE SEGMENTS	
☐ PROBABLY A GOOD CLUE	VERY STRONG CHANCE THAT CLUE MEANS SUBJECT IS IN THESE SEGMENTS	
☐ MAY BE A GOOD CLUE	STRONG CHANCE THAT CLUE MEANS SUBJECT IS IN THESE SEGMENTS	
☐ PROBABLY NOT A GOOD CLUE	BETTER THAN EVEN CHANCE THAT CLUE MEANS SUBJECT IS IN THESE SEGMENTS	
☐ VERY LIKELY NOT A GOOD CLUE	NO INFORMATION FROM THE CLUE TO SUGGEST SUBJECT IS OR **IS NOT** IN THESE SEGMENTS	
☐ DON'T KNOW	BETTER THAN EVEN CHANCE THAT CLUE MEANS SUBJECT IS **NOT** IN THESE SEGMENTS	
COPIES	STRONG CHANCE THAT CLUE MEANS SUBJECT IS **NOT** IN THESE SEGMENTS	
☐ PLANS ☐ ATTACH TO CLUE	VERY STRONG CHANCE THAT CLUE MEANS SUBJECT IS **NOT** IN THESE SEGMENTS	
☐ INVESTIGATIONS ☐ OTHER	VIRTUALLY 100% CERTAIN CLUE MEANS SUBJECT IS **NOT** IN THESE SEGMENTS	
☐ DEBRIEFING _____		

SAR 135 BASARC 3/98	14.PREPARED BY	15.CLUE & SEGMENT PROBABLITIES PREPARED BY

Appendix I. Dementia Evaluation Form

Purpose: Please use this form to provide information in case the person wanders away or becomes lost. Keep a copy of this sheet handy to give to law enforcement. All searches begin with an investigative component. During this time you will be asked dozens of questions to aid law enforcement and search teams determine where and how to look. This information is critical to the success of the search. Completion of this form, before an incident, allows the searching to start sooner and aids in collecting more accurate information.

Wanderer Information		
First Name:	Middle Name:	Last Name:
First or Nickname:	Name to call:	Social Security #
Home Street Address:	City:	State: Zip Code:
Local Street Address: *(if applicable)*	City:	State: Zip code:
Home Phone #:	Local Phone #: *(if applicable)*	

Contact Information (person providing information)		
First Name:	Middle Name:	Last Name:
Relationship to Wanderer:		Date Completed:
Home Street Address:	City:	State: Zip Code:
Local Street Address: *(if applicable)*	City:	State: Zip code:
Home Phone #:	Local Phone #: *(if applicable)*	
Cell Phone #: *(if applicable)* Pager #:	Work Phone #: *(if applicable)*	

Physical Description			
Date of Birth:	Age:	Sex:	Race:
Height:	Weight:	Build:	Hair Color:
Hair Length:	Hair Style:	Balding?	Mustache?
Beard?	Sideburns?	Facial Features/shape:	Complexion:
Marks/Scars/Tattoos:	General Appearance:	Eye Color:	

Notes:

Accessories and Equipment

Item	Owns?	Description	Missing?*
Glasses	Yes ❏ No ❏		Yes ❏
Dentures	Yes ❏ No ❏		Yes ❏
Hearing Aid	Yes ❏ No ❏		Yes ❏
Cane or walker	Yes ❏ No ❏		Yes ❏
Watch	Yes ❏ No ❏		Yes ❏
Jewelry	Yes ❏ No ❏		Yes ❏
Wallet/purse Contents	Yes ❏ No ❏		Yes ❏
Keys	Yes ❏ No ❏		Yes ❏
Safe Return Products	Yes ❏ No ❏		Yes ❏
Other items (tissue, tobacco, matches, lighter, items stuffed in pockets, etc)	Yes ❏ No ❏		Yes ❏

* Complete the shaded missing column only if a wandering incident occurs. If it appears the wanderer has the item with them check yes.

Clothing Worn When Last Seen

Fill in this section only if a wandering incident occurs. On a separate sheet of paper you might consider keeping an inventory of the person's clothing and footwear.

Item	Style/Description	Color
Hat/Cap		
Shirt		
Pants		
Dress		
Sweater		
Coat/Jacket		
Raingear		
Footwear		
Hose/Socks		
Underwear		
Other		

Notes:

Physical Health

Known Physical disabilities:	
Uncorrected Vision:	**Uncorrected hearing:**
Known Medical conditions:	
General Physical condition:	
Prescribed Medications:	
Over-the-Counter Medications:	
Consequences of not taking medication:	
General Physician: **Address:**	**Office Phone Number:**
Emergency Phone Number:	

Dementia/Alzheimer's Questions

Dementia Diagnosis: (Alzheimer's, Vascular, Parkinson's, etc)	
Neurologist/Gerontologist: **Address:**	**Office Phone Number:** **Emergency Number:**
MMSE Score (obtain from Physician)	**Date of Last MMSE test**

Pick the box below that best describes the subject

❑ Mild confusion and forgetfulness, short-term memory affected.	❑ Difficulty distinguishing time, place, and person. Some language difficulties.	❑ Nearly complete loss of judgment, reasoning, and loss of some physical control.

Complete the following questions on the basis of the last two weeks. Check yes if the activity is performed even once.

Questions for Dementia Disability Assessment	Yes	No	N/A
Undertake to wash himself/herself or to take a bath or shower.	❑	❑	❑
Undertake to brush his/her teeth or care for his/her dentures.	❑	❑	❑
Decide to care for his/her hair (wash and comb)	❑	❑	❑
Prepare the water, towels, and soap for washing, taking bath, or shower	❑	❑	❑
Wash and dry completely all parts of his/her body safely	❑	❑	❑
Brush his/her teeth or care for is/her dentures appropriately	❑	❑	❑
Undertake to dress himself/herself	❑	❑	❑
Choose appropriate clothing (with regard to the occasion, neatness, the weather, and color combination	❑	❑	❑
Dress himself/herself in the appropriate order (undergarments, pat/dress, shoes)	❑	❑	❑
Dress himself/herself completely	❑	❑	❑

Notes:

Questions	YES	NO	N/A
Decide to use the toilet at appropriate times	❑	❑	❑
Use the toilet without "accidents"	❑	❑	❑
Decide that he/she needs to eat.	❑	❑	❑
Choose appropriate utensils and seasonings when eating	❑	❑	❑
Eat his/her meal in the appropriate sequence	❑	❑	❑
Eat his/her meals at a normal pace and with appropriate manners	❑	❑	❑
Undertake to prepare a light meal or snack for himself/herself	❑	❑	❑
Adequately plan a light meal or snack (ingredients, cookware)	❑	❑	❑
Prepare or cook a light meal or snack safely.	❑	❑	❑
Attempt to telephone someone at a suitable time	❑	❑	❑
Find and dial a telephone number correctly	❑	❑	❑
Carry out an appropriate telephone conversation	❑	❑	❑
Write and convey a telephone message adequately	❑	❑	❑
Undertake to go out (walk, visit, shop) at an appropriate time	❑	❑	❑
Decide to use a mode of transportation (car, bus, taxi)	❑	❑	❑
Adequately organize an outing with respect to transportation, keys, destination, weather, necessary money, shopping list	❑	❑	❑
Go out and reach a familiar destination without getting lost	❑	❑	❑
Go out and reach a non-familiar destination without getting lost	❑	❑	❑
Safely take the adequate mode of transportation (car, bus, taxi)	❑	❑	❑
Return from the store with the appropriate items	❑	❑	❑
Show an interest in his/her personal affairs such as his/her finances and written correspondence	❑	❑	❑
Organize his/her finance to pay his/her bills (checks, bankbook, bills)	❑	❑	❑
Adequately organize his/her correspondence with respect to stationery, address, stamps	❑	❑	❑
Handle adequately his/her money (make change)	❑	❑	❑
Complete his/her financial transactions adequately	❑	❑	❑
Answer his/her correspondence adequately	❑	❑	❑
Decide to take his/her medications at the correct time	❑	❑	❑
Take his/her medications as prescribed (according to the right dosage)	❑	❑	❑
Shows an interest in leisure activity(ies)	❑	❑	❑
Takes an interest in household chores he/she used to perform in past	❑	❑	❑
Plan and organize adequately household chores that he/she used to perform	❑	❑	❑
Complete household chores adequately as he/she used to perform in the past	❑	❑	❑
Stay safely at home by himself/herself	❑	❑	❑
TOTALS			

	Yes	No
Does the subject know name?	❑	❑
Does the subject know where they are when at home?	❑	❑
Does the subject recognize the local neighborhood?	❑	❑
Does the subject recognize familiar faces?	❑	❑
Will subject answer to his/her name being called?	❑	❑
Is subject able to conduct a conversation?	❑	❑
Does the subject have the ability to tell time?	❑	❑

Notes:

	Yes	No	If yes please describe
Does the subject suffer from personality or emotional changes	❏	❏	
Does the subject suffer from delusions	❏	❏	
Does the subject suffer from paranoia	❏	❏	
Does the subject suffer from hallucinations	❏	❏	
Does the subject suffer from depression	❏	❏	
Has the subject experienced an emotional breakdown	❏	❏	
Has the subject shown violence towards others	❏	❏	
Is the subject registered in the Alzheimer's Associations' Safe Return program	❏	❏	If yes, please list ID #

Subject's Experience

Residence type	Address	City	State	Dwelling type	Years
Current					
Previous					
Previous					
Previous					
Previous					
Childhood					
Childhood					
Other					

Notes:

	Yes	No	If yes please describe
Is subject familiar with area where last seen?	❏	❏	
What is the subject's favorite area?	❏	❏	
Has the subject been involved with outdoor classes, scouting, military, overnight experiences, or outdoor recreation?	❏	❏	
Is the subject afraid of noises, crowds, dogs, traffic, water, horses, the dark, or other items?	❏	❏	
Will the subject talk to strangers?	❏	❏	
Is the subject dangerous to themselves or others?	❏	❏	

Please describe each incident where the subject wandered away. Please continue on additional pieces of paper if required. If possible, mark the location where the person was found on a map.

	Incident #1	Incident #2	Incident #3
Date			
Where the person was last seen			
What was the person doing when last seen			
Events that might have caused the person to have wandered			
What actions did you take			
Where was the person found			
How was the person found			
List any medical problems that resulted from being lost			
What was the distance from the point the person was last seen			

Notes:

Occupation and Hobbies

Please list job occupations/major volunteer work beginning with the current or most recent.

Job Occupation/Volunteer Work	Years

Please list hobbies and interests.

Hobby or interest	Years

Notes:

Walking Habits

Distance typically walked each day (during the past week.)		miles
Greatest distance walked during the past three months.		miles
Greatest distance walked during the past ten years.		miles
Number of walks during the past week		
Estimate the greatest distance you believe the person could walk		miles

Please rate the person's ability to walk

❑ Confined to bed, unable to walk	❑ Requires walker or cane to walk small distances	❑ Walks unassisted for short distances but shuffles or limps	❑ Walks with assistance	❑ Walks effortlessly

Please list any physical limitations to walking

Critical Wandering Patterns

Please answer the following questions in regards to the last 6 months

	Yes	No	If Yes, please describe
Does the person talk about a person or place that is out of town?	❑	❑	
Does the person talk about a person who is no longer alive?	❑	❑	
Does the person talk about visiting a person or place that is out of town?	❑	❑	
Has the person attempted to visit a person or place out of town without supervision?	❑	❑	
Can the person drive a car safely	❑	❑	
Can the person find keys and start a car	❑	❑	
Does the person desire to drive a car	❑	❑	
Does the person travel independently using public or private transportation	❑	❑	
Has the person attempt to travel independently on public or private transportation in the last 6 months	❑	❑	
Does the person walk or travel a considerable distance from home and return unaided.	❑	❑	
Does the person get lost or confused easily in an unfamiliar setting?	❑	❑	
Does the person get lost or confused easily at home/living quarters.	❑	❑	

Notes:

Please answer the following questions in regards to the last 6 months

	Yes	No	If Yes, please describe
Person wanders.	❏	❏	
Person wanders at night.	❏	❏	
Person wanders during the day	❏	❏	
Wandering appears goal-oriented	❏	❏	
Wandering appears random	❏	❏	
Person seeks out exits or tires to escape from present location	❏	❏	
Wandering pattern similar to pacing (back and forth)	❏	❏	
Wandering appears related to a search for a person or place.	❏	❏	

Photograph

Please obtain two recent photographs that could be released to law enforcement and the media if required. One photograph should be a facial photograph while the second should show the full body. The Alzheimer's Association Safe Return program requests one original photo, passport size or larger.

Date of Photo:	Changes since photo taken:
Is a Videotape available:	Location of Videotape:

Notes:

References

Alzheimer, Alois. 1906. A characteristic disease of the cerebral cortex. Trans. Konrad Maurer. 2002. In *Concepts of Alzheimer's Disease: Biological, Clinical and Cultural Perspectives* eds. Peter J. Whitehouse, Konrad Maurer, and Jesse F. Ballenger. Baltimore: Johns Hopkins University Press.

Alzheimer's Association. 2007. Behavioral and psychiatric Alzheimer symptoms. http://www.alz.org/documents/fs_behavioralandpsychiatric.pdf.

Alzheimer's Association. 2006. Behaviors. http://ww http://www.alz.org/documents/national/Behaviors10_5.pdf w.alz.org.

Alzheimer's Association. Safe Return®. http://www.alz.org/we_can_help_safe_return.asp.

Alzheimer's Association. 2003. Stages of Alzheimer's disease. http://www.alz.org/documents/national/FSstages.pdf.

American Psychiatric Association. 2000. *Diagnostic and statistical manual of mental disorders*, 4th ed., text revision. Washington, DC: American Psychiatric Association.

Boyer, Christopher and Ben Ho. 2001. *Scent behavior class for SAR dog handlers.* Privately printed.

Brown, Katherine, Robert D. Keppel, Joseph G. Weis, and Marvin E. Skeen. 2006. *Case management for missing children homicide investigation.* Washington, DC: Attorney General of Washington State and U.S. Department of Justice.

Caldwell, Marianne Dickerman. 1995. *Gone without a trace.* Forest Knolls, CA: Elder Books.

Castleman, Michael, Dolores Gallagher-Thompson and Matthew Naythons. 1999. *There's still a person in there: The complete guide to treating and coping with Alzheimer's.* New York: Penguin Putnam.

Colwell, Martin. 2001. Managing the urban search. http://www.sarinfo.bc.ca/ManagingTheUrbanSearch.doc.

Cook, Mike. Urban search. Edmonton, Alberta, Canada: Edmonton Police Service.

Cooper, Donald C., Patrick (Rick) LaValla, and Robert (Skip) Stoffel. 1999. *Search and rescue fundamentals: Basic skills and knowledge to perform wilderness, inland, search and rescue*, 3rd ed., revised. Tacoma, WA: ERI International.

Dest, Michael M., James Nunn, Gary Steffens. 1994. Operations of the Rim of the World Search and Rescue Teams from 1968 to 08/30/94. San Bernardino, CA: Rim of the World Search and Rescue Team.

Hanfland, Kenneth A., Robert D. Keppel, and Joseph G. Weis. 1997. *Case management for missing children homicide investigation.* Washington, DC: Attorney General of Washington State and U.S. Department of Justice.

Hill, Kenneth A. *Lost Person Behavior.* 1997. Ottawa: National SAR Secretariat.

Kelly, Kimberly R. 1998. Managing the search for the missing at risk Alzheimer's subject. *Law Enforcement Quarterly.* San Diego, CA: San Diego District Attorney's Office.

Kelly, Kimberly R. 2003. *Project far from home: Understanding and managing the missing at risk Alzheimer's search and rescue subject*, revised. San Diego, CA: San Diego County Sheriff's Department.

Kelly, Kimberly R. 2007. Missing at risk: Understanding and managing the search for the missing Alzheimer's subject. San Diego, CA: San Diego Sheriff's Department.

Koester, Robert J. 1999. *Lost Alzheimer's disease search management: A law enforcement guide to managing the initial response and investigation of the missing Alzheimer's disease subject; Instructor's manual.* Charlottesville, VA: dbS Productions.

Koester, Robert J. and David E. Stooksbury. 1992. Lost Alzheimer's subjects: Profiles and statistics. *Response—The Journal of the National Association for Search and Rescue* Volume 11, Number 4: 20-26.

Koester, Robert J. and David E. Stooksbury. 1995. Behavioral profile of possible Alzheimer's disease subjects in search and rescue incidents in Virginia. *Wilderness and Environmental Medicine* Volume 6: 34-43.

Kramer, John A. 1999. *A guide to urban searches.* Raleigh, NC: privately printed.

LaValla, Patrick (Rick), Robert (Skip) Stoffel, A. S. G. (Tony) Jones. 1997. *Search is an emergency: A text for managing search operations.* Olympia, WA: Emergency Response Institute.

Long, Chris. 1998. The William G. Syrotuck symposium on search theory and practice. *Response: The Journal of the National Association for Search and Rescue* Volume 16, Number 1: 33-34.

Mace, Nancy L. and Peter V. Rabins. 1992. *The 36-hour day.* New York: Warner.

Maurer, Konrad, Stephan Volk, and Hector Gerbaldo. 2000. Auguste D.'s case history. In *Concepts of Alzheimer's Disease: Biological, Clinical and Cultural Perspectives,* eds. Peter J. Whitehouse, Konrad Maurer, and Jesse F. Ballenger. Baltimore: Johns Hopkins University Press.

Mehrabian, Albert. 1981. *Silent messages: Implicit communication of emotions and attitudes.* Belmont, CA: Wadsworth.

Midence, Kenny and Louise Cunliffe. 1996. The impact of dementia on the sufferer and available treatment interventions: An overview. *Journal of Psychology* Volume 130, Number 6: 589-602.

Nussbaum, Paul David and Larry E. Beutler. Finding the lost Alzheimer's victim. *Training Keys* #381. Alexandria, VA: International Association of Chiefs of Police.

Pennington, Mark. 1993. Urban search and rescue. *Response 93—National Association for Search and Rescue Conference Proceedings*: 1-20. Chantilly, VA: NASAR.

Reisberg, Barry, et al. 1989. Global deterioration scale (GDS) stages. *Bulletin of Clinical Neurosciences* Volume 54: 95-112.

Reisberg, Barry, et al. Behavioral symptomatology in Alzheimer's disease. *Aging and AD Symptomatology*, 23-30.

Rowe, Meredith A. and J. C. Glover. 2001. Antecedents, descriptions and consequences of wandering in cognitively-impaired adults and the Safe Return (SR) program. *American Journal of Alzheimer's Disease and Other Dementias* Volume 16, Number 6: 344-352.

Rupf, Warren E. *Child abduction protocol—Contra Costa County Sheriff.* Contra Costa County, CA: Privately printed.

San Diego County Sheriff's Search and Rescue. Team operations and mission reports, 1982–1996, 1996 –2007. San Diego, CA: Privately printed.

Shenk, David. 2001. *The forgetting: Alzheimer's; Portrait of an epidemic.* New York: Random House.

Silverstein, Nina M. February 2005. Promoting safety and comfort in the patient who wanders. Lecture presented at NICHE Clinical Practice Conference, University of Massachusetts, Boston.

Silverstein, Nina M., Gerald Flaherty, and Terry Salmons Tobin. 2002. *Dementia and wandering behavior: Concern for the lost elder.* New York: Springer Publishing Company.

Silverstein, Nina M. and Gerald Flaherty. 2007. Wandering in hospitalized older adults. *Try This: Best Practices in Nursing Care for Hospitalized Older Adults with Dementia* Issue Number D6. New York: John A. Hartford Institute for Geriatric Nursing / Alzheimer's Association.

Silverstein, Nina M. and Terry Salmons. 1996. *He comes back eventually... wandering behavior in community residing persons with Alzheimer's disease registered with Safe Return.* Boston: Gerontology Institute, University of Massachusetts.

St. John, Michael. 2001. Missing children in urban areas and abduction searches. *Response 2001—National Association for Search and Rescue Conference Proceedings.* Chantilly, VA: NASAR.

St. John, Michael. 2007. Missing children and searching for victims of abduction with a potential sexual assault and homicide. *Technical Rescue* Issue 49: 38-42.

Stoffel, Robert (Skip), et al. 2006. *The textbook for managing land search operations.* Cashmere, WA: Emergency Response International.

Thomas, David W. 1995. Wandering: A proposed definition. *Journal of Gerontological Nursing,* 35-41.

Warner, Mark L. and Ellen Warner. 2000. *The complete guide to Alzheimer's proofing your home.* West Lafayette, IN: Purdue University Press.

Warner, Mark, et al. 2005. *In search of the Alzheimer's wanderer: A workbook to protect your loved one.* West Lafayette, IN: Purdue University Press.

Washington Explorer Search and Rescue Pierce County Unit. *Search techniques: Urban search type 1 and urban search type 2.* Pierce County, WA: Washington Explorer Search and Rescue Pierce County Unit.

Wehbring, John. 2000. *Non-wilderness search.* San Diego, CA: Mountain Rescue Association.

Young, Christopher S., Bay Area Search and Rescue Council (BASARC), et al. 1998. The suburban search process. *Response—The Journal of the National Association for Search and Rescue* Volume 16, Number 3: 249-274.

Young, Christopher S. and Kimberly R. Kelly. 2005. Urban search management. Lecture presented at the National Association of Search and Rescue (NASAR) Conference, Oakland, CA.

Additional Resources

Missing and Abducted Children

U.S. Department of Justice, Office of Justice Programs, Office of Juvenile Justice and Delinquency Prevention. May 2007. *What about me? Coping with the abduction of a brother or sister: Guide.* http://www.ncjrs.gov/pdffiles1/ojjdp/217714.pdf.

Sedlak, Andrea J., David Finkelhor, and Heather Hammer. 2005. *National estimates of children missing involuntarily for benign reasons.* Washington, DC: U.S. Department of Justice, Office of Justice Programs. http://www.ncjrs.gov/pdffiles1/ojjdp/206180.pdf.

U.S. Department of Justice, Office of Justice Programs, Office of Juvenile Justice and Delinquency Prevention. *When your child goes missing—A family survival fuide.* http://www.ncjrs.gov/pdffiles1/ojjdp/204958.pdf.

Products

Un-supported vinyl for plastic overlay covers from the Kittrich Corporation. Contact: 1.800.497.2867 or contactus@kittrich.com.

Acronyms

AC	Area Command
AD	Alzheimer's disease
ATV	all terrain vehicle
BOLO	Be On the Look Out
CISD	Critical Incident Stress Debriefing
CP	command post
EOC	Emergency Operations Center
ETNS	emergency telephone notification systems
FEMA	Federal Emergency Management Agency
FLIR	forward looking infrared
GIS	Geographic Information System
GPS	Global Positioning System
HAZMAT	hazardous materials
IAP	Incident Action Plan
IC	Incident Commander
ICS	Incident Command System
IPP	initial planning point
ISRID	International Search & Rescue Incident Database
LKP	last known position
MCP	mobile command post
MDC	mobile data computer
NCIC	National Crime Information Center
NCMEC	National Center for Missing and Exploited Children
NIMS	National Incident Management System
NLETS	National Law Enforcement Telecommunications System
OES	Office of Emergency Services
OPS	Operations Section
PIO	Public Information Officer
PLS	point last seen
POD	probability of detection
RP	reporting party
SAR	search and rescue
TENS	Telephone Emergency Notification System
UC	Unified Command
USGS	United States Geological Survey
UTM	Universal Transverse Mercator
USAR	Urban Search and Rescue

Index

Symbols

M

Made in the USA
Coppell, TX
21 January 2025

44778743R00193